Weight Training For Dummies

Cheat Sheet

Myths about Weight Training

Myth #1: You'll get huge unless you lift light weights.

Reality: The only way your muscles will burst the seams of your dress shirts is if you regularly lift extremely heavy weight repetitions — *and* if you have a body type that will even allow for the development of mega muscles.

Myth #2: You're the only one in the gym baffled by the equipment.

Reality: Nobody is born knowing how to operate the Assisted Dip Machine or perform a Decline Chest Fly! Weight training equipment can baffle even the sharpest of minds.

Myth #3: Weight lifting is dangerous.

Reality: If Dr. Ruth tried to hoist a 300-pound barbell overhead, that would be dangerous. But if you use good technique and common sense, you're likely to stay injury-free.

Myth #4: Thigh exercises will slim your thighs, and ab exercises will whittle your middle.

Reality: You cannot melt the fat off of any particular body part by performing exercises that target that area. There simply is no such thing as spot reducing.

Myth #5: Lifting weights won't help you lose weight.

Reality: Lifting weights is an essential part of a fat-loss program. Developing muscle is the only way to boost your metabolism, which can help you lose fat and keep it off.

Myth #6: Free weights are for muscleheads and machines are for beginners.

Reality: The free weight room of a gym is not a special club for bodybuilders; novices are welcome there and should make a point of learning to use dumbbells and barbells.

Great Weight Training Values

- **An adjustable weight bench:** Although you can perform dozens of exercises with dumbbells alone, a weight bench gives you far more versatility.

- **Weight lifting gloves:** Gloves give you a firmer grip on the weights, protect the skin on your palms, and make you look like a pro.

- **A personal trainer:** A gifted trainer can get you over the learning curve in a hurry and, in just a few sessions, teach you technique tips that last a lifetime.

- **Exercise tubing:** Rubber tubing fits easily into your carry-on bag or your desk drawer at work and gives you a better strength workout than you might imagine.

- **A weight training diary:** Tracking the details of your workouts provides you with valuable feedback and the inspiration to keep lifting.

How to Be a Good Personal Training Client

- **Show up on time.** Trainers are professional people with busy schedules and bills to pay, so show them some courtesy.

- **Have a good attitude.** Your trainer doesn't want to hear you whine about your boss or your latest speeding ticket.

- **Listen to your trainer.** When your trainer advises you to perform 12 repetitions per set, don't say, "My stockbroker said I should do 40."

- **Speak up.** Don't be afraid to ask why you pull a bar down to your chest rather than to your belly button.

For Dummies: Bestselling Book Series for Beginners

Weight Training For Dummies®

Cheat Sheet

Weight Training Etiquette

- ✔ Share the equipment. Don't take a nap on a machine you're not using.

- ✔ Keep the grunting to a minimum. A weight room isn't a public library, but neither is it a championship wrestling arena.

- ✔ Return your weights to their designated spot on the rack.

- ✔ Don't hog the drinking fountain. If the line behind you is longer than a World Series ticket line, don't fill your entire water bottle.

- ✔ Don't bring your gym bag into the weight room. You know those large, hollowed out cubes called lockers?

- ✔ Keep your sweat to yourself. Carry a towel and wipe off any bench or machine that you use.

- ✔ Treat the locker room like your own bathroom. Nobody wants to become personally acquainted with clumps of your hair.

What to Look for in a Fitness Trainer

- ✔ **Certification:** Your trainer should have a credential from one of the professional organizations we describe in Chapter 5.

- ✔ **A personality that's compatible with yours:** Do you prefer a cheerleader or a drill sergeant?

- ✔ **Good teaching skills:** Your trainer may have a Ph.D. in physiology and be more congenial than Rosie O'Donnell, but can he or she teach you to do a push-up?

- ✔ **Personal attention:** A trainer shouldn't give the same program to a 65-year-old woman and a professional hockey player.

Talk Like a Pro: A Glossary of Your Muscles

Slang	Translation	Slang	Translation
Pecs	Chest	Tris	Rear of upper arms
Traps	Upper back	Abs	Front midsection
Lats	Middle back	Glutes	Butt
Delts	Shoulders	Quads	Front thighs
Bis	Front of upper arms	Hams	Rear thighs

Hungry Minds™

For Dummies: Bestselling Book Series for Beginners

Praise, Praise, Praise for Weight Training For Dummies!

"From etiquette to execution, all of weight training do's and don'ts are here, presented just as dummies like it — straightforward and with loads of humor. Going to the gym has never been this much fun."

— Alec Harvey, Lifestyle/Entertainment Editor, *The Birmingham News*

"Once again you can benefit from the knowledge of two fitness insiders. *Weight Training For Dummies* provides a fun, easy-to-follow guide on the best way to fast results: strength training. Armed with info on gym jargon, etiquette, myth busting, choosing a trainer, and more, you'll never be intimidated by a weight room again."

— Peg Moline, Editorial Director, *Shape* magazine

"The new dynamic duo has done it again! I highly recommend this exercise bible: It's for anyone who's never walked into a weight room, but more importantly, it's for anyone who's ever walked out of a weight room feeling frustrated, injured, overlooked, or self-conscious. *Weight Training For Dummies* is an information-packed, educational, accessible accomplishment."

— Nicole Dorsey, M.S., West Coast Editor, *Fitness* magazine

NOTE: DO NOT SMASH NOSE... IT HURTS & BRUISES FOR LIFE.

Praise, Praise, Praise for the first edition of Fitness For Dummies!

"...a funny, irreverent, and very smart guide to wading through the confounding maze of fitness information and misinformation. If you've been waiting for an enjoyable and low-barrier entry into shaping up, here it is."

— *Cooking Light* magazine

"...an upbeat, crystal-clear overview of the big fitness components: exercise (both aerobics and strength) and nutrition."

— *The Dallas Morning News*

"*Fitness For Dummies* is one of the best exercise guides on the market."

— *The Columbus Dispatch*

"This book is a joy to read — written with wit and style, it comes as a welcome reassurance that both razor sharp accuracy and first-rate writing can co-exist in the same package."

— Jonathan Bowden, M.A.C.S.C.S., Senior Faculty, Equinox Fitness Training Institute and Contributing Editor, *Fitness* magazine

"This is one of the most comprehensive, authoritative — and entertaining — fitness books I've ever seen."

— *Men's Fitness* magazine

Weight Training

FOR

DUMMIES®

2ND EDITION

Weight Training

FOR

DUMMIES®

2ND EDITION

by Liz Neporent and Suzanne Schlosberg

Hungry Minds™

Best-Selling Books • Digital Downloads • e-Books • Answer Networks • e-Newsletters • Branded Web Sites • e-Learning

New York, NY ◆ Cleveland, OH ◆ Indianapolis, IN

Weight Training For Dummies,® 2nd Edition

Published by
Hungry Minds, Inc.
909 Third Avenue
New York, NY 10022
www.hungryminds.com
www.dummies.com (Dummies Press Web Site)

Library of Congress Control Number: 00-104219

ISBN: 0-7645-5168-X

Printed in the United States of America

10 9 8 7 6

2O/SY/QZ/QR/IN

Distributed in the United States by Hungry Minds, Inc.

Distributed by CDG Books Canada Inc. for Canada; by Transworld Publishers Limited in the United Kingdom; by IDG Norge Books for Norway; by IDG Sweden Books for Sweden; by IDG Books Australia Publishing Corporation Pty. Ltd. for Australia and New Zealand; by TransQuest Publishers Pte Ltd. for Singapore, Malaysia, Thailand, Indonesia, and Hong Kong; by Gotop Information Inc. for Taiwan; by ICG Muse, Inc. for Japan; by Intersoft for South Africa; by Eyrolles for France; by International Thomson Publishing for Germany, Austria and Switzerland; by Distribuidora Cuspide for Argentina; by LR International for Brazil; by Galileo Libros for Chile; by Ediciones ZETA S.C.R. Ltda. for Peru; by WS Computer Publishing Corporation, Inc., for the Philippines; by Contemporanea de Ediciones for Venezuela; by Express Computer Distributors for the Caribbean and West Indies; by Micronesia Media Distributor, Inc. for Micronesia; by Chips Computadoras S.A. de C.V. for Mexico; by Editorial Norma de Panama S.A. for Panama; by American Bookshops for Finland.

For general information on Hungry Minds' products and services please contact our Customer Care Department within the U.S. at 800-762-2974, outside the U.S. at 317-572-3993 or fax 317-572-4002.

For sales inquiries and reseller information, including discounts, premium and bulk quantity sales, and foreign-language translations, please contact our Customer Care Department at 800-434-3422, fax 317-572-4002, or write to Hungry Minds, Inc., Attn: Customer Care Department, 10475 Crosspoint Boulevard, Indianapolis, IN 46256.

For information on licensing foreign or domestic rights, please contact our Sub-Rights Customer Care Department at 650-653-7098.

For information on using Hungry Minds' products and services in the classroom or for ordering examination copies, please contact our Educational Sales Department at 800-434-2086 or fax 317-572-4005.

Please contact our Public Relations Department at 212-884-5163 for press review copies or 212-884-5000 for author interviews and other publicity information or fax 212-884-5400.

For authorization to photocopy items for corporate, personal, or educational use, please contact Copyright Clearance Center, 222 Rosewood Drive, Danvers, MA 01923, or fax 978-750-4470.

Hungry Minds™   is a trademark of Hungry Minds, Inc.

About the Authors

Liz Neporent: Liz's first set of weights (actually, her brother's) were made of blue plastic and filled with sand; when they started leaking sand all over the house, her mother relegated all weight lifting activities to the basement. Since that time, she has graduated into a well-known corporate fitness consultant, designing and managing fitness centers worldwide. Along the way, Liz also was a personal trainer, received a master's degree in exercise physiology, and got certified by the American College of Sports Medicine, National Strength and Conditioning Association, American Council on Exercise, and the National Academy of Sports Medicine. Recently she was named Club Industry Magazine's Woman Entrepreneur of the Year and was appointed to the board of directors and faculty of the American Council on Exercise. She is coauthor and author of several books including *Fitness For Dummies* and *Fitness Walking For Dummies* and writes frequently for *The New York Times, Family Circle, Shape,* and others. She currently hosts a daily internet radio show on eyada.com.

Suzanne Schlosberg: Suzanne's writing career began her freshman year in college, when she was assigned to cover a pre-season NBA game and found herself in a locker room interviewing a dozen tall, muscular, naked Boston Celtics. She decided she liked this writing stuff. Suzanne went on to become a newspaper reporter and magazine writer. Now a contributing editor to *Shape* and *Health* magazines, Suzanne is the coauthor, with Liz Neporent, of *Fitness For Dummies* and the author of *The Ultimate Workout Log.* She is also an instructor in the UCLA Extension Certificate in Journalism program.

Always happy when she has a barbell in hand, Suzanne has lifted weights in Zimbabwe, Morocco, Iceland, and Micronesia, among other locales. She is the women's record holder in the Great American Sack Race, a quadrennial event held in Yerington, Nevada, in which competitors must run 5 miles while carrying a 50-pound sack of chicken feed. The 22-inch trophy remains her crowning, and only, achievement in the realm of fitness competition. Suzanne also has bicycled across the United States twice and is a mediocre road racer. Although Suzanne cycles about 200 miles a week near her home in Los Angeles, she makes her daily half-mile trip to Starbucks in her sport-utility vehicle.

Authors' Acknowledgments

The authors wish to thank Richard Miller and The Gym Source of New York City for providing exercise equipment for many of our photos. We're also grateful to Arthur Belebeau and Daniel Kron for their wonderful — and speedy — photography and to Chris Gristanti, who generously donated several photos. Trotter Fitness Equipment provided additional photographs.

Many thanks to all the models who appeared in this book. Your time, patience, and of course, images are much appreciated. The models are Patty Buttenheim, Aja Certain, Terry Certain, Katherine Cole, James Gaspard, Debbie-Deb Hanoka, James Jankiewicz, Spike Jozzino, Subhash Mandal, Amy Ngai, Nancy Ngai, Alicia Racela, Fred Reid, Doris Shafran, Jay Shafran, Bob Weiter, Carrie Wujeik, and Norman Zinker.

Thanks, also, to Reebok for providing clothing and shoes. Some additional clothing was provided by Everlast, Nike, and Brooks.

Finally, thanks to Stacy Collins, Lisa Roule, and Colleen Esterline of Hungry Minds, Inc. for giving us the opportunity to write this book.

Acknowledgments from Liz

Much gratitude goes to my family, especially my husband Jay Shafran who is supportive beyond belief. Thanks to Suzanne Schlosberg the best writing partner ever. Ever! I would also like to acknowledge the following people who are forced to put up with me in some way: John Buzzerio, Nancy Ngai, Linda Strohmeyer, Patricia Buttenheim, Jimmy Buff, Jimmy Rotolo, Stephen Harris, James Jankiewicz, Bob Welter, Subhash Mandal, Holly Byrne, Grace De Simone, and Zoomer.

Acknowledgments from Suzanne

It would be impossible to find a better writing partner than Liz Neporent. She knows so much, works so hard, and accepts the fact that I will never, ever like her dog. I also want to thank my agent, Felicia Eth, for being on the ball. Alec Boga did a stellar job as my supervisor, and Nancy Gottesman was always there to entertain and distract me. As always, I'm grateful to my family for their support.

Publisher's Acknowledgments

We're proud of this book; please send us your comments through our Online Registration Form located at www.dummies.com.

Some of the people who helped bring this book to market include the following:

Acquisitions, Editorial, and Media Development

Project Editor: Colleen Williams Esterline

    (Previous Edition: Leah P. Cameron)

Senior Acquisitions Editor: Stacy S. Collins

Copy Editor: Colleen Williams Esterline

    (Previous Edition: Michael Simsic)

Acquisitions Coordinator: Lisa Roule

Technical Editors: Gina Allchin, Marlisa Brown, John Buzzerio, Holly Burne, and Grace De Simone

Editorial Manager: Jennifer Erhlich

Editorial Assistant: Carol Strickland

Editorial Administrator: Michelle Hacker

Cover Credit: Tony Stone © Terry Vine

Production

Project Coordinator: Nancee Reeves

Layout and Graphics: Beth Brooks, Brian Drumm, Jason Guy, Clint Lahnen, Tracy K. Oliver, Brent Savage, Jacque Schneider, Brian Torwelle, Jeremey Unger

Special Art: Medical Illustrations Dept., Indiana University School of Medicine

Proofreaders: Corey Bowen, Joel K. Draper, Charles Spencer

Indexer: Joan Griffitts

Photographers: Arthur Belebeau, Daniel Kron

Additional Photography: Chris Gristanti, Trotter Fitness Equipment

General and Administrative

Hungry Minds, Inc.: John Kilcullen, CEO; Bill Barry, President and COO; John Ball, Executive VP, Operations & Administration; John Harris, CFO

Hungry Minds Consumer Reference Group

    Business: Kathleen A. Welton, Vice President and Publisher; Kevin Thornton, Acquisitions Manager

    Cooking/Gardening: Jennifer Feldman, Associate Vice President and Publisher

    Education/Reference: Diane Graves Steele, Vice President and Publisher; Greg Tubach, Publishing Director

    Lifestyles: Kathleen Nebenhaus, Vice President and Publisher; Tracy Boggier, Managing Editor

    Pets: Dominique De Vito, Associate Vice President and Publisher; Tracy Boggier, Managing Editor

    Travel: Michael Spring, Vice President and Publisher; Suzanne Jannetta, Editorial Director; Brice Gosnell, Managing Editor

Hungry Minds Consumer Editorial Services: Kathleen Nebenhaus, Vice President and Publisher; Kristin A. Cocks, Editorial Director; Cindy Kitchel, Editorial Director

Hungry Minds Consumer Production: Debbie Stailey, Production Director

Contents at a Glance

Cartoons at a Glance

By Rich Tennant

"Okay, I know I need to start working out. Now, can I please have my soap-on-a-rope back?"

page 7

Scottish Home Gym

You spend good money on a nice piece of equipment, and now it just sits in the corner of the room collecting dust.

page 255

"READ THE ASSEMBLY INSTRUCTIONS," I SAID. BUT NOOOoo..."ONLY AN IDIOT READS THE INSTRUCTIONS." HE SAID.

HANG IN THERE, SIR. THE JAWS-OF-LIFE WILL BE HERE ANY MINUTE.

page 43

"When exactly was it discovered that fun house mirrors had accidentally been installed in the body sculpting room?"

page 331

MIKE'S GYM

"I heard it was good to cross-train, so I'm mixing my weight training with scuba diving."

page 283

Popeye's Weight Training Video

PHEW! THAT'S ENOUGH FOREARM WORK. LET'S GET BACK TO THOSE CALF MUSCLES BEFORE WE FINISH UP WITH—YOU GUESSED IT—MORE FOREARM WORK.

page 79

Fax: 978-546-7747
E-mail: richtennant@the5thwave.com
World Wide Web: www.the5thwave.com

Table of Contents

Introduction

*W*hen the first edition of *Weight Training For Dummies* was published, lifting weights was on the verge of becoming a mainstream phenomenon. Women, Baby Boomers, seniors — all of these groups were starting to get the message: Hoisting hunks of iron benefits everyone, not just bodybuilders with shoulders wider than the wingspan of a DC-10.

Now, four years later, weight training has become even more popular. Some 87 percent of all health clubs now offer personal training, compared to 66 percent in 1996. In the same period, four million women have started using weight machines. Health club memberships have more than doubled for people over age 55. One gym in Palms Springs, California, has even stopped playing rap music because of complaints from the gym's increasingly gray-haired membership.

However, just because weight training has become more popular doesn't mean it has become any less intimidating for novices. It's only natural for a beginner to be baffled by the equipment and the lingo. You may look at a barbell and wonder how you're going to lift the thing while remaining on good terms with your lower back muscles. You may stare at a weight machine and wonder which end the homemade pasta comes out of. You may wonder what it means when a trainer says, "Do three sets of eight reps on the Lat Pulldown and then super set with the Seated Row."

In this book, we give you the knowledge and the confidence to start a weight training program, either at home or at a gym. We describe more than 150 exercises suitable for rookies and veterans alike. Our brand-new chapter of advanced exercises is one of four new chapters in the second edition. This edition also updates you on the latest in weight training equipment, Web sites, videos, research, and gym classes. Plus, we address pressing questions, including

- ✔ What's the key to building strength and tone without getting bulky?
- ✔ Can any nutritional supplements actually help you build muscle or burn fat?
- ✔ Which gives you better results: free weights or machines?
- ✔ Should you do yoga and Pilates in addition to weight training?
- ✔ Should you wear a weight belt and gloves, or are these accessories just for show?
- ✔ Can you trust weight training information you read on the Internet?

✔ How do you distinguish the qualified trainers from the quacks?

✔ What should you say if a fellow gym member asks to use the machine you're using?

✔ If you're overweight, should you lose weight before you lift weight?

In *Weight Training For Dummies,* we tell you about safe weight lifting techniques, steer you toward equipment bargains, entertain you with stories about fellow lifters, and inspire you to keep pumping iron when you'd rather pump a keg and fire up the backyard grill. In fact, we take care of just about everything except lifting the weights. We figured we'd save that job for you.

What Weight Training Can Do for You

We all have different reasons for wanting to lift weights. Undoubtedly, many of these reasons have to do with looking better. Sculpted arms and toned "abs" have become somewhat of a fashion statement. But we can think of more compelling and, ultimately, more satisfying reasons to lift weights. Here's a reminder of what weight training can do for you:

✔ **Keep your bones healthy.** The average woman loses about 1 percent of her bone mass each year after age 35. Men are susceptible to brittle bones, too. Lifting weights can drastically slow the rate of bone loss — and may even reverse the process. With strong bones, you won't become hunched over as you age, and you'll lower your risk of life-threatening fractures. No matter what your age, it's never too late to start strengthening your bones.

✔ **Help control your weight.** When you lose weight through dieting and aerobic exercise (such as walking or bicycling), you lose muscle along with fat. This can be a problem: When you lose muscle, your metabolism slows down, so you're more likely to regain the weight. By adding weight training to the mix, you can maintain (or increase) your muscle and thereby maintain (or even boost) your metabolism. Although weight training is no magic bullet for weight loss, many obesity experts consider it to be an essential part of any weight-control program.

✔ **Increase your strength.** Lifting the front end of a fire truck may not be among your goals in life, but a certain amount of muscle strength does come in handy. Weight training makes it easier to haul your stacks of newspaper to the recycling bin and drag your kids away from a video game. Studies show that even 90 year olds can gain significant strength from lifting weights.

✔ **Boost your energy.** Forget about hokey dietary supplements. One of the best energy boosters around comes not in a bottle but on a weight rack. When you lift weights, you have more pep in your step. You can bound to the bus stop or sail through your company's annual charity walk-a-thon.

✔ **Improve your heart health.** For years we've known that aerobic exercise such as walking, jogging, and cycling can lower your risk of heart disease and high blood pressure. But new research suggests that weight training may offer these benefits as well. Specifically, studies show that lifting weights can lower your risk of having a heart attack or stroke by lowering your LDL ("bad") cholesterol and reducing blood pressure.

✔ **Improve your quality of life.** Any activity that accomplishes all of the above has to make you a happier, more productive person. (Research suggests that weight training can even relieve clinical depression.) Of course, hoisting hunks of steel is no instant cure-all, but you'd be surprised how much satisfaction a pair of 10-pound dumbbells can bring into your life.

How to Use This Book

You can use this book in several ways:

✔ If you're a novice, we suggest you start by reading Parts I and II — these parts get you comfortable with the equipment, the lingo, the safety basics, and the etiquette. Then skip to Part IV, which explains how to design a weight routine that meets your needs. (You may want to refer back to this part every now and then.) Then go back to Part III, which shows you the exercises. In your spare time, like when you're not busy lifting weights, hit Parts V and VI.

✔ If you already know an E-Z Curl bar from a horseshoe grip and know that in the weight training world, a circuit has nothing to do with electrical currents, you can go straight to Part III and find numerous exercises for each body part. You may also want to focus on Part IV, which describes how to combine these exercises into a routine that fits your schedule and your equipment preferences.

✔ No matter what your level of knowledge about weight training, you can always use this book as a reference. Flip to the index and look up any specific topic, such as hamstring stretches, fitness magazines, or high-protein diets.

How This Book Is Organized

Weight Training For Dummies is divided into six parts. In general, you can read each part — or any chapter within it — without having to read what came before. When you come to a section that does require prior knowledge, we refer you to the chapter that provides the background. Here's a rundown of each part.

Part I: Stuff to Know Before You Pick Up a Weight

Lifting isn't one of those activities like, say, checkers, that you can competently engage in after a one-minute explanation. Before you hop aboard the Leg Press, you need to know a bit of weight training jargon and understand key safety precautions. This part explains terms such as power cage, spotter, and plate-loaded weight machine — terms that you can use to impress guests at your next cocktail party. This part also teaches you how to test your own strength and chart your progress in a weight training diary.

Part II: Weight Training Wisdom

In this part, we offer insight into the less technical aspects of weight lifting. We clue you in to equipment bargains, help you size up health clubs, and warn you about smarmy salespeople. We tell you which video instructors to invite into your living room, which group strength training classes to avoid, and how to recognize a quality trainer. We also fill you in on the finer points of weight training etiquette, like what to do when a gym member is hogging the Butt Blaster.

Part III: The Exercises

We suspect this part is what prompted you to buy the book. Here we demonstrate a wide variety of exercises for all your major muscle groups. Each chapter includes a muscle diagram (so that you can locate your "quads" and your "delts") and an ever-so-brief physiology discussion. We demonstrate exercises for novices and veterans, home lifters and gym members. We also explain how to modify many of the exercises if you have trouble with your back, your knees, or other joints.

Part IV: Designing Your Workout Program

You can't combine any dozen exercises and call them a workout any more than you can throw on random articles of clothing and call 'em an outfit. To get good results and avoid injury, you need to carefully select your exercises. In this part, we explain the essential elements of any weight routine. Then we explain how to custom design a program so that it suits your goals and your schedule.

Part V: Beyond the Barbell

Pumping iron will get you only so far. To get healthier and look better, you also need to eat sensibly, regularly engage in aerobic exercise, and stretch your muscles. In this part, we explain how to balance your weight workouts with the other important components of fitness. We debunk myths about stretching, and we explain just how much walking, stairclimbing, or swimming you should do each week. We introduce you to yoga and Pilates, two popular disciplines that can compliment your strength workouts, and we show you several exercises to improve your balance and coordination. We also set the record straight on the pills, powders, and potions sold at gyms and health food stores.

Part VI: The Part of Tens

This part is a hodgepodge of important weight training subjects. We recommend ways to educate yourself about weight training, such as reading fitness magazines, participating in Internet advice boards, and spying on fellow health club members. We describe common weight training errors and warn you against bogus gizmos, including electrical stimulation devices that claim "You quickly shape up doing nothing at all!" This part contains a chapter new to the second edition: "Ten Myths and Misconceptions about Weight Training."

Icons Used in This Book

 The Myth Buster superhero rescues you from misleading notions, fighting for truth, justice, and a good weight training workout. For example, he points out that high-protein diets are *not* the key to weight loss and that abdominal training will *not* eliminate your love handles.

 When you see the Jargon Alert whistle, you know that there's mumbo jumbo up ahead — weight training terminology such as *rep, pecs,* and *abduction* (which, by the way, has nothing to do with kidnapping). We give you the English translation of terms commonly used by fitness trainers.

 We use this icon when we tell a true story, like the time Liz snapped her face with a rubber exercise band, the time Suzanne carried a 50-pound sack of chicken feed for 5 miles, and the time that one guy we know got stuck under a barbell — and waited for 20 minutes before calling for help.

The Warning icon cautions you to the hucksters lurking at the depths of the fitness industry, hawking useless gadgets like electronic muscle stimulators. We also use this icon to signal mistakes that can cause injury, such as bending your knees too far or lifting too much weight.

When you see the Tip icon, you know that we're pointing out an especially helpful weight training hint or giving you a heads-up on an effective strategy.

The check mark gives our stamp of approval to products we like, such as cleverly designed dumbbell kits and weight benches. This is the best of the stuff we've come across in our travels.

Special Icons

The following icons are used primarily in the chapters that demonstrate exercises: Chapters 8 through 14 and Chapter 25.

This officer is on the posture beat, reminding you about good technique so that you don't become the victim of an 11-80 (that's police code for "Accident — Major Injuries"). He tells you when to keep your shoulders relaxed, your abdominal muscles tight, and your knees bent.

This Joint Caution icon suggests that you skip or modify the exercise if you've ever injured the joint indicated, such as the knee or lower back. Even if you've never suffered an injury, pay special attention to the joints in question and make sure that you don't feel any discomfort.

Part I
Stuff to Know Before You Pick Up a Weight

The 5th Wave   By Rich Tennant

"Okay, I know I need to start working out. Now, can I please have my soap-on-a-rope back?"

In this part . . .

Part I takes the intimidation out of weight lifting. You get a description of the major weight training tools: dumbbells, barbells, weight machines, rubber tubing, and a few other mysterious contraptions you're likely to come across at a health club or a home equipment store. You also get a crash course in safety so that you don't crush your fingers in a weight machine or whack a fellow lifter in the ribs with a barbell. In addition, you find out how to track your progress in a weight training diary and how to test your muscle power on a variety of equipment. And for the few, the proud, the ambitious, we list the physical requirements for entrance into several fire and military academies.

Chapter 1

Tools of the Trade

· ·

· ·

*N*o question: The most intimidating thing about weight training is the equipment. You could examine a weight machine for half an hour — looking it up and down, walking circles around it, touching it, prodding it, even reading the instructional plaque posted on the frame — and still have absolutely no clue where to sit, which lever to push, or what possible benefit you could derive from using it. Heck, even a simple metal bar sitting on a rack can leave you scratching your head.

We have two points to make about the bewildering nature of weight equipment. First, relax. With a bit of practice, weight training contraptions are actually easy to operate. Second, be happy that you decided to take up weight lifting in the 21st century. Back in the 1800s, fitness enthusiasts took to lifting furniture, boulders — even cows! Although we personally have never tried hoisting farm animals overhead, we feel confident that today's weight training devices are a major improvement.

In this chapter, we introduce the basic strength-building tools found in health clubs and home equipment stores, including some high-tech contraptions that have become popular since the first edition of this book. We detail the pros and cons of each equipment category: free weights (dumbbells and barbells), machines, and rubber exercise bands and tubes. And we help you decide which type of equipment is right for you. We also answer the big questions: Should beginners stick to machines? Do barbells build bigger muscles? Can you get strong without using any equipment at all?

Jargon We Couldn't Resist

In fitness magazines, health clubs, and videos, you often hear weight equipment referred to as *resistance equipment*. We hate to clutter your brain with jargon right off the bat, but *resistance* is a word you should know. Resistance is an opposing force, like a weight or gravity; in order for your muscles to get stronger, you must work against resistance. *Resistance equipment* is actually a more accurate term than *weight equipment* because, as we explain later in this chapter, you can build muscle without using weights at all. Rubber exercise tubes, for example, don't weigh more than a couple of ounces, but they provide enough resistance to strengthen your muscles. Throughout this book, we use the terms *resistance training, weight training, strength training,* and *weight lifting* interchangeably.

A ...For Dummies Guide to Dumbbells and Other Free Weights

Free weights are the metal bars that have weighted plates welded or clipped onto the ends. Dumbbells are the short ones — you can lift them with one hand. Barbells are the long bars that you see Olympic weight lifters pressing overhead with both hands. Dumbbells and barbells are called free weights not because they're given away by philanthropic bodybuilders but because they're not attached to any pulleys, chains, or other machinery.

Some novices think that free weights are the domain of advanced weight lifters, equipment that's not to be fooled with until you've graduated from weight machines. Not true. Beginners have just as much to gain from using free weights as those guys and gals with necks the diameter of a tree stump.

Different kinds of dumbbells

Dumbbells come in pairs, and at most health clubs, they're lined up on a rack from lightest (as light as 1 pound) to heaviest (upward of 180 pounds). By the way, the super heavy dumbbells are mostly for show, considering that about .0000001 percent of the population is capable of lifting them. At some gyms, these weights sit untouched year after year, like the orange jelly candies in that bowl at Aunt Selma's house.

Dumbbells come in many shapes and materials. Some have hexagonal ends so that they don't roll around the floor. Some have contoured handles so they fit more comfortably in your hand. Some are made of shiny chrome; others are gray steel. Others are coated with rubber so that if some yahoo drops them, the weights won't dig a hole in the floor the size of Australia. Figure 1-1 shows an array of dumbbells.

Figure 1-1:
Gyms rack
dumbbells
in pairs.

Different kinds of barbells

Like dumbbells, barbells, also called *bars,* come in a variety of designs. The most popular is a straight bar — at most gyms, these bars weigh 45 pounds and are 6 or 7 feet long. (However, many gyms have bars in a variety of weights, sometimes as light as 15 or 20 pounds. If you're not sure how much a bar weighs, be sure to check with a staff member.) If you want to lift more than 45 pounds, as most people eventually do, you choose from an array of round plates weighing 1¼ to 45 pounds and slide them onto either end of the bar. (The *plates* have a hole in the center.) For example, if you want to lift 75 pounds, you slide a 10-pound plate and a 5-pound plate onto each end.

Some plates have additional holes cut into either side to make them easier to pick up and carry; the holes function like built-in luggage handles. We think these plates are a brilliant invention and have probably helped prevent many an accident and a backache.

Clip-like or screw-like devices called *collars* temporarily secure the plates onto the bars so that they won't rattle around or slide off as you push or pull the bar. Be sure to use these collars, as shown in Figure 1-2, at the gym and at home; many a mirror has been shattered by runaway weight plates. Some health clubs require that you use collars. At one of our favorite gyms, Dave's Power Palace in Carson City, Nevada, Dave himself will march over and stare you down if you forget to clip on the collar. Dave, a former power lifter and deputy sheriff, weighs about 280 pounds. He's not someone you want to argue with.

Figure 1-2:
Use a collar to prevent runaway weights.

In addition to straight bars, most health clubs and equipment dealers have a number of exotic-looking bars with various twists and bends in them. The most common is a W-shaped bar about 3 feet long called the EZ-Curl, which is designed to make certain triceps exercises more comfortable. Some gyms and equipment stores also have an array of straight and EZ-Curl bars with weight plates welded to the ends. These barbells are convenient to use because you don't have to slide weight plates on and off. If you want to switch from 75 pounds to 85 pounds, you simply put the 75-pounder back on the rack and pick up the 85-pounder. No muss, no fuss.

These welded bars are often shorter and less bulky than the traditional bars, so they're more comfortable for many arm and shoulder exercises. However, you typically won't find these *fixed-weight* barbells weighing more than 150 pounds. For many barbell exercises — particularly certain chest and leg exercises — you may need a lot more weight than 150 pounds. With traditional bars, you can pile on up to about 600 pounds (not that we expect you to do this).

The value of free weights

A friend of ours was lying on a weight bench holding two dumbbells overhead when his cat hopped up onto the bench. While trying to shoo the cat away by squirming around, our friend kept the weights overhead for so long that he tore a rotator cuff muscle. The point of this story isn't to scare you away from using free weights. In fact, we believe the best approach to strength training is to combine free weights and machines. Just know that barbells and dumbbells require plenty of concentration. If you follow the safety tips described in Chapter 2 (and if you avoid choosing your pet as a training partner), free weight training is perfectly safe. Here are several good reasons to use dumbbells and barbells:

✔ **Free weights are versatile.** With barbells and dumbbells, you can do literally hundreds of exercises that work virtually every muscle group in your body. Flip through Part III of this book, and you'll get an idea of just how handy they are. Most weight machines, on the other hand, are designed to perform only one or two exercises.

✔ **Free weights give your muscles more freedom to move.** Suppose that you're lying on a bench pushing a barbell above your chest (this is the Bench Press, shown in Chapter 9). You can press the weight straight up over your chest, or you can move your arms a few inches back so that you are pressing directly above your neck. Or you can position your arms anywhere between. All these movements are perfectly legitimate ways of doing the exercise, and some may feel more comfortable to your body than others.

✔ **Free weights involve several muscle groups at once.** For example, chest press movements are designed to work your chest, shoulders, and triceps. However, when you perform these movements with a barbell, you also call on your abdominal and lower back muscles to keep your body still and to keep the bar balanced as you press the weight up. With the equivalent machine, you don't have to worry about holding the bar still, so your abdominal and back muscles don't get much action. (However, as we explain in the "Don't Be Afraid of Weight Machines" section later in this chapter, the more limited action of a machine is sometimes a benefit.)

Making the choice: Dumbbells versus barbells

As we demonstrate in Part III, you can perform many movements with both dumbbells and barbells. For example, while sitting on a bench, you can either press a bar overhead (the Military Press) or press up two dumbbells (the Dumbbell Shoulder Press). Which is the better option? Actually, both have their benefits.

Dumbbells are helpful because they allow each arm to work independently. If one side of your body is stronger than the other — a common phenomenon — this imbalance is apparent when you're working with dumbbells. Your weaker arm may start wobbling, or may poop out sooner than your dominant arm. Using dumbbells can help correct strength imbalances because each side of your body is forced to carry its own weight, so to speak. By contrast, if you use a bar, your stronger side may simply pick up the slack for your weak side.

On the other hand, some exercises just don't *feel* as good when you use dumbbells. Any seasoned lifter can tell you that nothing is quite like doing the Bench Press — it's considered the quintessential meat-and-potatoes chest exercise. Even though the Dumbbell Chest Press is a perfectly good exercise, it may not deliver quite the same amount of satisfaction, probably because you can't lift as much total weight. For example, if you can do the Dumbbell Chest Press with a 20-pound dumbbell in each hand, there's a good chance that you can lift at least a 60-pound barbell.

Using a Weight Bench

A weight bench is what you'd expect: a sturdy, padded bench that you lie, sit, or kneel on to lift weights. To get the most out of free weights, benches are a must. Sure, you could lie on the ground, but many exercises will come to an abrupt halt when your elbows smack against the floor. As a result, your muscles won't get a chance to work to their fullest. (Your elbows might not feel so great, either.)

Benches come in a variety of designs. These are the four most common benches. Some benches can be adjusted to serve all four functions.

- **Flat:** A flat bench looks like a long, narrow piano bench, only with padding and metal legs. See the Dumbbell Chest Press exercise in Chapter 9 for an example.

- **Vertical:** A vertical bench looks like a really formal chair — with the seat back straight up. You wouldn't want to sit in one of these at the dinner table, but they're quite comfortable for weight lifting. The back support prevents you from straining your lower back muscles during exercises that you perform while sitting up. The Dumbbell Shoulder Press, shown in Chapter 10, uses this type of bench.

- **Incline:** The seat back of an incline bench is usually adjustable so that you can lie flat, sit up straight, or position yourself at any angle in between. (The angle you choose determines which muscles are emphasized.) The Incline Chest Fly, shown in Chapter 9, uses this type of bench.

- **Decline:** A decline bench is sloped downward so that you're lying with your legs higher than your head (the same direction that the bed was sloped at a ski condo Suzanne recently rented). A decline bench is primarily used to strengthen the lower portion of the chest muscles. We describe a few decline chest exercises as "options" in Chapter 9. Most lifters don't do much decline work because getting in and out of the position is awkward, especially when you're holding weights.

Weight lifting accessories

Here's a rundown of items that people carry in their gym bags. Even if you never set foot in a health club, these accessories can make your workouts more comfortable and, in some cases, safer.

✔ **Gloves:** Weight lifting gloves have padded palms, and the tops of the fingers are cut off. They prevent your hands from callusing and can prevent your hands from slipping off a bar. They also look cool. See Chapter 26 for details about gloves.

You may want to use weight lifting pads instead of gloves. These are spongy rubber squares or circles that you place in the palm of your hands like pot holders while you lift. Some people feel that pads offer more control than gloves because more of your hand is in contact with the weight. However, they're not as convenient as gloves because you have to carry them around as you work out. (Some come with clips so you can hook them to your shorts.)

✔ **Belts:** The controversy in the fitness community rages on: To wear a belt or not to wear a belt? Proponents of weight lifting belts maintain that belts protect your lower back. Opponents counter that a belt is like a crutch. If the belt does all the work to keep your body stable, then your abdominal and back muscles won't develop to their fullest potential, and you may end up with back problems down the line.

Who's right? We're not fond of belts. Although many casual lifters swear by them, we think that you don't need one unless you're a serious power lifter. Your abdominal and lower-back muscles will benefit from the work they do to support you during a lift.

✔ **Shoes:** Wear athletic shoes that have plenty of cushioning and ankle support. On occasion we see people wearing thongs or loafers when they lift weights. If you drop a weight when you're wearing sandals, your toes have NO protection. (Shockingly, some exercise books show people lifting weights in bare feet.) And if you wear shoes without rubber soles, your footing won't be secure enough. We've even seen weight-lifting videos in which the models wear high heels. We cringe at the thought of what these people are doing to their ankles and knees — and the accidents waiting to happen when they pick up a heavy weight and lose their balance.

✔ **Clothing:** Suzanne made the mistake of wearing running shorts to her first weight lifting session. The error became apparent when the trainer told her to hop on the outer-thigh machine, which required spreading her legs. The lesson: Wear tight shorts. Or at least long ones. On top, wear a T-shirt or tank top. Forget the multilayered, northern Alaska look, and certainly don't wear one of those vinyl exercise suits. Heavy clothing only traps your sweat and leads to dehydration; it can also impede your movement and hide mistakes in your posture that you'd be able to see if you weren't dressed for an expedition to the North Pole.

✔ **A towel:** Do you want to lie down in a pool of someone else's sweat? We didn't think so. Be courteous. Use a towel to frequently wipe off your body and the equipment you use.

✔ **A water bottle:** Every gym has a drinking fountain, but you'll drink more water while weight lifting if you have a bottle by your side. If you exercise at home, a water bottle is a must.

✔ **A weight training log:** Recording your workouts in a journal keeps you motivated and helps you assess your fitness goals. For suggestions on what to write down, see Chapter 3.

Don't Be Afraid of Weight Machines

Attach a few bars onto a large metal frame, add a cable and a pulley or two, weld a seat and a few pads onto your creation, and presto! A weight machine is born. Of course, weight lifting machines are a bit more sophisticated than this definition suggests, but you get the idea. There are countless ways to put these various elements together — flip through Part III and you'll see that weight machines look wildly different. Here's a look at the varieties of machines:

- **Weight-stack machines:** Traditional weight machines have a stack of rectangular weight plates, each weighing 5 to 20 pounds. Each plate has a hole in it; to lift 50 pounds, you stick a metal pin in the hole of the weight plate marked *50*. When you perform the exercise — by pushing or pulling on a set of handles or levers — the machine picks up the plate marked 50, plus all of the plates above it. These machines are great time-savers because it's so simple to change the amount of weight you're lifting.

- **Plate-loaded machines:.** Plate-loaded machines are a hybrid of traditional machines and free weights. They have a large frame and protect you from dropping any weight onto the floor, but they aren't attached to a stack of weight plates; instead, you place any number of round weight plates onto large pegs.

  We think some of these plate-loaded machines are gimmicky. They offer no benefits over traditional machines — unless you happen to enjoy carrying weight plates around the gym. However, we do like the plate-loaded machines that let you work each side of your body separately. We also like the varieties that have "free-floating" levers. Instead of forcing you to move through a fixed pathway, the machines let you move pretty much any way you want. These machines mimic the feel of free weights (for the most part) while retaining most of the safety benefits of a weight machine.

- **Hydraulic and air pressure machines:** This is another machine category that doesn't have a weight stack. Hydraulic and air pressure machines have a series of pistons that create resistance by pumping oil, gas, or fluid. These machines are fine — some are very well designed — but some exercisers don't feel motivated when they use them because there is no weight stack moving up and down or any clanging of steel. All you hear is a sound that's similar to a can of hair spray in action. You tend to see these machines at larger gyms with a wide variety of different equipment. Gyms with limited space or budgets don't usually spring for these.

- **Electronic machines:** These high-tech contraptions may be the future of weight machines. Some varieties, such as TechnoGym, have computers built right in. You swipe an ID card into the machine, which automatically sets the resistance based on your last workout. As you do your set, the machine sends you technique tips. Other electronic systems, such as Fitlinxx, are attached to regular weight training machines. You punch in a code and the machine retrieves your personal information.

The advantage of electronic machines is that they store all of your information. This feature is great for beginners, who may be too overwhelmed to remember how much they lifted last time. These systems also run a variety of extensive reports so that you can analyze your training in depth. For instance, you can compare your progress on the Leg Press to your progress on the Leg Extension. Serious athletes may find this information useful.

However, what's new isn't always better. Electronic machines slow down the pace of the gym and remove some of the human element involved in working out. Instead of interacting with the staff and other members, you interact with a machine. Also, if the system goes down, the repair process generally takes longer than it does with your basic weight-stack machine. And, the electronic systems aren't connected with free weights, so computer-dependent lifters may be discouraged from experimenting with dumbbells and barbells.

Smith machines and power cages

Make special note of two contraptions that come in handy for some of the advanced exercises shown in Chapter 14.

✔ **The Smith machine:** The Smith machine — named for an influential 1970s fitness figure named Randy Smith — features a regular free-weight bar trapped inside a track so that the bar must travel straight up and down. The Smith machine increases the safety of exercises such as bench presses, overhead lifts, and squats because you don't have to worry about the bar wobbling or slipping from your grip. At the same time, the machine retains the feel of free weights. Many Smith machines possess another safety feature: self-spotting pins jutting out from the frame. These pins prevent the bar from being lowered below a certain point, so there's no chance you'll get crushed under the bar if the weight is too heavy.

Smith machines use a traditional 45-pound bar, but in some cases the bar is balanced on springs to negate most or all of its weight.

The purpose is to add smoothness to the movement. Many lifters don't like this feature because it takes away from the macho spirit of weight lifting. Also, the movement is a bit too smooth, removing all of the coordination and extra muscle usage associated with lifting free weights.

✔ **The Power Cage:** A power cage is a large steel frame with a series of stanchions affixed to the sides. You stand in the center of the cage and place your bar on the stanchions that are at the right height for your lift. A power cage doesn't offer as much safety as a Smith machine because once you lift the bar from the stanchions, you're on your own. Still, the cage does offer an extra measure of protection during heavy lifts or lifts that require a lot of balance. And if your muscles give out, the stanchions catch the weight before it crashes to the floor.

What weight machines can do for you

Like every machine ever invented, from the Cuisinart to the calculator, weight machines are designed to provide advantages over the low-tech contraptions that came before. Here are some of the ways that weight machines can top dumbbells and barbells:

- **Weight machines are safe.** There's no chance they'll come crashing down on you, so you need less instruction and supervision than you do with free weights.

- **Weight machines are easy to use.** Machines don't require much balance or coordination, so you can get the hang of an exercise more quickly. Also, you're more likely to use proper form because the machine provides so much guidance. However, machines don't guarantee good form. You can still butcher an exercise on a machine, which can lead to injury or at the very least cheat your muscles out of a good workout.

- **Weight machines enable you to *isolate* a muscle group.** In other words, machines enable you to hone in on one muscle group to the exclusion of all others. For example, very few free weight exercises isolate your hamstrings, your rear thigh muscles. Usually, you can't exclude other muscles — such as your front thighs, butt, or lower back — from getting involved.

  On the other hand, numerous machines can isolate your hamstrings. This feature of weight machines is helpful if you have a particular weakness or are trying to build up one body part.

- **Weight machines help you whip through your workout in minutes.** You put in the pin, do the exercise, then move to the next machine. This process also makes it easy to work out with a friend who is either stronger or weaker — you don't have to load or unload weight plates off a bar. But keep in mind that you do need to adjust each machine to fit your body. In Chapter 2, we explain how to adjust machines.

- **Weight machines challenge your muscles throughout the entire motion of an exercise.** Many (although not all) modern-day weight machines compensate for the fact that your muscles aren't equally strong throughout a particular motion. Consider the Triceps Kickback exercise, shown in Chapter 11. This exercise is relatively easy at the start, but by the time your arm is halfway straightened out, your muscle is being challenged a lot more. By the end, your triceps again has better leverage, so you finish feeling strong.

Weight machines can manipulate the resistance at various points in the exercise by using a kidney-shaped gizmo called a *cam*. When you're at a weak point during the exercise, the cam lightens the load. When your muscle has good mechanical advantage, the cam gives it more work to do. This way, your muscles are working to their fullest throughout the motion. Otherwise, you're limited to a weight you can move only at your weakest point, as you are with free weights.

Arthur Jones, inventor of Nautilus machines, was the first person to use the cam in exercise machines, and he became a multimillionaire for it. The term *Nautilus machine* has become a generic term like *Band-Aid* or *Jell-O.* When people refer to Nautilus machines, they may be talking about any one of the major brands, including Cybex, Body Masters, Hammer Strength, Galileo, or Icarian.

Cable machines: A different breed

Not all machines use a cam. A class of contraptions called cable machines use a typical round pulley. A *cable machine* is basically a vertical metal beam, called a *tower,* with a pulley attached. You can adjust the height of the pulley so that it's close to the floor, up over your head, or anywhere in between. Some cable machines have two towers (for an example, see the Cable Crossover exercise shown in Chapter 9). Cable machines are more versatile than Nautilus-type machines. Clip a new handle onto the pulley and you instantly create a new exercise.

Consider the Triceps Pushdown, described in Chapter 11. Pressing down with a rope feels considerably different than pressing down with a V-shaped bar. You may prefer one attachment over the other, or you may want to use both for variety. See the sidebar, "Cable attachments," for a rundown of the most popular attachments. In Part III of the book, we recommend certain attachments for certain exercises.

Stretching Your Workout

Giant rubber bands and rubber tubes provide resistance for just pennies. You can't get as strong or measure your progress as precisely as you can with machines and free weights, but bands do challenge your muscles in different and effective ways. For example, bands provide resistance during both the up and down motions of an exercise. With most free weight and weight machine exercises, on the other hand, you typically feel resistance only during the lifting portion of the exercise.

Rubber bands and tubes are also convenient and portable. (You can't exactly pack a bunch of dumbbells into your overnight bag.) If you don't have access to machines, bands are a great supplement to free weights because they allow you to do exercises that just aren't possible with dumbbells and bars. Chapter 25 shows you ten exercises that you can perform with bands and tubes.

Cable attachments

At most gyms, you see a large heap of metal bars and handles sitting in a plastic container or milk crate. This may look like a pile of junk, but actually it's more like a treasure chest. By attaching these handles to a cable pulley, you create an unlimited variety of exercises.

Some people are afraid to go near this pile, so they simply settle for using whatever bar happens to already be attached to the cable. But if you frequently switch the handles, your workout will be a lot more fun. Here's a rundown of the most popular cable attachments:

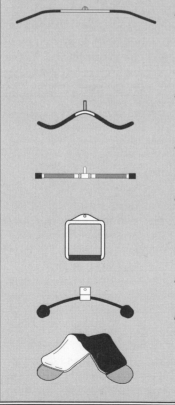

✔ **Long bar:** These bars come in various lengths and are commonly used for back exercises that involve pulling the bar to your chest, such as the Lat Pulldown, shown in Chapter 8. You can pull these bars with an underhand or overhand grip, and you can place your hands as far apart or as close together as you like.

✔ **Curved short bar:** Some of these are U-shaped and some are V-shaped. Both varieties are used almost exclusively for triceps exercises, such as the Triceps Pushdown.

✔ **Straight short bar:** This bar is used in triceps exercises, biceps curls, and rows. We especially like to use this bar for the Triceps Pushdown and the seated Cable Row.

✔ **Horseshoe:** Unlike with the other bars, you grasp the horseshoe with one hand. It's used for numerous chest, arm, and back exercises in which you work each side individually. Try the horseshoe with the Triceps Pushdown, the seated Cable Row, and the Cable Lateral Raise.

✔ **Rope:** This attachment is most commonly used for triceps exercises such as the Triceps Pushdown.

✔ **Ankle collar:** You clip this wide leather ankle bracelet to the pulley to perform exercises such as leg lifts, back kicks, and leg curls. It's great for strengthening your inner and outer thighs while you're standing. We don't use the ankle collar in this book, but a trainer can fill you in.

Lifting Your Body Weight

Why is it that certain exercises can be quite challenging even though you're not holding any weights or using a machine? (The Lunge, shown in Chapter 13, is a good example.) In these cases, you're not lifting *no* weight, you're lifting your body weight. With a number of exercises, moving your own body weight offers plenty of resistance, especially for beginners.

The effectiveness of a no-equipment exercise depends on how much of your weight you actually have to move, and how hard you have to work to overcome the force of gravity. Consider the Push-up, shown in Chapter 9. In the *Military* version, you have to push your entire body upward, directly against the force of gravity. The *Modified* version, where you're balanced on your knees rather than your toes, factors out the weight of your legs so that the exercise is easier. Neither exercise requires you to hold a weight, but both versions can be tough.

Chapter 2

How to Avoid Dropping a Weight on Your Toe and Other Safety Tips

• •

In This Chapter

▶ The universal laws of weight lifting

▶ The art of spotting and being spotted

▶ Avoiding injury while lifting weights

▶ What to do if you are injured

• •

Suzanne has a grandmother who refuses to believe that weight lifting is safe. Speaking to this woman, you would think that hoisting a 20-pound barbell is a risk on par with operating a wood chipper without safety goggles.

Forget what Grandma says. The truth is, there's nothing inherently unsafe about weight machines or barbells. It's what you *do* with these contraptions that can leave you with smashed toes, ripped hamstrings, and torn tendons. If you pay attention, use good form, and don't get too macho about how much weight you lift, you can go for years without even a minor injury. In fact, one of the best reasons to lift weights in the first place is to *reduce* your risk of injury in daily life by strengthening your muscles and bones. Follow the safety tips in this chapter, and you'll walk out of the weight room the same way you entered it: in one piece and under your own power.

The Universal, Immutable Safety Laws of Weight Lifting

We said that weight training is safe, but this doesn't mean that you won't feel occasional muscle soreness — especially if you're new to the game or haven't worked out in a while. A little bit of post-workout soreness is okay; chances are, you'll feel the tightness or achiness 24 to 48 hours after your workout, rather than right away. (This is called Delayed Onset Muscle Soreness, for those of you who feel more comfortable when your pain has a name.) The following guidelines can help you keep this soreness to a minimum.

Warm up before you lift

Before you pick up even a 2-pound dumbbell, you need to warm up your muscles with at least five minutes of easy aerobic exercise. Your warm-up increases the temperature of your muscles, making them more pliable and therefore less susceptible to injury. If you have a particularly heavy weight workout planned, warm up for 10 minutes. Active Isolated stretching (AI), a technique we explain in Chapter 19, is also an acceptable way to warm up.

Walking, jogging, stairclimbing, and stationary biking are excellent warm-up activities for the muscles south of your waistline. But to prepare your upper body muscles, you need to add extra arm movements to these activities. So, swing your arms fairly vigorously as you walk, jog, or use the stairclimber. When you ride the stationary bike, gently roll your shoulders, circle your arms, and reach across the center of your body. Better yet, use an aerobic machine that exercises your entire body, such as a rower, cross-country ski machine, or stationary bike with arm handles. (Many gyms have the Cybex Upper Body Ergometer; ask a trainer where you can find the U.B.E.)

Start with an easy set

If you're planning to do more than one set of an exercise, start by performing 8 to 10 repetitions with a very light weight. A warm-up set is like a dress rehearsal for the real thing, a way of reminding your muscles to hit their marks when you go live. Even monstrously huge bodybuilders do warm-up sets. Sometimes you'll see a human hunk of muscle bench-pressing with just the 45-pound bar. Just as you're thinking, "What a wimp," he piles on so many weight plates that the bar starts groaning. Then you realize: That first set was just his warm-up.

Lighten up

If you go too heavy, you may lose control of the weight and drop it on yourself or on someone else. Or you may strain so hard to lift the weight that you tear a muscle. Or you may end up so sore that you can barely lift your feet up high enough to climb stairs.

Observe the speed limit

Lifting weights too quickly is a good way to injure yourself. When you're pressing, pushing, lifting, or extending at the speed of a greyhound, you can't stop mid-rep if weight plates come loose, you're positioned incorrectly, or something just doesn't feel right. So take at least two seconds to lift a weight and two seconds to lower it. Some experts feel you should move even slower than that. If you're causing any banging and clanging, slow down your pace.

Don't hold your breath

We're not suggesting you should inhale and exhale with the gusto of a Lamaze student, but on the other hand, don't hold your breath. Lifting weights temporarily causes your blood pressure to shoot up, which normally isn't a problem. But when you hold your breath, your blood pressure rises even higher — and then suddenly comes crashing down. This drastic drop may cause you to pass out and, if you have a heart condition, could put you in serious jeopardy.

Use proper form

In addition to heeding the general safety tips we present here, be sure to follow the specific tips we give you for each exercise. Even subtle form mistakes, such as overarching your back or cocking your wrist the wrong way, can lead to injury.

Cool down

If you've done a fairly fast-paced weight workout (such as a weight circuit, described in Chapter 15), complete the workout with five minutes of slow aerobic exercise. The aerobic cool-down gives your pulse, blood pressure, and breathing a chance to slow down before you hit the showers. If you've been lifting weights at more of a plodding pace, with plenty of rest between sets, a few minutes of stretching can suffice as a cool-down. Ending your workout with an easy set also helps you cool down.

Rest a muscle at least 48 hours

You're welcome to lift weights on consecutive days — just don't exercise the *same muscle* two days in a row. When you lift weights, you tear apart your muscle cells. They need a rest day to repair themselves so that they come back even stronger. If you ignore this rule, weight lifting may make you weaker rather than stronger. At the very least, your muscles will feel too tired to perform at peak operating levels. In Chapter 16, we explain how you can lift weights four to six days a week without ever hitting the same muscle group on consecutive days.

Weight Machine Safety Tips

One of the selling points of weight machines is that they're safer than free weights. And it's true — you're in no danger of being crushed by a 100-pound barbell. Still, if you're not careful, you can injure yourself.

Custom fit each machine

Some machines require a single adjustment, such as the seat height. Others require two or more adjustments: For instance, with some versions of the Leg Extension Machine exercise, shown in Chapter 13, you have to adjust the back rest as well as the leg bar. Don't worry, you don't need a plumber's license to adapt these machines to your body. Usually, you just pull a pin out of a hole, lower or raise the seat, and then put the pin back in place. Some machines are so simple to adjust that they don't even involve a pin. With practice, fitting the machine to your body becomes second nature.

Don't get lazy about making adjustments. Using a weight machine that doesn't fit your body is like driving a car while sitting in the back seat: uncomfortable, if not downright dangerous. When you strain to reach a handle or sit with your knees digging into your chest, you're at risk for pulling a muscle or wrenching a joint. After you make an adjustment, jiggle the seat or the back-rest to make sure you've locked it securely in place. You don't want the seat to suddenly drop to the floor with you on it.

Watch your fingers

Occasionally, a machine's weight stack gets stuck in midair. Don't try to rectify the situation yourself by fiddling with the plates. Instead, call a staff member for help. We once saw a gym member try to fix a weight stack himself. The thing came crashing down, sandwiching his fingers between the weight plates. We've seen other people get clumps of hair caught in the stacks. And we heard about a guy who got his genitals stuck between weight plates. We don't know the details and don't want to, but we did hear the story from a reliable equipment dealer who witnessed the ordeal.

Buckle up

If a machine has a seat belt, use it. The seat belt prevents you from wasting any muscle power squirming around to stay in place as you move the bar or lever of the machine. You're most likely to find seat belts on older models of the inner/outer thigh, pullover, seated leg curl, and triceps dip machines.

Don't invent new uses for the machinery

You wouldn't use your best sweater to dust the house, right? You wouldn't use your television as a step-stool to reach the top cupboard. So don't use a chest machine to strengthen your legs. People are constantly inventing new — and unsafe — ways to use weight machines. For example: In order to release the chest bar on the Vertical Chest Press machine (described in Chapter 9), you must use your feet to press down on a bar near the floor. Well, we've seen people ignore the chest press altogether and use this floor bar to exercise their thighs or arms. If you dream up new uses for a machine, you may be asking for injuries.

Free Weight Safety Tips

We know one guy who arched his back so severely over years of bench-pressing that he finally was forced to retire as a police officer. So keep in mind the following during your free weight workouts:

- ✔ **Use proper form when you lift a weight off the rack.** Always bend from your knees — not your hips — when you lift a dumbbell or barbell off a rack or when you lift a weight plate off a weight tree. Get in close to the rack and keep your arms bent. Figure 2-1 shows you how not to lift a weight off the rack.

- ✔ **Pay attention when carrying weights around.** Always hold heavier weight plates with *two* hands (as shown in Chapter 24), and keep the plates close to your body when you carry them. When you carry bar-bells, watch where you're going. Making a U-turn while hauling around a 7-foot bar can cause some serious destruction. When carrying a dumb-bell in each hand, keep your elbows slightly bent.

- ✔ **Use collars.** As we explain in Chapter 1, a collar is a clamp-like device that you use to secure a weight plate onto a bar. Often, when you per-form a barbell exercise, the bar tilts slightly to one side; without a collar, the plates may slide right off and land on somebody's toes or crash into the mirrors on the wall. We know one woman who was knocked uncon-scious when a collar flew off a guy's weight bar and hit her in the head.

- ✔ **Don't drop weights onto the floor.** After you complete a dumbbell exer-cise on a bench (such as the Chest Fly or Dumbbell Chest Press, described in Chapter 9), bring the weights to your chest and then gently rock yourself up into a sitting position. Some people simply let go of the weights, which is not only unnerving to the other gym members but is also unsafe.

- ✔ **Safely return weights to the rack.** When you finish using dumbbells, barbells, or weight plates, don't just lean straight over with locked knees and plunk the weights back on the rack. Bend your knees, pull your abdominals in, and hold the weights close to your body before you release them. And be careful not to smash your fingers when placing the weights back on the rack. We've done that. Ouch!

Figure 2-1:
The wrong
way to lift
weights
from the
rack.

The Art of Spotting and Being Spotted

A spotter is someone who stands close by, ready to grab your weights in case your muscles give out. You don't need a spotter hovering over you for every free weight exercise; otherwise you'll feel smothered, as if your mom is chaperoning you on a date. But do call upon a spotter when . . .

✔ **You're trying an exercise for the first time.** Even if you're not lifting much weight, the weights may wobble when you perform a new movement. A spotter can gently help guide you through the motion until you have the confidence and the muscle memory to do it yourself.

✔ **You're attempting a heavier weight than usual.** If you've never bench pressed 100 pounds, try it first in the presence of a spotter. The moment the bar comes crashing down on your chest is not a good time to find out you weren't ready for the lift. Lifting heavy weights without a spotter is a lot like a trapeze artist working without a safety net. You may be fine the first nine times, but the tenth time. . . .

✔ **You want to eke out extra reps.** Sometimes you're just not sure whether you have one more repetition in you. If you have a spotter, there's no danger in trying. A spotter also can help you with machine exercises, assisting you, for instance, on the last few inches of a heavy Leg Curl or Arm Curl.

Briefing your spotter

Prepare your spotter for the mission ahead. Explain how many repetitions you're aiming to complete and how many reps you think that you can do before you'll need the spotter's assistance. Be honest! If you think you may need a spot on the sixth repetition, say so. This way, your spotter can start paying extra close attention around the fourth rep.

Also, make it clear to your spotter whether you need help lifting the bar off the rack or getting the dumbbells into position. If so, you need to set up a specific plan, like whether the spotter will help you *on* the count of three or *after* the count of three. Tiny misunderstandings can lead to big injuries.

Something else you need to tell your spotter: Thank you. Offer your gratitude both before and after your set.

When you're the spotter

When people recruit you as a spotter, you have a big responsibility to perform your job correctly. So be realistic. If you weigh 90 pounds soaking wet, don't attempt to spot someone doing a 350-pound Bench Press. If you have any doubt you can pull it off, don't take on the assignment. The moment that the lifter's arms give out is not the moment to realize you're out of your league.

If you do accept the job, pay close attention so that you are ready at the precise moment your spottee needs help. You know it's time to step in when the weight stops moving for more than a split second or if it begins traveling in the wrong direction. Of course, if a lifter screams, "HELP!" that's also an indication you'd better stop scratching your nose. Do not foist a lift-or-die mentality upon your spottee. Just because he or she may have planned to complete five reps doesn't mean that you should withhold assistance if the lifter starts struggling after three. On the other hand, don't offer your spottee too much help too soon. This defeats the purpose of spotting and annoys the heck out of the person being spotted.

Don't lean so close to your spottee that you impede or distract his or her movement. We don't enjoy bench-pressing when someone's face is directly over ours and we can see up the person's nostrils. Finally, be a cheerleader. There's no need to jump up and do the splits, but people appreciate support — and may even lift more weight — if you offer an enthusiastic "You're almost there!" or "It's all you! You've got it!"

Where you stand when spotting someone can make the difference between being a great help and being useless in an emergency. The following list offers spotting tips for a variety of common exercises:

- ✔ **Bench Press:** Stand behind the bench with your hands above or underneath the bar but not touching it. When the lifter needs you, lean in and get a quick grip on the bar.

- ✔ **Chest Fly and Dumbbell Chest Press:** For these dumbbell exercises (and versions performed on an incline bench) place your hands close to the person's wrists, not the weights. (You may see people spot underneath the elbows, which is not a crime but not as safe, either.) When spotting flat-bench chest exercises, kneel on one knee behind the bench and follow the movement with your hands. For incline exercises, you may find it more comfortable to stand with your knees bent.

- ✔ **Barbell Squat:** Stand behind your spottee and be prepared to assist at the hips or underneath the arms. Your spottee may not want to be spotted at the hips unless you happen to be that person's spouse or significant other. If you're squatting with an especially heavy weight, you may want two spotters, one standing on either side of the bar.

- ✔ **Pull-up and Dip:** Stand behind your spottee and offer assistance by holding his or her shins or waist and guiding them upward.

- ✔ **Machine exercises:** Spot at the bar or lever of the machine, never by placing your hand underneath the weight stack. For example, if you're spotting someone on the Cable Row (pictured in Chapter 8), stand slightly behind and to the side of your spottee. Grasp one of the handles and gently assist it the rest of the way.

Common Weight Training Injuries

Accidents happen, even to careful lifters. So, here's a primer on weight training injuries in case you do run into one.

First, some terminology. When you *strain* or *pull* a muscle, you actually overstretch or tear the *tendon,* the tough, cord-like tissue at the ends of the muscle where the muscle tapers off and attaches to the bone. A strain can happen when you push up the bar too forcefully during the Bench Press or stand up too quickly out of the Squat. Strains are often accompanied by a sudden, sharp pain and then a persistent ache.

A *sprain* is something different altogether. It happens not to a muscle but to a joint, such as your ankle or wrist. When you sprain a joint, you have torn or overstretched a *ligament,* the connective tissue that attaches one bone to another. You may feel pain and throbbing and notice some swelling and bruising. You can sprain just about any joint in your body; ankles and wrists seem to take the most beating.

Depending on the severity of the injury, the healing process may take anywhere from a couple of days to a couple of months. If your injury does not appear to be healing, see your doctor. Here's a rundown of injuries commonly caused by lifting weights:

✔ **Torn rotator cuff:** The muscles of your rotator cuff (described in Chapter 10, along with Suzanne's maddening rotator cuff injury) are often injured during Bench Presses and Shoulder Presses. You may have torn your rotator cuff if you feel a persistent ache or a sharp pain deep within your shoulder at a specific point during the exercise. Another sign of a torn rotator cuff is being unable to raise your arm in front of you and over your head. If you have injured your rotator cuff, stop performing any exercises that cause you pain or soreness in that area. To be safe, skip all overhead pressing movements for a while and lighten up your load on the Bench Press. You may also want to limit the distance you move the bar — or skip the exercise altogether. Review your form: Make sure you're not bouncing the weights up and down or taking the exercise past the safe finish point.

The rotator cuff exercises shown in Chapters 10 and 26 can help prevent injuries to these muscles. These exercises are a must if you lift heavy weights, if you lift frequently, or if you participate in a sport that uses the upper body, such as tennis, rock climbing, or swimming.

✔ **Sore knees:** Knee injuries come in so many varieties and have so many different causes that pinpointing the source of the problem can be hard. Often, the injury is caused by something you did outside of the weight room. Still, certain weight training mistakes, such as those described in Chapter 13, are likely culprits. Runners, walkers, and cyclists can ward off many common knee injuries by performing quadriceps exercises.

If any leg exercise causes you pain, skip it or modify it by following our instructions. Some people try to protect their knees from injury by wrapping them in yards of bandages. We don't love the idea of knee wraps unless you're into some serious power lifting. A wrapped knee may mask a problem that needs immediate attention.

To help protect your knees, make sure that you strengthen both your front and rear thigh muscles — the muscles that support your knee joint. Stretching is also very important to keep all of the muscles that surround the knee loose and limber.

✔ **Sore wrists:** Some people injure their wrist muscles by bending their wrists too much when they lift weights, so pay attention in Part III when we describe the proper wrist position for various exercises. To prevent wrist injuries, do Wrist Curls and Reverse Wrist Curls (see Chapter 11) on a regular basis.

✔ **Lower back pain:** If you have a history of back problems, you can just as easily throw out your back reaching for an apple in the fridge as you can pumping iron. But the weight room is an especially great place to trigger an old back injury — or to develop a new one. Always take precautions for your lower back when you lift weights. One important preventive measure (that we mention repeatedly throughout this book) is to pull your abdominals inward. By tightening your abs, you create a sort of natural girdle to support and protect your lower back.

Overcoming Injuries

We don't yet have a cure for the common cold, but we do have a pretty good cure for most minor sprains and strains. It's called RICE, which is an acronym for: Rest, Ice, Compression, and Elevation. RICE is most effective if you begin the process within 48 hours of injuring yourself. Here's a rundown on each of the elements:

✔ **Rest:** Stop doing activities that aggravate your injury. (Notice that we didn't say stop all activity — that's rarely the solution.) Wait until you've had two completely pain-free days before doing exercises that involve the injured area.

✔ **Ice:** Contrary to popular belief, it's ice, not heat, that helps reduce the pain and swelling of most common injuries. Ice your injury for 15 to 20 minutes, three or four times a day, for as long as you feel pain. You can apply ice with a pack, a plastic bag full of cubes, even a package of frozen strawberries. But don't allow ice to sit directly against the skin. (You may end up with ice burns.)

Two areas may not respond well to icing: your neck and back. These injured areas may be so sensitive to the cold that you may tense up. If that's the case, a moist heating pad or wet, warm towel is best for treating the injury.

✔ **Compression:** Put pressure on the injury to keep the swelling down. Use a damp elastic bandage or buy a special brace or wrap for your knee, elbow, or wrist. Wrap it tightly enough that you feel some tension but not so firmly that you cut off your circulation or feel numb.

✔ **Elevation:** Elevating your injured body part drains away fluids and waste products so that the swelling goes down. If you've hurt your ankle, you don't need to lift it up over your head. Propping up your ankle on several pillows or books does the trick.

Sometimes, however, RICE isn't sufficient to treat an injury. If the pain is truly excruciating or is bothersome for more than a few days, it probably needs more aggressive treatment and possibly medical attention. If you experience excessive swelling, discoloration, or bleeding, you may need a trip to the emergency room. Use your judgment. If you see a bone fragment sticking out of your ankle, don't simply stick an ice pack over it.

Chapter 3

Testing Your Strength and Tracking Your Progress

• •

• •

*B*ack in 1912 in the desert town of Wabuska, Nevada, there lived a ranch owner named Harry Warren who was something of a braggart. One day Harry's ranch hands bet their boss $1,100 that he couldn't carry a 120-pound sack of wheat from Wabuska to Yerington, 10 miles away. Harry promptly hoisted the sack onto his shoulders and proved his employees wrong. Every few years since, the town of Yerington has hosted a quasi-reenactment of Harry's feat: the Great American Sack Race. In this event, female participants must complete a 5-mile course with a 50-pound sack perched on their shoulders. Men must carry a 100-pound sack.

We mention this race because Suzanne entered it a few years back, figuring it would provide motivation for her workouts and a good test of her fitness. The Sack Race did indeed provide motivation, particularly after Suzanne shelled out $100 for the entry fee, $80 for new walking shoes, and $50 for the 25-, 40- and 50-pound sacks of chicken feed that she carried around her neighborhood while training.

The race itself was even more of a test than Suzanne had bargained for. As it turned out, the event was a *running* race — a fact that Suzanne learned at the starting line. Somehow — propelled by adrenaline, a strong upper body, and fear of humiliation — Suzanne went on to win the women's division, a feat that earned her $1,000 and an article in the Mason Valley News, known as "The Only Newspaper in the World That Gives a Damn About Yerington."

Now, we're not suggesting that novice weight lifters try out for the Sack Race, the Navy Seals, or the Green Bay Packers, but we do recommend that you put your strength to the test from time to time. Strength tests are particularly important when you begin a weight training program. You need to know your starting point so that you can set realistic goals and design a workout program that reflects your current abilities. In this chapter, we describe a variety of strength tests that are appropriate for beginners, and we explain how to track your progress in a workout diary. Just for fun — and for veteran lifters who want to see how they stack up against the nation's finest — we also include the physical fitness requirements for a handful of law enforcement agencies and branches of the armed forces.

The Safest Way to Test Your Strength

When you start an exercise program, you need to test more than the strength of your muscles. It's also important to evaluate your cardiovascular fitness (on a stationary bike or treadmill, for example), as well as your flexibility. However, considering that this book is called *WEIGHT TRAINING For Dummies,* we're going to focus on tests of muscular strength. You can consult a qualified medical professional or fitness trainer (or our book, *Fitness For Dummies,* also by IDG Books Worldwide, Inc.) for details about other fitness tests.

The term *strength testing* is somewhat of a misnomer. Strictly speaking, your *strength* refers to the maximum amount of weight that you can lift one time — also called your *one-rep max.* For example, if you can squeeze out only one Shoulder Press with 45 pounds, that's your one-rep max for that exercise. In general it's not such a hot idea to go around testing your one-rep maxes, especially if you're a beginner. Some veterans like to go all out sometimes, but they typically test their one-rep max for just one or two exercises in a given workout. Pushing to the max places a lot of stress on your body parts and can cause extreme muscle soreness, even in experienced weight lifters.

A safe alternative to testing all-out muscle strength is testing your *muscular endurance;* you use a lighter-than-max weight and perform as many repetitions as you can. Most health clubs choose to do this type of testing. You can safely test your muscular endurance at home, too.

Table 3-1 contains a list of exercises that you can use to test the muscular endurance of each muscle group. (Actually, you can use any exercise you want, but these are some of our favorites.) We haven't included a machine option for abdominals because we believe that exercises performed on the floor are more effective. The results simply give you a reference point. Strength improves quickly once you begin lifting weights regularly.

We can't tell you how much weight to use for your strength tests because everyone's abilities are different, but we offer this helpful guideline: For each exercise, choose a weight that you think you can lift at least six times. If the weight still feels exceptionally light after six repetitions, put it down and rest a couple of minutes. Then try a weight that's a few pounds heavier.

For exercises that use no weight — such as the Abdominal Crunch and the Push-up — simply perform as many repetitions as you can.

Table 3-1	Sample Exercises to Test Your Strength	
Body Part	*Free Weight Option*	*Machine Option*
Butt and Legs	Squat	Leg Press
Front Thigh	Quad Press	Leg Extension
Rear Thigh	Kneeling Leg Curl	Lying Leg Curl
Calf	One-leg Calf Raise	Standing Calf Raise
Upper Back	One-arm Dumbbell Row	Lat Pulldown
Lower Back	Back Extension	Back Extension on a Bench
Chest	Push-up	Vertical Chest Press
Shoulders	Dumbbell Shoulder Press	Shoulder Press
Biceps	Dumbbell Biceps Curl	Arm Curl
Triceps	Bench Dip	Triceps Dip
Abdominals	Abdominal Crunch	

Once you test your strength, use the results to design a weight training program that will help you reach your goals.

Tracking Your Progress

Lots of people set goals. Many of them even set realistic ones. But too often, people don't fulfill their ambitions — because they didn't stick with their workout program or because their routine was improperly designed. One way to address both problems is to log your workouts in a notebook or weight training diary.

What to write down in your log

Some people benefit so much from recording their weight routines (and cardiovascular workouts) that they do it on a daily basis. Other people find the paperwork annoying and prefer to keep a log for, say, one week every couple of months as a reality check. No matter how often you use your log, jotting down many or all of the following details is a good idea:

- ✔ **Your goals:** At the start of each week, jot down specific workout goals such as, "Push extra hard on back and biceps" or "complete eight Push-ups."

- ✔ **The name of each exercise:** We're talking specifics. Don't just write "chest;" write "Incline Chest Fly" or "Vertical Chest Press." This way, you know whether you're getting enough variety. Plus, you'll be forced to learn the name of each exercise. We know people who have worked out for years and still refer to the Dumbbell Shoulder Press as "that one where you push the dumbbells up."

- ✔ **Sets, reps, and weight:** Note how many repetitions you performed and how much weight you lifted for each set. Suppose that you did three sets of leg curls — first 12 reps with 30 pounds, then 10 reps with 40 pounds, and then 7 reps with 50 pounds. You can note this by writing: "3" in the set column, "12, 10, 7" in the reps column, and "30, 40, 50" in the weight column.

- ✔ **How you're feeling:** We're not asking you to pour out your emotions like a guest on *Oprah*. Just jot down a few words about whether you felt energetic, tired, motivated, and so on. Did you take it easy, or did you act like you were in Basic Training?

- ✔ **Your cardio routine:** Record how much cardiovascular exercise you did — whether it was a half hour walking on the treadmill at 4 miles per hour or 15 minutes on the stairclimber at level 6. Also note whether you did your cardio workout before or after you lifted weights.

- ✔ **Your flexibility routine:** Record the amount of time you spent stretching and how it felt. If you're feeling really ambitious, you can record the names of the stretches or come up with names for your standard stretching routines.

Analyzing your workout log

Your journal gives you positive reinforcement on a daily basis. Watching your progress over time is also a big boost. If two months ago you could barely eke out 10 repetitions using 30 pounds on the Leg Extension machine and now you can easily perform 10 reps using 50 pounds, you know you've accomplished something.

Not only can a diary keep you motivated, but recording your workouts can also help you get better results. If you're dedicating plenty of time to your weight training but aren't getting stronger or more toned, your workout diary may offer clues as to why you're not seeing results. Scrutinize your diary and ask yourself the following questions:

- ✔ **Am I getting enough rest?** Maybe you've been lifting weights every other day, but your body actually needs two rest days between workouts. An extra day of rest may give you more oomph when you lift.

Daily Workout Log

Day of the week	Date			
Goals				
Cardiovascular Training	Time			Distance
Strength Training	Weight	Sets	Reps	Notes
Stretching	Notes			

✔ **Am I working each muscle group hard enough?** Your log may indicate that you've been neglecting a particular muscle group. Maybe you're averaging only four sets per workout for your legs compared to six or seven sets for your other body parts. Perhaps that's the reason your leg strength seems to be lagging.

✔ **Am I getting enough variety in my workout?** When you flip through your diary, maybe you see the words "Biceps Curl" three times a week for the past three months, but you rarely see any other arm exercise. Maybe you've fallen into a rut. You could add new exercises or vary the number of sets and repetitions you've been doing. Or you could mix up the order of your exercises.

✔ **Am I lifting enough weight?** Maybe you never write down the words "tough workout." Perhaps picking up the 10-pound dumbbells for your biceps curls has become such a habit that you forgot to notice that those 10-pounders now feel light.

✔ **Am I doing my cardiovascular exercise before my weights or after?** Maybe you've been doing 30 minutes on the stairclimber before your weight sessions — and are, therefore, pooped out before you even lift a single weight.

Be All That You Can Be

Arresting thugs, steering a submarine, and pulling people out of burning buildings may not be among your aspirations in life. However, you might get a kick out of knowing whether you're strong enough to be a Marine or a fire-fighter. The following sections include tables that show you the physical fitness requirements for a handful of academies.

U.S. Marine Academy

Marines are looking for a few *strong* men and women. Even after you become a Marine, you must continue to take fitness tests periodically. Tables 3-2 and 3-3 outline the performance requirements for men and women in the Marines.

Table 3-2   U.S. Marine Academy Physical Requirements for Men

Activity	Ages 17-26	Ages 27-39	Ages 40-45
Minimum Performance Level			
Pull-ups	3	3	3
Sit-ups (1 minute)	40	35	35
3-mile run	28 minutes	29 minutes	30 minutes

Activity	Ages 17-26	Ages 27-39	Ages 40-45
Superior Scores			
Pull-ups	20	20	20
Sit-ups	80	80	80
3-mile run	18 minutes or less	18 minutes or less	18 minutes or less

Table 3-3 U.S. Marine Academy Physical Requirements for Women

Activity	Ages 17-26	Ages 27-39	Ages 40-45
Minimum Performance Level			
*Flexed-arm hang	16 seconds	13 seconds	10 seconds
Sit-ups (1 minute)	22	19	18
1.5-mile run	15 minutes	16.5 minutes	18 minutes
Superior Scores			
Flexed-arm hang	70 seconds	70 seconds	70 seconds
Sit-ups	50	50	50
1.5-mile run	10 minutes or less	10 minutes or less	10 minutes or less

During the flexed-arm hang, you must remain in uppermost chin-up position, with your arms bent. After your chin lowers underneath the bar, the test is finished.

The United States Air Force

The United States Air Force has a detailed training program that you can either send away for or download from the World Wide Web at www.usafa.af.mil. See Tables 3-4 and 3-5 for some sample tests.

The following list describes the exercises in the USAF physical fitness tests:

- ✔ **Pull-ups:** Start from a full hang and grip the bar with your hands about shoulder-width apart. No rocking, kicking, or cheating allowed.
- ✔ **Sit-ups:** Do as many bent-knee Sit-ups as you can do in two minutes.
- ✔ **Push-ups:** Perform Military Push-ups as described in Chapter 14.

Table 3-4	USAF Candidate Fitness Test Data for Men	
Exercise	Minimum	Average
Pull-ups	4	10
Sit-ups (2 minutes)	49	69
Push-ups (2 minutes)	24	41
300-Yard Shuttle Run	*65 Sec	*60 Sec

*Maximum time limit

Table 3-5	USAF Candidate Fitness Test Data for Women	
Exercise	Minimum	Average
Pull-ups	1	2
Sit-ups (2 minutes)	46	68
Push-ups (2 minutes)	9	24
300-Yard Shuttle Run	*79 Sec	*69 Sec

The Seattle Fire Department

Here are the physical requirements that the last American heroes must meet to win the privilege of saving lives and hauling hundreds of pounds of equipment into burning buildings. These standards apply to both men and women. Applicants must do the following:

- Complete a steep Incline Press (Shoulder Press about 30 degrees below vertical) with a 95-pound barbell. Arms must be fully extended.

- Perform a Biceps Curl with an 85-pound barbell, arms fully extended and back and shoulders against the wall.

- Lift an 80-pound ladder mounted five feet high, carry the ladder 40 feet, and place it on a sawhorse.

- Hoist 80 pounds of equipment to the seventh floor of a building, either alternating hands or yanking with both hands at once.

- Run up seven flights of stairs with an 85-pound hose while wearing a 25-pound mask.

STREND: A New Trend

We know muscleheads around who couldn't run three miles even if it meant a lifetime supply of protein bars and wiry speedsters who couldn't bench press a broomstick. But it's a rare person who has both strength and endurance. If you're one of these people, you may want to try a STREND competition (or at least test yourself at home). *STREND* is an acronym and registered trademark derived from the first three letters of the words *STRength* and *ENDurance*. The STREND Fitness Challenge was founded in 1992, to test those who practice both strength and cardiovascular disciplines.

The STREND Fitness Challenge consists of six events. The first five test upper-body muscular strength: Bench Press, Pull-up, Shoulder Press, Chin-up, and Bar Dip. (For Chin-ups, your palms are facing you and close together; for Pull-ups, you hold the bar a little wider than shoulder width with palms facing away. The Shoulder Press is performed behind the neck — a variation that we think is extremely risky. In fact, Suzanne seriously injured her rotator cuff training for this very event.) The sixth event — a three-mile run — tests cardiovascular endurance. Your *STREND Factor* is determined by adding up the number of repetitions performed correctly for the five upper-body tests and then dividing that total by your time in the run. The greater your STREND Factor, the better you place in the competition and the larger your trophy.

The competition has three divisions: Elite, Open, and Basic. The Basic division is intended for people who are unable to perform an unassisted Pull-up, Chin-up, or Bar Dip. Entrants in the Basic category use specially designed equipment to perform modified versions of these exercises. For each of the strength tests, all competitors must lift a weight based on a percentage of their body weights. Competitors have three minutes per event to perform as many consecutive repetitions as possible. They use the remainder of the three minutes to rest for the next event. After the final strength test, the contestants rest three minutes and then run three miles on a circular track.

Tables 3-6 and 3-7 indicate how much weight you must lift depending on your gender and the division you enter.

Table 3-6   STREND Competition Weight Requirements for Males

Based on percentages of body weight

Test	Elite	Open	Basic
Bench Press	115%	100%	50%
Pull-up	115%	100%	modified
Shoulder Press	60%	50%	30%
Chin-up	115%	100%	modified
Bar Dip	125%	100%	modified

Table 3-7 STREND Competition Weight Requirements for Females

Based on percentages of body weight

Test	Elite	Open	Basic
Bench Press	80%	50%	30%
Pull-up	100%	100%	modified
Shoulder Press	40%	30%	20%
Chin-up	100%	100%	modified
Bar Dip	100%	100%	modified

Part II

Weight Training Wisdom

In this part . . .

Part II is free of technical mumbo jumbo. This part helps you decide whether to lift weights at home or at a gym and shows how to save money either way. We recommend strength equipment to fit every budget and caution you against health club hucksters. We help you choose a weight training mentor, whether you go for a personal trainer, a body-sculpting teacher, or an exercise video instructor. We also give you the lowdown on weight training etiquette: Just because you may be wearing tight shorts, dripping with sweat, and stinking up the joint doesn't mean that you can't show some courtesy.

Chapter 4

Joining a Gym or Exercising at Home: Which Is for You?

. . . .

In This Chapter

▶ Choosing a health club

▶ Designing a home gym

▶ Buying free weights and machines

▶ Lifting weights when you travel

▶ Buying rubber exercise bands

. . . .

*I*s it better to lift weights at a health club or at home? That's like asking whether it's better to drive a half-ton pickup truck or a four-door sedan. The answer depends on your personal needs.

In this chapter, we help you decide whether to invest in a gym membership or weight equipment for your home — or to cover your bases and do both. We help you size up a health club's equipment, staff, atmosphere, and facilities, and we tell you how to avoid getting suckered by an unscrupulous salesperson. On the home-gym front, we help you decide which gadgets to buy, where to shop, and how much to spend.

Join the Club

For the uninitiated, walking into a health club for the first time can be plenty intimidating. Californian Kim Smith laughs when she recalls her first visit to the club she now belongs to. "I was sure that everyone was staring at me — I could feel the walls closing in. I looked at the equipment and said, 'No way. I can't do it.' I thought I'd break the machines and they'd make me pay for them." Even though the club's staff treated her kindly, she was too overwhelmed to join. "I walked out and said I'd be back on Monday," Smith recalls. "But I didn't come back until four years later."

You may feel overwhelmed when you walk into a club, but don't let those feelings prevent you from signing up. Within a few sessions, your terror of the triceps machine will seem unwarranted, and the club will start to seem as familiar as your own neighborhood. Here are a few of the many great reasons to become a health club member:

- **Equipment choices:** Even if you buy a top-notch multigym for your home, it's going to have only one or two stations for training each muscle. At a health club, you may have a half dozen machines for your back muscles alone, including newfangled contraptions that haven't yet reached the consumer market or are too expensive or too large for home use.

- **Advice:** At a good gym you have staff members walking around who can remind you how to do the perfect Back Extension or how to adjust the calf machine. You also have a room full of members with healthy egos who love to spew advice.

- **Safety:** Weight training isn't inherently dangerous, but if you do happen to get stuck underneath a 100-pound barbell, at least you have people around to rescue you. You also have plenty of spotters to choose from; at home your only option may be to drag your uninterested spouse in from watching *The Sopranos*. As we explain in Chapter 2, you want a spotter with a bit more enthusiasm than that.

- **Motivation:** Once you're inside a health club, you've eliminated all of your excuses not to exercise. There's no laundry that suddenly needs to be folded, no hard drive that needs defragging this instant, no lint crying out to be picked up off the rug. Pretty much your only option is to work out. Besides, the atmosphere of a club makes you *want* to work out. You see people of all shapes and sizes pumping and pushing and pulling, and you can't help but be inspired to do the same.

- **Cost:** A typical health club membership costs $250 to $2,000 a year, depending on where you live and what type of facilities the club offers. Home weight equipment may cost you less over a period of years, but unless you're *a* Silicon Valley multimillionaire you probably can't afford to update your equipment as often as health clubs replace their contraptions. In order to stay competitive, many gyms turn over at least some of their equipment every year, if not more often. So if you like having new toys to play with, joining a gym is a good idea.

- **Relaxation:** Ironically, a health club may be just the remedy for busy people who say that they don't have time to go to one. At the gym, you're free from stress and distractions. The phone doesn't ring. Your kids don't beg you to watch *The Lion King* for the 127th time. Your boss can't assign you a last-minute report.

- **Other facilities:** Weight training is only one component of fitness. As we explain in Chapter 18, aerobic exercise is equally important. At a gym, you have an array of treadmills, stationary bikes, stairclimbers, and other elliptical trainers. You might also find a sauna, a steam room, a swimming pool, and a snack bar that serves fresh-fruit smoothies.

Lifting Weights at Home

Great as we think health clubs are, they're not the right choice for everybody. Here's when to consider working out at home:

✔ **You live too far from a gym.** Although there are more than 13,000 fitness centers in this country, not everybody lives near one of them. If you don't live or work within 10 minutes of a club, lifting weights at home may be your best option. Or if you can afford it, join a club that you can get to on days when you have time, but also invest in some basic weight equipment at home for days when you're too busy to make the drive.

✔ **Your schedule.** If your club doesn't have child care or you can't leave the house for some other reason, buying your own equipment makes sense. The same applies if you work wacky hours and the gym's schedule doesn't jibe with yours. If your den is equipped with dumbbells and a bench, you can exercise at 4 a.m. on Sunday if you want.

✔ **You're self-conscious.** If you can't bear the thought of exercising in front of other people — or just need a little time to get used to what you look like in a pair of athletic shorts — by all means, work out at home. Videos (or a trainer) can give you instruction and help keep you motivated. However, don't let self-consciousness keep you away from a club for too long if you have other compelling reasons to go. For the most part, health club members are too busy looking at themselves in the mirror to notice what you look like.

✔ **You don't like crowds.** Some people simply like to be alone with their dumbbells.

Choosing a Health Club

Many people have no choice. If your neighborhood has only one club, that's the one you probably need to join, even if the facilities aren't top-notch. You're more likely to use the mediocre club around the corner than the first-rate gym that's 45 minutes away. If you learn a routine of basic exercises, you can get a good workout in just about any facility that calls itself a gym.

Of course, there are exceptions: Suzanne once was in the weight room on the ship of a cheap cruise line that shall remain nameless. The dumbbells weren't marked, so you had to pick up each weight and say, "Well, this *seems* like it weighs about 20 pounds." Worse, some dumbbells were missing their mates, so you couldn't do exercises like chest presses or lateral raises. The experience was so frustrating that Suzanne abandoned her workout and instead went to try karaoke in the Tahiti lounge.

Don't be scared off by the name of a health club or the size of the people who work out there. Among the general public, Gold's Gym franchises seem to have a reputation of catering only to serious bodybuilders. In reality, Gold's clubs — like any other chain clubs — cater to people of all ages and ability levels. We know a 94-year-old woman who belonged to a Gold's Gym in Sacramento. Sure, some gyms attract more serious lifters than others, but believe us, at virtually every gym in America, there are people like you. Besides, you can learn a lot from hanging around veteran lifters.

On the other hand, if you do have a choice of clubs, weigh your options carefully. When you tour a club, you may want to bring the following checklist of factors to consider. Walking into a new gym can be overwhelming, and you may get distracted while fending off a relentless sales pitch. Take your time: Don't let your tour guide rush you through the weight room or the locker area. Here are some points to keep in mind as you consider joining a gym:

- **Hours of operation:** Some gyms are open 24 hours a day, seven days a week; others close at noon on weekends. Make sure that the hours of operation fit your schedule.

- **The cancellation, freeze, and refund policies:** Many gyms let you put your membership on hold for medical or maternity leave. Some will refund your remaining membership if you move more than 25 miles away. Most states have laws that allow you to cancel within three days of joining with a full refund. However, some clubs are so stingy that you may have to threaten legal action to get them to comply with this law.

- **Qualifications of the staff:** At a gym that Liz manages, she placed an advertisement for trainers and received at least two applications from residents of the state correctional facility. It wasn't so much the felony convictions that bothered her; it was the fact that these people's only experience was pumping iron in the prison yard. Liz's club turned down their applications, of course, but you never know where these people might have landed a job upon their release.

- **Cleanliness:** Make sure that there are no substances in the showers that resemble anything you grew in a test tube in high school biology class. Remember that you're joining a gym to *improve* your health, not destroy it. We have been in clubs where seeing a roach crawling across the locker room was pretty much a daily occurrence. Ugh.

- **Equipment quality:** The quality of free weights doesn't vary much, but it's *not* a good sign if the plates on the dumbbells rattle around or you see lots of "Out of Order" signs scattered around on various contraptions. High-quality weight machine brands include Cybex, Nautilus, Galileo, Body Masters, Hammer Strength, and Icarian. Try out a few machines. Do they move smoothly? Is the weight stack rusted? These are subtle signs relating to how well the management takes care of the gym.

- **Friendliness of management:** Do the gym staffers behind the front desk greet you with a smile or are they standing in a clique gossiping about the members? If the staff isn't accommodating before they've made a sale, think about how they'll act *after* you've signed on the dotted line. Even if you're not dependent on trainers, you may need them at some point. Maybe they'll waive the $2 penalty on the day that you forget your membership card. Or maybe they'll allow your visiting sister to sneak into the club for free.

- **Cost:** Cheaper isn't always better. If the club's machinery is always broken or the bathrooms are cleaned monthly, you may pay more in doctor's bills for injuries and infections than you do for your monthly membership.

- **Extra conveniences:** Some gyms have blow dryers in the locker rooms, Internet access on the cardiovascular equipment, membership competitions, and special guest instructors — little extras that keep you motivated over the long haul.

- **Affiliation with other clubs:** If you travel a lot, consider joining a club that is affiliated with gyms around the country. Large chains may not have the most qualified staff or offer the most personalized attention, but you can save money on guest passes.

Designing a Home Gym

Just as you don't want to rush into buying a health club membership, you should put some time and thought into creating a home gym. Before you purchase any equipment, consider the following questions. (This section deals only with weight training equipment; you need to consider any cardiovascular equipment, such as a treadmill or stationary bike, separately.)

How much space do you have?

If you have virtually no space for weight equipment, your best bet is a set of rubber exercise tubes that come with door handle attachments. However, we think that you can build greater strength and size using dumbbells and a weight bench, so make room for these gadgets if at all possible. You can conserve space by buying clever dumbbell products such as Power Blocks, Smart Locks, or Plate Mates, which are all described in the "Nifty dumbbell products" sidebar in this chapter.

When a "deal" isn't a steal

A friend of ours walked into a large, New York City health club and asked one simple question: How much does a yearly membership cost? "The lady behind the counter refused to tell me," he recalls. "She said, 'I have to take you on a tour of the weight room, and then you have to see the locker rooms, and then you have to speak with the manager.' She acted like I was asking for classified information that might compromise national security."

Getting the facts you want from a health club often requires persistence and savvy. Here are some tips to prevent you from getting ripped off:

✔ **Stand your ground.** Health club salespeople may quote what seems like a reasonable price, but by the time you get finished adding in all the options like locker space and towel service, they've doubled the price of admission. (Some clubs are as chintzy as restaurants in Rome that charge you for the use of your table cloth and silverware.)

✔ **Ask what the price includes.** If it doesn't include an item you want, such as an extra training session, ask if the salesperson will toss it in to make the sale. As our mothers always say, you never know until you ask. Also, don't let the salespeople cheat you out of the advertised price. If you see an ad in the paper, bring it with you to the club. If you heard an ad on the radio, note the station and the time it aired.

✔ **Don't be insulted.** Some salespeople try to assault your self-esteem to get you to join or to sign up for extra training sessions. They may imply that you're fat and that the only way you could go out in public without embarrassing yourself is to lose weight at their health club. Remember, many health club salespeople work on commission, so they'll say just about anything to make a sale.

Our friend from New York City managed to get a decent membership price, but he wasn't off the hook so quickly. "During my free training session, my trainer asked what my goals were, and I told him I wanted to stay healthy. He said, 'Well, most guys want to get big.' And I said, 'Well, I don't want to get big. I just don't want to get fat.' He didn't really feel satisfied with my answer. He wanted me to sign up for a whole bunch of training sessions so that I could get big."

✔ **Don't rush into your decision.** The gym will be there tomorrow. And if it isn't, you'll be glad you didn't sign up, right? Not long ago, a New York City health club was selling memberships right up until the day before it closed its doors. This happens more frequently than we care to think.

✔ **Don't pay an initiation fee if you can help it.** Some gyms waive this fee during certain times of the year or if you join with a family member — or if you're persistent enough.

✔ **Don't sign up for more than a year.** Many states have laws that forbid lifetime and long-term memberships. But there are loopholes in the law, and even when there aren't, disreputable salespeople may try to snow you. You don't know where you'll be a year from now — and more importantly, you don't know where the gym is going to be a year from now. Many gyms have monthly memberships that are slightly more expensive than buying a whole year, but these month-to-month deals may be a better deal for you if your life is in flux.

✔ **Join with a friend and ask for a discount.** And know that the best sales are usually in the slower summer months and right after Christmas. Some clubs give you a rebate or free months if you recommend a friend to join.

What are your goals?

Make sure that you buy equipment that can help you reach your goals. If you want to build some serious muscle, a couple sets of dumbbells isn't going to cut it. In fact, you may need to buy a dozen pairs of dumbbells and purchase a free weight bench. Just make sure your goals jibe with the amount of space you have available: If you live in a tiny apartment but want to live in a body like Jackie Chan's, you may have to unload your bed, coffee table, television, refrigerator, and stove in order to make space for your weight equipment. (We know people who have done this.) If your goal is to develop moderate strength and muscle tone, your best bet is to buy an adjustable weight bench and several pairs of dumbbells.

How much money can you spend?

The cheapest (and smallest) weight training gadget you can buy is a rubber exercise band, which will set you back less than $3. However, as we explain in Chapter 1, there are limits to the amount of muscle strength you can develop for the price of a McDonald's Happy Meal. On the other hand, you don't need to raid your retirement account in order to build a firm, strong body. For $200 to $500 you can buy an adjustable weight bench and more than enough dumbbells. If you have an extra thousand or two lying around, go ahead and purchase a multigym for variety. By the way, if you're tight on money, don't even think about buying any weight training gizmo off of the TV. Read Chapter 26 and you'll understand why.

Will you be using videos?

If you plan to use weight training videos, we suggest you invest in dumbbells and an adjustable weight bench (or at least a step aerobics platform, which can double as a bench). Many videos also use rubber exercise bands, ankle weights, barbells, or physioballs. So when you buy new tapes, make sure that you have (or are willing to buy) the necessary equipment.

Free Weight Options

If you're just starting out, dumbbells are a more practical purchase than barbells because they're more versatile. You may want to save barbells for your next shopping spree. In terms of quality, where you buy free weights doesn't much matter, whether you go to a sporting goods store, department store, specialty shop, or garage sale. A specialty weight shop may offer the best selection, but prices may be higher.

Strength training on the road

If you're looking for an excuse to skip your weight training workout, vacations and business trips won't cut it. You can keep your muscles strong no matter where you go, whether your destination is Cut Bank, Montana, or the Mongolian desert.

Of course, you may not always find a health club with 14 shoulder machines and aromatherapy baths. While touring Micronesia, Suzanne worked out at Yap island's only gym — a tin shack where the locals hoist rusty barbells while chewing betel nut, a mild narcotic that stains your teeth red. In Nairobi, she lifted weights at a club where staff members had to boil water on a stove in the weight room because the water wasn't safe to drink. The bottom line: You can always make do.

Strength training on the road is well worth the effort. Even fitting in one short workout a week can help you maintain the strength you've worked so hard to build. Here are some tips for getting in a strength training workout away from home:

✔ If possible, book a hotel with a gym. Some hotel gyms have facilities that rival those at regular health clubs, including personal trainers, towel service, and massage. And these days, even many of the less posh hotel gyms offer a decent array of free weights and weight training machinery.

✔ Look for a gym in the neighborhood. If your hotel doesn't have a gym, ask the concierge, or simply open up the phone book and look under "health club" or "fitness." Expect to pay $5 to $10. Some upscale Los Angeles and New York clubs charge as much as $25 — we say go elsewhere.

The best bargain in the West is Dave's Power Palace in Carson City, Nevada, a clean, well-equipped club that charges $2 per workout. Our favorite East Coast bargain is Fifth Avenue Muscle, in Brooklyn, New York, which charges $4.

✔ When you work out away from your home club, expect to sign a waiver essentially saying that any torn muscle, broken bone, or smashed toenail you sustain is your fault and yours alone. If you are in a gym that's foreign to you, stick to free weight exercises and machines that you recognize (unless you ask someone on staff to help you). This isn't the time to test whether you have a knack for figuring out how weight training contraptions work.

By the way, one of the best reasons to find a local gym has nothing to do with your muscles. "You get to meet the locals and find out about the least crowded beaches, and the best place to go for a beer," says Alec Boga, an avid traveler from California, who has lifted weights in Thailand, Costa Rica, Zimbabwe, Venezuela, and Fiji, just to name a few countries. "The equipment might be good or bad, but you just ad lib and enjoy talking to the people."

✔ If you have no access to weight equipment, pack a rubber exercise band. You can perform dozens of exercises with a single band, which takes up about as much space as your travel toothbrush. See Chapter 25 for band exercises.

✔ As a last resort, lift your own body weight. If you get stuck without even a band, you can do no-equipment exercises such as push-ups, crunches, back extensions, squats, and lunges. On a South Pacific island that had no gym at all, Suzanne did push-ups and lunges in her hotel room; she had to perform them naked because the place had no air conditioning and was far too hot and humid for her to even have considered exercising while clothed.

Buying dumbbells

The biggest mistake people make when buying dumbbells is investing in a pair of 10-pound weights and then using them for every exercise. We suggest starting with eight pairs. For women who are beginning lifters, we recommend dumbbells weighing 2, 3, 5, 8, 10, 12, 15, and 20 pounds. For novice men: 8, 12, 15, 20, 25, 30, 35, and 40 pounds. As we explain in Chapter 15, to get good results you need to lift precisely the right amount of weight for each exercise.

So what's all of this going to cost? The answer depends on how fancy you want your weights to be. Dumbbells cost about $.50 to $2 per pound, depending on which part of the country you live in, where you buy them, and whether you catch a good sale. (That would mean $150 to $300 for the women's set and $300 to $600 for the men's.) Hexagonal dumbbells (called *hexes* by those in the know) tend to be less expensive. Plastic-coated dumbbells are cheaper, but we're not fond of those because the plastic tends to rip over time.

Liz once owned a pair of dumbbells that started to leak; every time she pressed the dumbbells overhead, a few grains of sand would fall into her mouth or eye. The most expensive dumbbells are the shiny chrome ones with contoured handles. You can see your reflection in the ends of the really top-drawer ones. You find these in ritzier health clubs and in home gyms that try to emulate ritzy health clubs.

We recommend buying a rack to store your dumbbells. Racks save space, and they keep your house looking tidy so that your mother won't have to step over your weights if she stops by unannounced. Also, a rack can save you from injury because you don't have to constantly bend over and lift the dumbbells off the floor. Don't be surprised if a rack costs more than the dumbbells you're storing. A $200 to $300 rack should be adequate, but you can pay up to $800 for a three-tiered, chrome rack.

If you're short on space or money and buying eight pairs of dumbbells is impossible, consider an adjustable dumbbell kit. You get two short bars and a number of round plates that you clamp on with collars. Just beware: The plates tend to rattle around, and you may find it annoying to constantly pop off the collars and add or subtract weight plates. Making these adjustments can add precious minutes to your workout. Worse, you may be tempted to skip the adjustments and use the same weight for several exercises. See the sidebar "Nifty dumbbell products" for clever alternatives to the ones we discuss in this section.

Nifty dumbbell products

If you're in the market for dumbbells and want to save money and/or space, here are a few inventive gadgets that might suit your needs:

✔ **Plate Mates:** These are like oversized refrigerator magnets that you stick onto both ends of a dumbbell to increase the weight. Plate Mates come in four weights: 5/8 pound, 1¼ pound, 1⅞ pound, and 2½ pounds. Prices range from about $19 to $28 per pair. They enable you to save big bucks on dumbbells because you have to buy only half of the weights you otherwise would. For instance, you can transform a set of 5-pounders into 6¼-pound dumbbells or 7½-pounders simply by sticking a Plate Mate onto each end. Plate Mates bond to the weights quite well. You can shake the dumbbell up and down, and the magnet won't fall off. Removing a Plate Mate requires nothing but a quick twist.

✔ **Smart Locks:** These are a nice improvement to adjustable dumbbells. They're short bars that come with spring-loaded collars that easily pop on and off. The collars lock the plates onto the bars so tightly that they don't rattle around or slide off. For less than $200, you can buy a set that can build up to two 40-pound dumbbells.

✔ **Power Blocks:** These are clever but strange-looking adjustable dumbbells. Each block consists of a series of weighted, rectangular frames, each smaller one nesting inside one slightly larger. Holes run along the outside frame: You stick a two-headed pin in the hole that corresponds to the amount of weight you want to lift, and the pin locks in the number of frames you need to lift. Power Blocks save you time — it's a lot quicker to stick a pin in a hole than it is to clamp on new weight plates. For $600, you can buy a set that builds up to two 90-pound dumbbells. They fit into a corner of the room and take up no more space than your nightstand. A similar product, Probells, is easier to use but only goes up to 30 pounds. Probells sell for $299 a pair; their stand costs an additional $149.

Buying barbells

Unless you're related to the Sultan of Brunei, you'll probably find it too expensive and too space-consuming to buy a whole array of fixed-weight barbells, as we recommend you do with dumbbells. It's more practical to buy an empty bar and clip on the weights yourself. You can buy bars that weigh 15 to 30 pounds, although the most popular bars are the heavier bars used in health clubs.

Barbells cost about the same per pound as dumbbells, but if you're lucky, you may find them as low as a nickel a pound. Most stores sell variety packs, often called Olympic packs, which come with a whole assortment of plates weighing a total of 200 to 300 pounds.

As with dumbbells, we recommend buying a barbell rack. Vertical racks ($100 to $200) take up less space and are less expensive than horizontal racks ($300 to $700). However, it's more awkward to place a bar into a vertical rack. You can store your plates on a weight tree, a contraption that has several rungs. Weight trees come in an astonishing variety of shapes and sizes and typically cost $75 to $200.

We also recommend buying collars to keep the weight plates from sliding off the bar. The sturdiest and most user-friendly collars are made by MCR. You slip the collars onto the bar and twist a small lever, locking them in place. They cost $20 a pair.

Buying a bench

If you want to buy a bench for your home, your best bet is an adjustable incline bench — one that adjusts from a flat position all the way up to vertical. The decline feature shouldn't be a high priority because you won't use it very often, if at all. Before you buy a bench, sit on it, lie on it, drag it around, adjust it, and inspect it. Look for a high-quality Naugahyde, leather-like material used to cover all seat and back pads.

Good flat benches start at around $100 and run upward of $400 for extra-thick padding and high-quality hardware. Adjustable incline and decline benches are in the $200 to $600 range. Make sure the incline mechanism is secure and easy to manipulate. With some cheap brands, the pin that holds the back rest upright tends to slip out or even worse, break off. Good bench brands include Hoist, York, Icarian, Paramount, and Tuff Stuff. These are the brands you're also likely to encounter at the gym, along with Galileo, Cybex, and Body Masters.

Investing in Weight Machines

Obviously, it's not practical to put an entire line of weight machines in your home, unless you're willing to take out a second mortgage to pay for the weights and for the new wing of the house you'll need to build. A more reasonable alternative is a multigym (see Figure 4-1), which combines several weight lifting stations into one frame. Most multigyms have one or two weight stacks, meaning that one or two people can work out at a time. Good multigyms give your muscles a sufficient workout, although most models don't feel as smooth or as solid as health club machines.

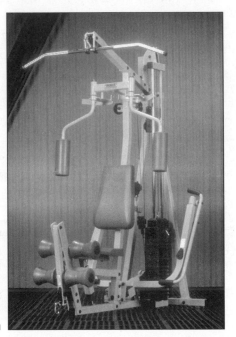

Figure 4-1:
You can buy a multigym to work out at home.

A decent multigym will cost you at least $1,000. Buy from equipment specialty stores, not from department stores and certainly not from TV infomercials. Visit several stores to compare prices. If you don't live near a specialty store, call the manufacturers and ask for the dealer closest to you. Most top brands have a dealer in every nook and cranny in the country, as well as many parts of Europe, Asia, and Africa. In some cases, it's cheaper to buy directly from the manufacturer. Good multigym brands include Parabody, Paramount, Universal, Vectra, Pacific, Hoist, and California Gym. Here are some tips for buying multigyms:

✔ Look for sturdy and thickly padded seats that are covered with durable material.

✔ Look for machines that use plastic-coated cables as opposed to chains or giant rubber bands. Check all cables for imperfections and fraying.

✔ Try out every exercise station. Some may feel comfortable, while others make you feel like your arm is about to be ripped out of its socket. Look for a weight stack that moves smoothly up and down. Some machines that move smoothly at heavier weights become wobbly and sticky when you're lifting only one or two plates.

✔ Make sure that the parts are easy to adjust. You don't want to waste half your workout fiddling with the arm and seat adjustments so that the machine fits your body.

✔ Look for free assembly. Forget about those "easy-to-follow" directions. Trying to put some of these contraptions together yourself is like trying to build a space shuttle with a step-by-step manual.

Buying Bands

Make sure that you buy bands or tubes specifically designed for exercise, instead of the kind you use to keep your mail together in the office. Office rubber bands aren't strong enough for you to constantly pull on, so there's a pretty good chance of getting popped in the face when one breaks. See Chapter 25 for a complete band workout and helpful tips on using bands and a description of our favorite band products.

TIP

Join your own home gym

Even if you're not interested in joining a health club, you may want to incorporate aspects of the gym experience into your home workouts. Adding the following health club features to your home gym can boost your motivation and sense of purpose.

✔ **A sign-in sheet:** When you go to the health club, you have to sign in at the front desk to prove you were there. We suggest you record your attendance at your home gym in a work-out log or even create your own attendance sheet that you can tape to the door or keep on top of your filing cabinet. Signing in at the beginning of your session reinforces your commitment to weight training.

✔ **A mirror:** The purpose of a mirror is not simply so you can smile at your reflection and admire your new and improved body. You need a mirror to check your form, especially when you're doing free weight and band exercises. Just make sure you watch where you put your dumbbells and barbells. If you leave them on the floor, they may roll around and crack the mirror. (We've never been to a gym that *didn't* have a mirror crack at one time or another. The best way to avoid this problem is investing in a dumbbell rack.) Any mirror will suffice as long as it's big enough for you to see your entire body when you're standing with your arms spread wide.

✔ **A stretching mat:** A mat is useful for doing strength training exercises on the floor, such as abdominal crunches and side-lying leg lifts. (And, of course, it's useful for stretching.) You can substitute a towel or blanket, but these tend to bunch up. Most stretching mats can be folded up and placed in a corner or underneath your weight rack. A good mat costs $20 to $100. There's little difference between the cheap mats and the expensive ones, except in the thickness of the padding, the quality of the surface covering, and the way they store (the cheap ones roll, the better ones fold). The mat should be long enough so that it fits your body from the top of your head to your tailbone. The padding should be cushy enough so that your knees don't dig into the floor when you do the Modified Push-up and other exercises that require kneeling.

✔ **A rubber mat to place under the equipment:** These mats look like the rubber mats on the floor of your car. They help cut down on noise and vibration to the floors below, and they help protect your floors and rugs. Mats are particularly good to put under equipment that leaks oil, such as multigyms and treadmills. Some mats are custom-designed to fit under specific pieces of equipment.

✔ **Proper attire:** Health clubs require you to wear freshly laundered exercise clothing so that the grime from your jeans, leather belts, and work shirts doesn't soil the pads on the weight equipment. Follow the same rule at your home gym, too. You'll prolong the life of your equipment. Plus, it's a lot more motivating to work out when you're wearing lycra shorts and a T-shirt than when you're trying to do the Bench Press in a business suit.

Chapter 5

Choosing Your Guru: Trainers, Videos, and Exercise Classes

*E*liza Doolittle had Henry Higgins. The Sweathogs had Mr. Kotter. Who's going to be *your* mentor? If you're a weight training rookie, you can progress more quickly if you have a seasoned professional to follow — someone who can teach you the ropes and keep you motivated when you'd rather scan the latest Internet postings on flyfishing.com. Even veteran lifters have a lot to gain by checking in with a pro from time to time. In this chapter, we introduce you to a variety of mentor options, including a fitness trainer, a body-sculpting instructor, and a video leader. We tell you who's qualified to teach you and who isn't. We explain what qualities to look for in a weight training guru and what you can expect to learn from a trainer, a class, or a video.

Everything You Need to Know about Trainers

This book offers detailed instructions for dozens of exercises and plenty of ideas for designing your own workouts. Still, we think that getting personal instruction at least three times is valuable for anyone who lifts weights. If you join a club, you should automatically get a free training session on top of a fitness evaluation. Ask in advance, and you may even get extra free sessions. If you lift weights at home, you can hire a trainer for a couple of sessions to get you up and running. (If a trainer isn't an option for you, a good video can augment what you learn in this book, although when you're an absolute beginner, a video is no substitute for hands-on instruction.)

What a fitness trainer can do for you

Fitness trainers have become famous for firming up fleshy actors and actresses for their roles as river-rafting guides, prize fighters, and psychopaths. Here's what a good fitness trainer can do for *you*.

Perfect your technique

A trainer can offer subtle pointers to improve your weight lifting form. Even if you do your best to follow instructions like "Keep your arm parallel to the floor," you may not be able to tell whether your arm is in precisely the right position. Once you know what it feels like to perform an exercise the right way, you're likely to keep using good technique when you're on your own.

Show you alternative exercises

A trainer can help you build on the exercises in this book, showing you additional moves that meet your specific needs and preferences. If you become enamored with the cable machine, a trainer can show you enough cable exercises to keep you entertained for eons. If you're pregnant, a trainer can show you how to perform abdominal exercises without lying on your back and hamstring exercises without lying on your stomach.

Introduce you to the equipment

Each brand of equipment has its own quirks. The seat adjustment for one Lat Pulldown machine (see Chapter 8 for a description) may work by a different mechanism than it does for another, even though the machines strengthen your back muscles in the same way. A trainer can teach you about the intricacies of each machine in your health club or home gym.

Design or update your program

If you wanted to, you could come up with a new routine every day for the rest of your life. A trainer can help you expand on our workout suggestions and design routines that fit your specific schedule, whether you work out three days a week for 20 minutes or twice a week for an hour. Trainers also come in handy if you're working toward a specific goal; preparing for ski season requires a different type of routine than getting ready for a backpacking vacation.

Keep you motivated

Some people would not even consider getting out of bed, let alone lifting a weight, if they did not have a trainer standing over them saying, "Okay, Marvin, ten shoulder presses, *now!*" Others can get by with a motivational boost every month or two, working out on their own the rest of the time. And then there are those who rely so much on their trainers for inspiration that they actually bring them along on vacation. We kid you not. Elizabeth Crutchfield, the owner of Homebodies, a New York personal training service, says that clients are paying upwards of $500 a day to bring their trainers along on vacation.

Who's a qualified trainer?

Fitness trainer is about as meaningful a term as *internet consultant* or *marketing liaison*. In terms of skills and education, it doesn't mean a darn thing. We know a group of private trainers who hang a large sign outside their gym that says "World Class Personal Trainers." Only one of the group's half dozen trainers is even certified by a single professional organization. Here are some tips to help you find a trainer you can trust. It's not always possible to assess a trainer in one interview or even in a couple of sessions, so if you start to sour on the first trainer you choose, don't hesitate to find another one.

Look for certification

Although there are no laws on the books requiring trainers to have any particular training or certification, more and more trainers are becoming certified by professional organizations and university programs. Many health clubs now require their trainers to have at least one certification, and as the personal training profession becomes increasingly competitive, many private trainers are earning certifications in order to stay ahead of the competition. This surge in certifications is good news for the consumer. A certification doesn't necessarily mean that a trainer is the most knowledgeable and skilled in the field, but it does show that your trainer considers fitness a serious career choice, not just a way to pay the rent between acting gigs or when the auto repair business is slow.

A number of certifications require several days of seminars taught by fitness experts and a passing grade on a written exam. Some exams require trainers to analyze videotaped exercises, pointing out which muscles are working at various points in the exercise and any technique mistakes the lifter may have made. But beware: We recently came across a certification offered over the Web that involved answering a few questions and paying $90. You could take the test as many times as you wanted and didn't have to pay until you passed — at which point you would be issued a fancy certificate saying you are a "Certified Kickboxing Instructor" or "Certified Personal Trainer." The Web site even bragged "No teaching experience necessary!"

Here's a list of some of the most reputable certifying organizations:

- American College of Sports Medicine (ACSM)
- National Strength and Conditioning Association (NSCA)
- American Council on Exercise (ACE)

Hire an experienced trainer

Don't be shy: Ask for references and call a few of the trainer's other clients. Do as good a job screening potential trainers as you'd do checking out potential employees. You should even ask for a résumé.

Make sure your personalities mesh

Trainers are human beings, which means that they come in all different personality types. Some are enthusiastic. Some are downright perky. On the other end of the spectrum are trainers who missed their calling as maximum security prison guards.

Interview a few trainers and choose one who makes you feel comfortable. Your trainer doesn't need to be your best friend. In order to act as an objective professional, your trainer — like your doctor or lawyer — may need some distance from you.

Expect good teaching skills

Even if your trainer has a Ph.D. in physiology and is more congenial than Rosie O'Donnell, there's no guarantee that he or she can teach you to perform a Push-up correctly. The ability to get a point across is a skill in and of itself. Good trainers speak to you in your native tongue, not in jargon. If you don't understand something, a trainer should be able to find another way of explaining the point. Also, good trainers prepare you to venture out into the world alone. They make sure that you understand not only how to adjust the seat on the Leg Extension machine, but also why you are adjusting it that way.

On the other hand, beware of trainers who talk too much. Some trainers give so many pointers that you feel as if you're a surgical resident performing your first intubation. The human brain can absorb only so much information.

Count on personal attention

Your trainer should shower you with questions about your goals and should thoroughly evaluate your health, strength, cardiovascular fitness, and flexibility. Some trainers will give a 65-year-old woman the same basic program that they'd give to a professional hockey player. Look for evidence that you're getting a custom-designed routine. If you find that you're performing exercises that are either far too difficult or way too easy (and the trainer doesn't seem to notice or care), you've been given the trainer's same old song and dance.

Many trainers specialize in certain types of clients, such as seniors, children, pregnant women, multiple-sclerosis patients, or ultra-endurance athletes. If you have a specific goal in mind or have special circumstances, it's wise to seek out a trainer who has the training and experience to meet your needs.

A few words about fees

Hollywood stars may pay $200 per weight training session, but you don't need to. Fees vary widely depending on what part of the country you live in, but in many places, you can find a trainer for about $30 an hour. Expect to pay $50 to $150 per hour if you live in big cities such as New York City, Los Angeles, or Chicago. You usually can save money by purchasing five or ten sessions at once. You also can save by hiring a trainer who works at your health club, but don't forget that you're also paying the club's monthly dues. Many trainers offer semi-private sessions for a reduced fee. If you go this route, try to hook up with a buddy whose goals and abilities are similar to yours.

By the way, after you sign up with a trainer, do not complain about his or her fee. Andrea Leonard, a trainer in Maryland, has one client who lives in a million-dollar home, drives an $80,000 BMW, and has a wardrobe larger than the cast of a Broadway musical. This client has gotten tremendous results, dropping two dress sizes, losing 15 pounds, and developing firm, sculpted muscles. "But," says Andrea, "every time we meet the woman says, 'I can't *believe* how much I spend on you. I tell my friends how great you are, but they're not *about* to spend *that* kind of money. By the way, my husband was wondering why you won't give me a discount.'"

Insist on liability insurance

Make sure that your trainer carries liability insurance. Of course, we hope you never find yourself in a position where insurance matters. But you do need to face the realities of the modern world. If you get hurt, you may be looking at thousands of dollars in medical bills, even if you have medical insurance. A trainer's liability coverage may foot the bill if you can prove your injury is a direct result of the trainer's negligence. Many insurers award coverage only to trainers who are certified, so liability insurance is often an indication that your trainer has some credentials.

How to act during a training session

Take an active role in your training sessions, especially if you're going to have just a few of them. Follow these tips to get the most out of your training sessions:

- ✔ **Show up on time.** Trainers are professional people with busy schedules and bills to pay, so show them some courtesy. Honor your trainer's cancellation policy (and avoid chronic cancellations). Most trainers require at least 24 hours notice when you can't make it to your session. They may let you slide the first time, but they do have the right to charge you for missed sessions.

- ✔ **Have a good attitude.** Your trainer doesn't want to hear you whine about your boss or your latest speeding ticket. Working out is fun — we would swear to it under oath.

- ✔ **Speak up.** The more questions you ask, the more information you're likely to remember. When you perform the Lat Pulldown, don't feel stupid about asking why you pull the bar down to your chest rather than to your belly button. A good trainer will have coherent answers on the tip of his or her tongue and won't say, "Because I'm the trainer — *that's* why."

✔ **Listen to your trainer.** When your trainer advises you to perform 12 repetitions per set, don't say, "My stockbroker says it's better to perform 40 repetitions." Trust that your trainer has more experience than you do. Of course, you should always ask questions if you don't understand something, and if your trainer's advice sounds out of line, you needn't heed it. But then, if your trainer's advice sounds out of line, you should find yourself another trainer.

An Introduction to Strength Training Classes

Some people thrive on one-on-one instruction. Others really respond to the atmosphere of a class, even if they can afford a private trainer. If you're uncomfortable with someone scrutinizing your every move, as a personal trainer does, then a class is a good way for you to learn good weight training technique while still blending into the crowd. And if you're short on self-motivation, a class can keep you pumping those weights when you'd prefer to go home and change the oil in your car. Even if you're the type of person who enjoys working out alone, you can pick up new moves by taking an occasional class.

Body sculpting

Body sculpting, sometimes called *body shaping,* is the classroom buzzword for weight training and calisthenics. We think that teachers started these terms because they figured *weight training* would scare away people who are afraid of lifting weights. Some people say, "Oh, I hate weight training, but I love body sculpting," which is like saying that you hate sweet potatoes but love yams.

Body sculpting classes use dumbbells and exercise bands, as opposed to weight machines. A class typically lasts about 45 to 90 minutes and works all the major muscle groups in the body. Most clubs also offer 15- to 30-minute body sculpting classes, such as "Abs Only" or "Lower Back Care," that focus on a particular area of your body. If you take a focused class, just make sure that you don't neglect the rest of your body.

Although we wholeheartedly endorse body sculpting classes, we do want to point out two flaws that commonly plague these classes: performing too many repetitions and failing to use enough weight. Just because you're in a classroom doesn't mean that the basic rules of weight training go out the window. You still need to lift enough weight for each exercise so that the muscle in question is fatigued by the 15th repetition.

Some body sculpting instructors have their students use 2-pound weights for every exercise and perform dozens of repetitions. These instructors tell you that this method results in long, lean muscles as opposed to big, bulky ones. The truth is, if you're using a weight so light that you can lift it 40 times, you won't get much in the way of results at all. Your muscles may be exhausted, but they won't have been challenged in a way that will build significant strength or muscle tone. If you're using dumbbells, you may need four or five different pairs to give each muscle the appropriate challenge. With bands, you may need to frequently adjust the tension.

What to expect from your instructor

In general, the quality of instruction has drastically improved in recent years, because most clubs demand certification and because poorly attended classes get dropped from the club's schedule. If you don't like one instructor, try another one if your schedule permits it. Also, mention your concerns to the club's management. Look for the following when evaluating an instructor:

- ✔ **Certification:** Your teacher should be certified as an exercise instructor by the American College of Sports Medicine, the American Council on Exercise, or the Aerobics and Fitness Association of America. Instructor certifications are different from personal training certifications. Typically, the exams aren't as difficult in the areas of physiology and general fitness knowledge as they are for personal trainers, but they focus more on the skills that instructors need for class situations.

- ✔ **Concern for newcomers:** A good instructor will ask whether anyone is new to the class and whether anyone has any injuries or special problems. If you fit the bill, you may want to arrive a few minutes early and explain your situation to the instructor. The teacher may give you a special place to stand so that he or she can keep an eye on you. At the very least, you should get a little extra attention.

- ✔ **Clear instructions:** A good instructor will teach you important terminology without overloading you with jargon. We know one instructor who says things like, "Raise up on your phalanges," which in English means "Stand up on your tiptoes."

Don't be afraid to walk out of any class that doesn't feel right. Liz once bailed on a step 'n' sculpt class because the teacher had the class members flying all over the step with weights in their hands. The uncontrolled activity caused a near-collision between Liz and the student next to her. Don't worry about hurting the teacher's feelings. Your priority is keeping your body intact.

✔ **Motivation:** Instructors shouldn't act like they're on autopilot. One friend of ours regularly took a 6 a.m. body sculpting class. The instructor would stumble into the room with a cup of coffee. Without even taking off her coat, she'd sit in a corner, shouting directions to the class as she sipped her coffee and munched on her bagel. If your instructor is too lazy to participate with his or her own class, complain to the management.

✔ **Individual technique tips:** Instructors can't possibly give a personal training session to all 20 members of the class, but they should offer some evidence that they're paying attention. They need to let you know if you happen to hold your arms too wide during Chest Fly exercises or if you throw your body around when you do Biceps Curls.

✔ **A warm-up, cool-down, and stretch:** Every weight training class should have a warm-up that consists of at least 10 minutes of light aerobic exercise. The class should end with a 3- to 5-minute aerobic cool-down followed by a stretching segment lasting 5 to 10 minutes.

✔ **An intensity check:** During the class, the instructor should check to make sure that people aren't pushing themselves too hard (or taking it too easy to benefit from the workout). The *intensity check* can be something as casual as "Hey, how's everyone doing so far?" For details on how and why to check your pulse, see Chapter 18.

All About Weight Training Videos

No video instructor can pop out of the TV set and tell you to stop arching your back or to lift your dumbbells higher. Clearly, a video isn't a substitute for a real-live trainer. However, a video can still teach you a lot about weight training that a book or magazine can't. You can witness an exercise being performed from start to finish, and you can learn new routines. Some videos even feature fancy graphics that indicate which muscles you're working during each exercise.

But perhaps the main reason that exercise videos are so popular is the convenience. "I don't have to worry about waiting for the equipment or using it after people have sweated all over it," says Californian Kim Smith, who owns 32 weight training videos. "And I can look as gruesome as I want to look. When I'm working my legs, I wear a thong leotard with my butt hanging out. And I can grunt and curse all I want."

With a weight training video, you also have the convenience of matching the difficulty of your workout to how you feel that day, whereas in a live class, you pretty much have to exercise at the instructor's pace. (You can modify moves, but you can't turn an advanced class into a beginner's session, or vice versa.) "Sometimes I'm in the mood for some real heart pounding," Kim says. "Other times I want to do a lightweight, pansy workout."

Kim changes her weight training routines on a monthly basis. When we last spoke to her, she was doing a *split routine*: a chest, shoulders, and triceps tape on Tuesdays; a thighs, hips, and butt tape on Wednesdays; and a back and biceps tape on Thursdays. On Sundays, she goes to a health club and works all her muscle groups. Some people might get bored listening to the video instructor utter the same exact words day after day. Not Kim. "I talk along with the instructors — I have their whole schpiel memorized. I feel like I know them, like they're my best friends."

Different types of weight training videos

You can find weight training tapes that use dumbbells, barbells, rubber exercise bands, rubber balls, machines — or a combination of these gadgets. Also, many tapes use the training techniques we discuss in Chapters 15 and 16, such as pyramids and super sets. Some videos combine strength training with aerobics or step aerobics routines. Many are suited to beginners; others you can grow into. And if you find instructors who you really respond to, chances are they'll continue coming out with new tapes to keep you hooked.

Where to buy videos

Actually, we suggest renting a video before you buy it. After all, if you buy a tape and the instructor annoys you or the workout is too easy or too confusing, the only way you'll use that tape is as a coaster at your Super Bowl parties. (Most stores don't let you return a tape simply because you didn't like it.) Large video stores such as Blockbuster carry a fairly wide array of workout videos. Try several different instructors until you find a few that you like and *then* invest in tapes of your own.

Perhaps the best way to buy weight training (and other) videos is through a catalog called *The Complete Guide to Exercise Videos* (www.collagevideo. com). The *Guide* includes some 300 videos, many of them weight training tapes. The catalog offers tapes by all the major instructors plus many excellent videos led by fitness experts who aren't household names.

The catalog and Web site give you the complete lowdown on each tape — how long each workout lasts, what types of exercises it includes, what type of music is played, how tough the workout is, and how the tape has been rated by major fitness magazines. The site also helps you sift through the offerings to find videos that meet your goals.

Dummies-approved instructors

Video devotee Kim Smith has formed strong opinions about which instructors she likes and which she doesn't. "I don't want a cheerleader," she says. "I want someone who's going to put me through the paces. Some of these instructors are so phony. They say, 'Are ya smilin'? Are ya havin' fun?' If I could, I would reach through the TV set and choke them."

We can't guarantee that you'll respond to the personalities of the following instructors, but we can say that you'll get a safe, solid workout with their videos. For consumer reviews of more than 100 video instructors, go to www.videofitness.com.

✔ **Kari Anderson:** She's one of the few instructors to use words like alignment and posture and then explain what they mean. One of Kari's other strong suits is that she often offers easier and more difficult variations on basic exercises.

✔ **Cory Everson:** Cory is a six-time Ms. Olympia body-building champion. She has a meat-and-potatoes approach to weight training — no fancy moves or silly jokes.

✔ **Gin Miller:** Gin usually demonstrates excellent form, and she doesn't treat exercise like it's brain surgery. More than many other instructors, she has the ability to make exercise seem fun.

✔ **Donna Richardson:** Donna is quite creative. She always comes up with that certain little twist on old, standby exercises. Her tapes are for experienced lifters.

✔ **Richard Simmons:** Richard is one of the few fitness stars to embrace the needs of exercisers who are very overweight or very out of shape. He instructs with compassion and humor.

✔ **Kathy Smith:** Kathy's tapes are ideal for beginners and intermediates. The routines are straightforward — nothing fancy. Many of her routines are designed by experts in the field, and Kathy is an expert at passing along their information.

✔ **Karen Voight:** Karen is one of the best instructors in the business, although she never, ever smiles. Her directions are always clear, concise, and correct. Her workouts can challenge even the most fit exercisers, so beginners should start out with another instructor.

✔ **Keli Roberts:** An advanced, energetic instructor, Keli's moves are unique and stylish, although probably too complex for real beginners.

If you want personal attention, you can call the catalog's *video consultants*, who will talk to you toll-free and help you select a video that's right for you. The consultants try out new videos every week, and they know what they're talking about. If you ask, they're willing to offer their unadulterated opinions on various instructor's methods. One advantage of ordering through this catalog is that if you're unhappy with the tape for any reason — including a personality conflict with the instructor — you can return the video without a hassle.

You can also buy videos from Amazon.com (`www.amazon.com`), which posts customer reviews, and Fitness Wholesale (`www.fwonline.com`), which offers descriptions of the videos but not reviews. Another option is Video Fitness (`www.videofitness.com`), an excellent Web site that doesn't sell tapes but allows you to trade videos through the site's Video Exchange. You post a "wish list" and a list of the tapes you're willing to exchange; then you negotiate trades (no money is involved).

Video Fitness (`videofitness.com`) is also a great place to go for reviews; more than 700 tapes are reviewed by video exercisers nationwide. The site's Beginner's Corner helps you set appropriate goals and select suitable videos, and the Mentoring Program matches video novices with veterans who are willing to offer motivation, support, and advice via e-mail. If you have the slightest interest in exercise videos, definitely check out this site.

Chapter 6

Weight Training Etiquette

• •

In This Chapter

▶ Minding your manners in the weight room

▶ Courtesy in weight training classes

• •

Suzanne was performing squats at a crowded health club not long ago when suddenly she was jolted off balance by an earsplitting thud. Moments later, the room was rocked by another deafening clunk. Simultaneously, dozens of heads turned toward the source of this unnerving noise: a large man hoisting a 500-pound barbell. Apparently, this guy did not have the strength to be lifting that much weight. Midway through each repetition — when he had the bar about two feet off the ground — he'd lose control and the 500 pounds would come crashing to earth, nearly sending the rest of the club's members into cardiac arrest.

This is what you call rude — and potentially dangerous — behavior. While weight training doesn't require the same level of concentration as, say, reading Faulkner, it does happen to be an activity that's difficult to perform with bomb explosion-type noises going on in the background. Finally, Suzanne politely asked the guy to lose the sound effects so that the rest of us could work out in peace. Judging from the snarl on his face, he didn't appreciate the constructive criticism. But he *did* cut out the clanging.

Even at a health club — a place where tank tops, profuse sweating, and mild grunting are perfectly acceptable — there are rules of etiquette. Sure, the social graces expected in a weight room are a bit different from those expected at the symphony or the Louvre, but manners are important just the same. In this chapter, we explain the rituals and customs that are unique to gyms. Some of these may seem odd at first, but once you learn how you're expected to act, you'll feel a lot more at home in your club — actually, in any club. By the way, if you witness a flagrant etiquette violation, don't be afraid to inform the club staff. You're not being a snitch. The rules are for everyone, whether you're the Queen of England or one of her loyal subjects.

Share the Equipment

In a gym, weight equipment is considered communal property, so don't sit on a machine while you rest between sets. Especially don't sit there reading a magazine, talking on your cell phone, or rehearsing an opera. (We've witnessed all three.) Instead, stand up and let a fellow gym member *work in* with you — in other words, let the member alternate sets with you. The same rule applies if you're using a pair of dumbbells. When you complete a set, place the weights on the floor so that someone else can sneak in a set while you rest. (If you place the weights back on the rack, you're likely to lose possession of them altogether.)

If someone else is using a machine or free weights that you have your eye on, feel free to say, "Mind if I work in with you?" Anyone who says no is astonishingly rude. Suzanne recently encountered such a person at her health club. The woman finished a set of shoulder exercises with 8-pound dumbbells, placed the weights on the floor, and then picked up a pair of 10-pounders to do a different exercise. When Suzanne asked permission to use the 8s, the woman shrieked, "Oh! No! I'm still using those!" Suzanne pointed out that the woman was in fact *not* still using the 8-pound dumbbells, as she was holding in her very hands a pair of 10-pound dumbbells. The woman fought bitterly to retain custody of the 8s, so Suzanne took the high road and walked away.

Liz once had to physically pick up a woman and carry her off a bench to make her share it with other members. Although the woman was upset, the incident made both her and Liz legendary in the gym. Fortunately, they later became friendly. The only time it's appropriate to retain possession of weight equipment while you rest is when you're using a barbell stacked with weight plates. Suppose that you're bench-pressing 75 pounds — that's the 45-pound bar with a 10-pound and a 5-pound weight plate on each side. Someone else, meanwhile, wants to bench press 225 pounds — the bar plus two 45-pound plates on each side. You can see what a hassle it would be for the two of you to work in with each other; between each set, you'd have to slide eight plates on and off the bar. So you're under no obligation to let the other person work in with you. (However, if people are waiting for the equipment, have the courtesy not to perform 15 sets.)

Extra Credit: If you see someone hovering around the machine you've been using for the last 15 minutes, say, "Would you like to work in with me?" Some people are shy and may not feel comfortable asking to work in with you. By the way, if you're working in with a person or group of people don't forget to wipe the equipment down before you trade places.

Unload Your Weight Bar

After you finish using a bar, leave it completely empty. Don't assume that everyone can lift the same amount of weight you can. Removing weight plates from a bar takes a fair amount of strength as well as good technique. Don't assume that the next person who comes along has the ability (or desire) to clean up after you. Suzanne recently encountered a man who left 45-pound weight plates on either side of the bench press bar and started to walk away. When she asked if he would clear the bar, he sneered, "I already did." Suzanne then pointed out that in the English language, the word "clear" means to "empty completely" — and that leaving 90 pounds of weight on a bar did not meet that particular definition. The man seemed irked that anyone could be so weak as to bench press less than 135 pounds (90 plus the 45-pound bar). Suzanne made it clear that it was the man's _attitude_ that was irksome.

By the way, this clear-the-bar rule doesn't just apply to heavy lifters. Even if you're using only a 10-pound plate, you still need to clear your bar. If the next person who comes along wants to use 45s, he or she will not want to be bothered with removing your 10-pounders. And don't leave it to the club's trainers to clear your bar.

Extra Credit: If you see someone walk away from a loaded bar, politely ask them to remove the plates. This person may not become your best friend, but the other health club members and the staff will thank you.

Return Your Weights to the Right Place

When you have removed a weight plate from a bar or when you are finished using a pair of dumbbells, return the weights to their designated spot on the rack. No one should have to waste 10 minutes hunting for the 15-pounders, only to find them sitting between the 40s and the 50s. Typically, clubs have dumbbells sitting in order. And on a weight plate tree, the light plates usually sit on the top rungs while the heavier ones go on the bottom. It's frustrating when people pile the plates indiscriminately on top of one another. Invariably, you have to slide off three 45-pound plates and two 25-pounders just to get to the 10-pound plate.

Never leave dumbbells or barbells on the floor when you're finished using them. Someone may trip on the weights. If you leave dumbbells on the floor between sets, criss-cross them or butt them up against the wall or the bench so that they can't roll away.

Extra Credit: If someone else has misplaced weights, do the club a favor and put them back in the right place — if you can safely lift them, of course. No sense in giving yourself a hernia just because someone else had bad manners.

Keep Your Sweat to Yourself

Carry a towel and wipe off any bench or machine you use. Nothing is quite as icky as picking up a slippery weight or lying down in a stranger's pool of sweat. If you forget to bring a towel, use your sweatshirt or the paper towels provided by the club.

Extra Credit: Wipe up the pool of perspiration you may have left on the floor surrounding your machine or bench. Otherwise, the next person may inadvertently do a third-base slide into the machinery.

Don't Block the Flow of Traffic

As we mentioned earlier, you shouldn't camp out on the equipment while you're resting between sets. However, neither should you should clog the pathways between machines — or congregate with a dozen of your buddies in the free weight area. Many members are too timid or polite to point out that the weight room should in no way resemble the floor of the commodities market, so they end up taking a detour halfway around the gym to get to a dumbbell rack that's six feet away. Some people are so oblivious to the traffic jam they have caused that breaking up their party is a feat akin to parting the Red Sea.

Liz was recently working out at a gym and wanted to use a machine that was blocked by a gaggle of women sharing the latest gossip about a cute trainer. Several times she asked them to move but eventually had to gently shove her way through the group.

Extra Credit: This rule applies outside the weight room, too. If you're going to flirt with the receptionist at the front desk, make sure you're not blocking the sign-in sheet.

Don't Hog the Drinking Fountain

Don't stand at the drinking fountain trying to catch your breath when the line behind you is longer than the line for World Series tickets. Take a drink, then get back in line. Better yet, carry a water bottle in the weight room. For some reason, many people who use a water bottle on the stationary bikes and stairclimbers don't think of carrying one around the strength training area. When you do fill up your bottle, let everyone else in line get a drink first; do not hold up the entire gym membership while you fill a gallon-sized water jug. And — this should be obvious, but club staffers report otherwise — don't spit your gum into the fountain. Actually, don't spit *anything* into the fountain. No one wants to stick their face into a big gob of phlegm.

Extra Credit: If you see a wad of gum in the fountain, grab a paper towel and remove it. Okay, maybe that's a lot to ask, but this *is* the extra credit section. At least ask a staff member to remove the gum.

Keep the Grunting to a Minimum

A weight room isn't a public library, but it's not a championship wrestling arena either, so keep the hooting and hollering to a minimum. If you're lifting some heavy poundage, you may feel the need to make some sort of audible noises. Just don't bellow like Godzilla. People who roar when lifting weights sound foolish and distract the people around them.

Extra Credit: If someone's grunting is assailing your ear drums, kindly ask him or her to lower the volume. Chances are, any noise that bothers you is distracting other club members, too. If you don't feel comfortable approaching the offending lifter, let a staff member know about the problem.

Don't Tote Around Your Gym Bag

Some people carry their bag from machine to machine, as if they're walking around an airport terminal and don't want to leave their luggage unattended. You know those large hollowed-out cubes called lockers? That's where you store your gym bag. At most gyms, the machines are only a few feet apart; by dumping your bag on the ground you're hogging precious floor space. Many gyms forbid members to bring their bags into the weight room because less honest members may walk out with lovely parting gifts, like dumbbells, cable handles, and other small items. Someone recently stole all of the collars from a gym that Liz manages, creating a real safety issue until the collars were replaced. (We define collars in Chapter 1.)

Extra Credit: Bring as few items as possible onto the gym floor. We see people walking from machine to machine carrying their coat, their headphones, their weight belt, their gloves, their newspaper, and their lunch. Transporting all this stuff slows down your workout and creates clutter that other members have to step over and around.

Don't Be Afraid to Ask for Advice

If you can't remember how to adjust a machine or perform an exercise, don't be afraid to ask for help. People who lift weights love to give advice; in fact, sometimes you can't shut 'em up. Remember that these people were once beginners, too. You may feel more comfortable asking a staff member for help, and you may get better advice. However, at some clubs, the staff trainers don't have any special education and may be of no more assistance than experienced club members.

Although you shouldn't be shy about asking questions, you also don't want to make a pest out of yourself. So use common sense. If someone is in the midst of raising 150 pounds overhead, don't tap him on the shoulder and ask how to adjust the inner thigh machine. And if a member has headphones on loud enough for you to discern which song he or she is listening to, chances are this person doesn't want to be bothered.

Extra Credit: When asking for help, include some flattery in your request. Say something like, "You really look like you know what you're doing. Would you mind showing me how to use this machine? I'd really appreciate it."

Be Careful When You Offer Unsolicited Advice

Regina Goodwin of Colorado was performing a back exercise one day after undergoing breast reconstruction surgery. Because one of her major back muscles had been removed during the operation, she was not able to perform this particular exercise in the traditional way. After witnessing Regina's unusual technique, a bodybuilder sauntered over and said, "Honey, let a *man* show you how it's done." Unfortunately, this man wasn't watching where he was standing, and Regina inadvertently whacked him between the legs with her dumbbell. "He screamed, and I dropped the weight on his foot," she recalls. "He has not been seen in the gym since."

Don't misunderstand: We're not saying that you can never offer unsolicited help in the gym. Just don't offer advice unless you know what you're talking about.

Extra Credit: Sometimes the knowledge you've gained can be a great help to a lost soul. For instance, you may see someone holding a workout card, glancing from the machine to the card and back to the machine. If the person looks particularly confused or hesitant, you may want to say, "Hi. I'm new here, too, and I had a tough time figuring that one out myself. Need any help?" The person might be grateful that you stepped in.

Don't Dress Like a Porn Star

Neither of us lives the life of a nun, and we are not easily shocked or offended. Still, we're often taken aback by the skimpy attire worn by members at the gyms we frequent. A few women at Suzanne's gym spend more time putting their body parts back into their workout wear than they spend actually lifting weights. Liz even had to evict a drunk woman who came to the gym wearing her lace lingerie. The only body part that was actually covered was the woman's head; for some reason, she was wearing a baseball cap.

Men sometimes pump iron while wearing offensive clothing as well. Our friend Amy worked out at a gym where immense bodybuilder types wore pink and turquoise striped shorts that extended only about a centimeter below their private parts. "The stripes got stretched in all sorts of shapes, depending on their curves," Amy observed. Nor are we fond of bodybuilders who cut out the middle and sides of their tank tops so that the tops are essentially held together by a strand of spaghetti.

Treat the Locker Room Like Your Own Bathroom

Even more so than the weight room, the locker room is the place where your true colors emerge. Women are on equal standing with men in this arena: Men may be more likely to hog dumbbells in the weight room, but women can clog the shower drain with the best of 'em.

- ✔ **The shower:** Don't take a marathon shower if people are waiting. With the exception of sweat, what you take into the shower should come out with you when you leave; this goes for biological as well as non-biological matter. Nobody needs to become personally acquainted with clumps of your hair, your empty shampoo bottle, your used razor, or your slimy sliver of soap. At some gyms people deliberately shove personal items — such as tissues, tampons and even socks — down the drain. The drain is not a garbage disposal!

- ✔ **The vanity area:** Don't hog the mirror or the blow-dryer. If you brush your hair and 200 strands of hair fall on the counter, wipe them off with a paper towel (wipe them into the towel, not onto the floor). Don't leave globs of shaving cream or makeup all over the vanities. Liz was getting dressed for a meeting and got a nice blob of mascara on the elbow of her dress. And don't drink the Listerine straight from the bottle. (We've witnessed this personally.)

- ✔ **The locker area:** Don't take up three lockers and spread your clothing over the entire bench, forcing other people to put on their socks while standing up. Shut your locker when you leave so that the locker room doesn't look like it's been ransacked by a band of hoodlums.

Limit yourself to one or two towels. We know one guy who regularly uses six: one under each foot, one around his waist, one over each shoulder, and one for his hair. Now, would he do that if he had to do the laundry? And how would he feel if he had to dry himself off with a paper towel because some inconsiderate boob hogged all the towels? After you're done using your towels and other paraphernalia, place them in the laundry or trash bin instead of dropping them on the floor. No one wants to sit on a bench strewn with soggy towels, pantyhose packages, and gnarled bobby pins. The staff isn't particularly thrilled to clean up those items, either.

Don't leave your belongings in lockers overnight unless you have permission from your gym to do so. Most gyms will empty out unsanctioned lockers at the end of every day and won't guarantee the safe return of your personal items.

If the lockers at your gym require a key, return it at the end of your workout. Keyed lockers are a convenience to members so that they don't have to carry a lock of their own. However, members often walk away with the keys, rendering the lockers unusable and creating a big expense for the facility, which has to keep replacing the keys.

Extra Credit: Let the staff know if the locker room is running low on towels, toilet paper, or some other item that the gym provides. Don't use an accusatory manner. A simple "Hey, did you know you're out of shampoo?" will suffice.

Courtesy in class

Remember that "Gets Along Well with Others" category on your grade school report card? Well, no one is going to grade your behavior in a weight training class, but the principle still applies: You must be courteous to your fellow students. Here's how to win friends and the teacher's approval in a body sculpting class. Some of these rules also apply to step aerobics and other types of classes.

✔ **Follow the teacher:** You're not just renting the weights for an hour; you're there to participate with the group. When the class is trying to listen to the instructor's explanation of the Shoulder Press, you shouldn't be off in your own world doing a set of biceps curls. This can be distracting to both the class members and the instructor.

✔ **Choose the appropriate class level:** If you're a flat-out beginner, don't venture into the Monster Muscles advanced body-sculpting class. It's not fair to the teacher, who is supposed to be challenging the other students, to have to stop to explain the basics to you. (Also, it's not fair or safe for

you.) On the flip side, if you're an advanced student slipping into a beginner body sculpting class, know that you won't be as challenged. Don't bother complaining to the instructor that the class is too easy for you.

✔ **Don't disorganize the weights or benches:** We sometimes see class members arrive early, pick through the weights to find the ones they want, and reserve their favorite spot in the class. This wouldn't be a problem if they didn't throw their reject equipment all over the floor.

✔ **Respect other students' personal space:** Place your equipment far enough from your neighbors that you don't smack into them during the exercises. If the class is too crowded, the teacher is obligated to turn people away or modify the routine so that nobody ends up black and blue.

✔ **Don't show up late:** Most teachers don't let students in after the warm-up period. You shouldn't miss this segment, anyway.

Part III
The Exercises

In this part . . .

Part III is the meat of the book. It's where we tell you how exactly to tone those triceps or build that butt. First we introduce the format for the exercise instructions and get you familiar with the muscles you'll be working. Each of the next six chapters focuses on a body area. The last chapter in Part III, new to the second edition, shows you advanced exercises for all of your muscle groups.

For each of your major muscle groups, we offer a brief physiology lesson and a rundown of important slang so that you can go around saying things like "I had a killer *lat* and *delt* workout." Then we describe exercises that use both free weights and machines. Throughout this part of the book, we nag you with instructions like "Don't arch your back," "Tighten your abdominals," and "Don't eat too much bread or you'll spoil your dinner." Just kidding on that last one.

Chapter 7

How to Read the Exercise Instructions

Don't be alarmed by the fact that we have devoted an entire chapter to reading the exercise instructions. This doesn't mean that the instructions are complicated. You won't feel like you're slogging through a tax preparation guide or one of those do-it-yourself shelving manuals. We simply want to introduce you to some basic terms used frequently in this part of the book. We also help you choose the exercises that are most appropriate for you, given your fitness level and the equipment available to you.

Introducing You to the Exercises

For every muscle group presented in this book (such as back, chest, or shoulders), we first show you exercises that don't require machines — that is, moves involving dumbbells, barbells, or no equipment at all. Then we present the exercises that do require weight machines. We include at least one machine per muscle group (except the abdominals, for reasons we explain in Chapter 12). Figures 7-1 and 7-2 show you the major muscle groups in your body.

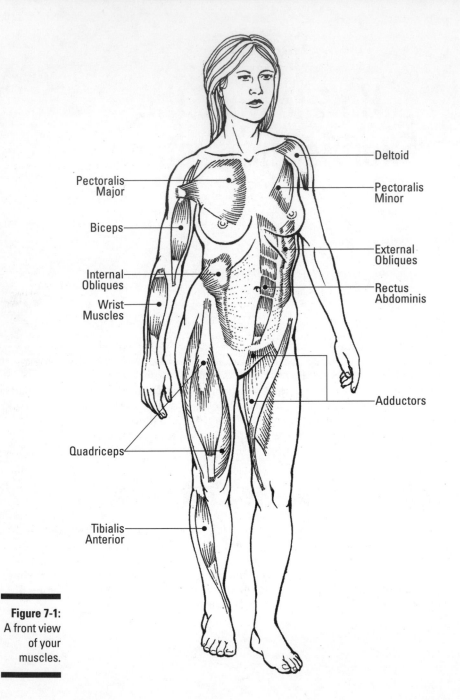

Deltoid

Pectoralis
Major

Pectoralis
Minor

Biceps

External
Obliques

Internal
Obliques

Rectus
Abdominis

Wrist
Muscles

Adductors

Quadriceps

Tibialis
Anterior

Figure 7-1:
A front view
of your
muscles.

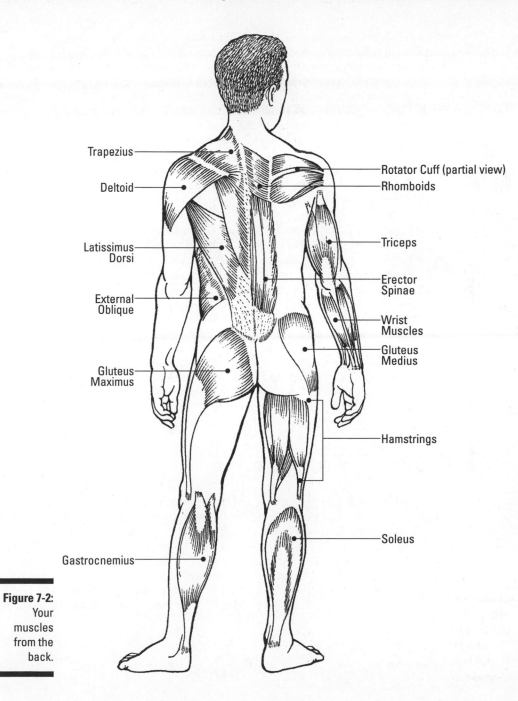

Trapezius

Deltoid

Latissimus Dorsi

External Oblique

Gluteus Maximus

Gastrocnemius

Rotator Cuff (partial view)

Rhomboids

Triceps

Erector Spinae

Wrist Muscles

Gluteus Medius

Hamstrings

Soleus

Figure 7-2:
Your
muscles
from the
back.

If we tried to show you every exercise in existence, this book would be thicker than the unabridged edition of the Oxford English Dictionary. So, we've chosen to present the most common, basic exercises — classic moves that are safe and appropriate for beginners but also are standard moves for veteran exercisers. New to this edition of the book is Chapter 14, "Advanced Exercises," which features moves that you may want to incorporate into your routine once you have mastered the basics.

If you have knee, hip, back, or other orthopedic problems, look for the Joint Caution icon; this icon alerts you to exercises that you may want to avoid or modify. We give you instructions on how to adjust many of the exercises to work around your joint problems.

After presenting each exercise, we describe a number of other versions, labeled "Other Options." Some of the options are easier than the basic version, requiring less coordination or strength. Others are tougher. Some options are neither easier nor harder than the basic version; they simply work the muscle from a different angle.

Once you feel comfortable with the basic version, expand your horizons by experimenting with the options. You may discover, for example, that you prefer to do the Dumbbell Shrug (Chapter 8) with a barbell instead. Or maybe you enjoy both versions and want to alternate them in your workouts. However, don't go bonkers and try all options of an exercise in a single workout. Experiment with one or two new options each time you work out, and concentrate on mastering the movement.

Our Favorite Phrases

Everyone has their pet phrases. Parents like to say "Eat your vegetables!" and "Don't forget to take a jacket!" (even if their children are 45 years old). Dentists like to say "Don't forget to floss!" and "Brush in all the corners!" Fitness experts have their favorite sayings, too, such as "Pull in your abdominals!" We use these phrases not to annoy you (we'll leave that job to parents and dentists), but to keep your joints and muscles from getting injured and to make the exercises more effective. Here's a rundown of the phrases we use repeatedly in Chapters 8 through 14. Chances are, you'll hear these same phrases in exercise videos and classes and when you work out with a fitness trainer.

"Pull in your abdominals."

Place your hand over your belly button and gently pull your belly button in and away from your hand; that's what it feels like to pull in your abdominal muscles. Don't try to create a vacuum or suck your stomach into your ribs.

Just hold your abs slightly in toward your spine. Tightening your abs helps hold your torso still when you exercise and keeps your back from arching or rounding, mistakes that can lead to back injury.

"Stand up tall with square shoulders and a lifted chest."

In other words, keep your head centered between your shoulders and don't round your shoulders forward. Your chest should be comfortably lifted, not forced; you needn't stand like a soldier at attention.

"Don't lock your joints."

We use the phrase "Don't lock your joints" in reference to your elbows and your knees. *Locking a joint* means straightening it so completely that it moves past the point where it normally sits at rest. For example, you don't normally stand with your *quadriceps* (front thigh muscles) as tight as can be with your kneecaps pulled up; that's a locked knee. Locking your knees is not only bad news for your knee joints, but it also can cause lower back pain. And it's a way of cheating when you perform exercises in a standing position, such as the Lateral Raise (Chapter 10) and the Barbell Biceps Curl (Chapter 11).

Locking your elbows places excessive pressure on your elbow joints, tendons, and ligaments. Constant elbow locking can cause *tennis elbow* (an inflammation of the elbow tendons), even if you've never held a tennis racket in your hand. Locking your elbows also can cause bursitis by rupturing the little lubrication capsules (the bursa) located in your joints. Bursitis results in swelling, pain, and tenderness at the elbow. Snapping your elbows also is a form of cheating because it temporarily takes the weight off the muscle that's supposed to be working.

"Keep your shoulders and neck relaxed."

If your shoulders are hunched up near your ears, you need to relax. We think that hunched shoulders are a vestige of holding the phone to your ear or sitting at your computer all day long. If you're prone to hunching, think about lengthening your shoulder blades, as if they are dropping down your back, and try to keep them there as you perform the exercise.

"Tilt your chin toward your chest."

Tilt your chin just enough to fit your closed fist between your chest and your chin. This position lines up the vertebrae of your neck with the rest of your vertebrae. (Because your neck is a continuation of your spine, it should stay in the same general line as the rest of your vertebrae.) So, don't tilt your chin back or drop it toward your chest like you do when you sulk. These two movements strain your neck and place excess pressure on the top of your spine.

"Don't shoot your knees past your toes."

We use the phrase "Don't shoot your knees past your toes" and similar phrases often when describing butt and leg exercises, such as the Squat and Lunge (Chapter 13). If your knees are several inches in front of your toes, you're placing your knees under a great deal of pressure. Also, you probably have too much weight distributed on your toes and not enough on your heels, which means the exercise won't strengthen your butt as effectively.

"Don't bend your wrists."

When you bend your wrists too far inward or outward (that is, when you don't keep your wrists in line with your forearms), you cut off the blood supply to the nerves in your wrists. If you do this frequently enough, you can give yourself a case of carpal tunnel syndrome. Sometimes we use the phrase "Keep your wrist in line with your forearms."

"Maintain proper posture."

Proper posture is an all-encompassing phrase that includes everything that we've mentioned in this section. We use this phrase often because good posture is so important — and because our posture often goes down the tubes when we focus on lifting and lowering a weight.

Good posture isn't automatic for most of us, so give yourself frequent reminders. And if you exercise with correct posture, you'll train your muscles to hold themselves that way in everyday life. Throughout these chapters, we use the Posture Patrol icon to remind you to maintain good posture.

Breathing Lessons

The exercise descriptions in this book do not include breathing instructions because we feel that extra instructions would amount to information overload. Nevertheless, proper breathing technique is important, so here are the general rules:

✔ Exhale deeply through your mouth during the most difficult part of the exercise, also known as the exertion phase. During the Bench Press, for example, pressing the bar up is the exertion phase, so exhale as the bar travels upward.

Exhaling protects your lower back by building up pressure that acts as a girdle to hold your spine in place. Exhaling also ensures that you don't hold your breath so long that you pass out.

✔ Inhale deeply through your nose to bring in a fresh oxygen supply during the less difficult part of an exercise (such as when you lower the weight during a Bench Press). Inhaling provides the spark of energy for your next repetition.

Before we get irate letters from the hard-core weight lifting contingency, we should explain that these breathing directions are for *non*-maximal lifts. We're not talking about world-class power lifting here. If you plan to compete in power lifting, you need to use a slightly different breathing technique than the one described above. Because we don't think that many of you plan to enter such competition, we won't bore you with the details.

Chapter 8

Working Your Back

*W*e think that back muscles have gotten the shaft. Nobody writes songs about them. No epic poems are written about them. They rarely take center stage in lingerie ads. Despite their lowly status, however, back muscles are quite worthy of your attention.

We divided this chapter into two sections: upper back and lower back. Even though these muscle groups reside in close proximity to each other, they have very different job descriptions and require different workout routines. Many upper back exercises involve lifting a fair amount of poundage; lower back exercises, on the other hand, require more subtle movements, usually without any free weights or machinery. We explain why you need to perform both types of exercises. We also tell you which popular back exercises have fallen out of favor with fitness experts and which moves get you the best results.

Upper Back Muscle Basics

Pull up a chair and let's talk about your upper back muscles. There. You just used 'em. In fact, you use your upper back muscles whenever you pull anything toward you, whether it's a piece of furniture, a stubborn golden retriever on a leash, or the mountain of chips you won at your Thursday night poker game.

The largest muscles in your back are the *latissimus dorsi.* They run from just behind each armpit to the center of your lower back. You can call these muscles your *lats.* Don't call 'em your lattes, as one of Suzanne's editors recently did; someone might think you're referring to an overpriced coffee drink. Don't call them your laterals, either — a mistake made by one of the country's largest health magazines!

The main purpose of your lats is to pull your arms toward your body. Above these muscles are your two *trapezius* muscles, or your *traps.* Together, your traps look like a large kite that runs from the top of your neck to the edge of your shoulders and narrows down through the center of your back. Your traps enable you to shrug your shoulders, like when your spouse asks how you could have forgotten to pay the phone bill. Your rhomboids cover the area between your spine and your shoulder blades. Along with your traps, you use your *rhomboids* for squeezing your shoulder blades together. You have to call them your *rhomboids* since *boids* somehow never caught on. Figure 8-1 highlights the muscles of your upper back.

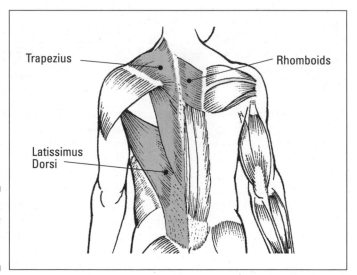

Figure 8-1:
The upper back muscle team.

Why You Need a Strong Upper Back

Okay, so well-developed lats aren't going to get you a starring role in any television dramas. But building up your back muscles does have its advantages.

- **Real-life benefits:** With a strong upper back, you'll find it easier to drag your kids into the dentist's office or lug your suitcases through endless airport terminals.

- **Injury prevention:** Strong lats help keep your shoulders healthy. Since they're the largest muscle north of your waistline, your lats do a good job of handling most of the work in pulling movements so you don't overstress your shoulders. For example, well-developed upper back muscles could save you from injury when unfolding the sofabed for a house guest.

- **The babe/hunk factor:** Upper back exercises can make your back more broad, which, in turn, makes your waist, hips, and legs appear smaller. Don't worry: You won't get so wide that you'll get stuck in any doorways.

Keys to a Great Upper Back Workout

Upper back exercises fall into three general categories: pulldowns and pull-ups, rows, and pullovers. Later in this chapter, we show you a variety of exercises in each category. For the most complete upper back workout, we suggest doing at least one exercise from each category, although you needn't do all of these exercises in the same workout.

- **Pulldowns and pull-ups:** With a pulldown, you grab a bar that's attached to an overhead pulley and pull it down; with a pull-up, you grasp a bar above you and pull yourself up. (See, this exercise stuff isn't so complicated!) We lump pulldowns and pull-ups into one category because they work your back in the same way. Both types of exercises involve your lats, traps, and rhomboids, but they also rely pretty heavily on your biceps, shoulders, and chest muscles. If you're looking to develop a broader back and improve your posture, emphasize pulldowns and pull-ups.

✔ **Rows:** This probably won't come as a shock, but rowing exercises mimic the motion of rowing a boat. You can perform rows with a barbell or dumbbell, a set of machine handles, or a bar that's attached to a low cable pulley. Rowing exercises use the same muscles as pulldowns and pull-ups except that they don't involve your chest. Rows are particularly helpful if you want to learn to sit up straighter; to perform a row correctly, you have to sit up tall.

✔ **Pullovers:** When you do a pullover, your arms move up and down in an arc, like when you pull an ax overhead to chop wood. Pullovers rely mainly on your lats, but they also call upon your chest, shoulder, and abdominal muscles. Like the other upper back exercises, pullovers help with posture. A pullover is an ideal transition exercise from a back workout to a chest workout. In other words, you can use a pullover as the last exercise of your back workout and as a prelude to your chest exercises because your chest will be warmed up.

Whether you're performing pulldowns, pull-ups, rows, or pullovers, remind yourself that these exercises are designed first and foremost to strengthen your back muscles, not your arms. Think of your arms merely as a link between the bar and your back muscles, which should do the bulk of the work. Concentrate on originating each exercise from the outer edges of your back. This bit of advice may be difficult to relate to at first, but as you get stronger and more sophisticated, you'll learn where exactly you should feel each exercise.

Most of the upper back exercises we show in this chapter involve weight machines or cable pulleys. If you work out at home and you don't have a multigym (a home version of health club machinery, described in Chapter 1), you can use a rubber exercise band to mimic the pulley machine. See Chapter 26 for a back exercise that you can do with a band.

Mistakes to Avoid When Working Your Upper Back

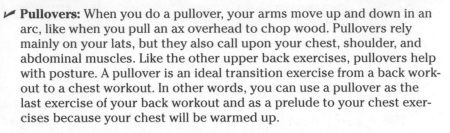

The upper back is one area where we see a lot of attempted heroics. With pulldowns and rows especially, people tend to pile on more weight than they can handle and end up contorting their bodies wildly in order to complete the exercise. This sort of behavior isn't going to get you anywhere. We know one trainer who tried to impress an entire gym full of people by doing a pulldown using the entire stack of weights on the machine. Rather than pulling down the bar, however, he was hoisted up out of his seat and left dangling in the air for a few seconds, like Liberace used to do on stage, only with a lot less flair.

The trainer was forced to let go of the bar when he tore a shoulder muscle. We suspect you won't get yourself into that kind of trouble. Nevertheless, here are some tips to avoid injury when you train your upper back:

- ✔ **Don't rock back and forth or wiggle around.** In an effort to pull the weight toward them, many people squirm around to build up momentum, but that's the last thing you want; instead, you should rely on your own muscle power. If you find yourself shifting around in order to lift and lower the weight, drop down a few plates.

- ✔ **Don't lean too far back.** You may be able to lift more weight when you lean way back, but that's because you have better leverage, not because your back muscles are getting a better workout. A more upright posture will ensure that your back muscles are in the prime position to do maximum work. Anytime you pull something toward you, squeeze your shoulder blades together and sit up tall. With pulldowns, you can lean back ever so slightly, but for rows you need to be sitting as tall as you do when your flight attendant demands that you return your seat back to its full upright position with your seat belt fastened and tray table locked.

- ✔ **Don't pull a bar down behind your neck.** There are endless variations of the pulldown exercise, but one now frowned upon by many exercise experts is the behind-the-neck pulldown. Critics of this exercise say that your arms are twisted so far back that your upper arm bones get jammed into your shoulder sockets, which could overstretch your ligaments and strain those delicate rotator-cuff muscles we describe in Chapter 10. Perhaps the dangers of this exercise are a bit overstated, but why take the chance? Unless you're a rock climber, an avid rower, or a swimmer who favors the butterfly stroke, front pulldowns will suffice.

Upper Back Exercises in This Chapter

Here's a preview of the upper back exercises shown in this chapter:

- ✔ One-arm Dumbbell Row
- ✔ Dumbbell Shrug
- ✔ Machine Row
- ✔ T-bar Row
- ✔ Lat Pulldown
- ✔ Cable Row
- ✔ Assisted Pull-up

One-arm Dumbbell Row

The One-arm Dumbbell Row targets your back, but also emphasizes, your biceps and shoulders. Be especially careful if you have **lower back** problems.

Getting Set

Stand to the right of your weight bench and hold a dumbbell in your right hand with your palm facing in. Pull your abdominals in and bend forward from your hips so that your back is naturally arched and roughly parallel with the floor and your knees are slightly bent. Place your left hand on top of the bench for support and let your right arm hang down. Tilt your chin toward your chest so that your neck is in line with the rest of your spine. See photo A in Figure 8-2.

The Exercise

Pull your right arm up, keeping it in line with your shoulder and parallel to the ceiling. Lift until your hand brushes against your waist. Lower the weight slowly back down. See photo B in Figure 8-2.

Do's and Don'ts

- ✔ DO remember that, although your arm is moving, this is a back exercise. Concentrate on pulling from your back muscles (right behind and below your shoulder) rather than just moving your arm up and down.

- ✔ DO keep your abs pulled in tight throughout the motion.

- ✔ DON'T allow your back to sag toward the floor or hunch up.

- ✔ DON'T jerk the weight upward.

Don't round
your back.

Figure 8-2:
Focus on
using your
back
muscles
rather than
just lifting
your arm.

Other Options

Rotation Row: As you lift the dumbbell, rotate your arm so that your palm ends up facing backward. This gives the exercise a different feel and places extra emphasis on your biceps.

Barbell Row: Place a barbell on the floor and stand about a foot away from it. With your knees bent, bend down and grasp the bar in an overhand grip with your hands a little wider than your shoulders. Pull your abs in tight and don't let your back arch. Keeping your hips bent so that your torso is at a 45-degree angle to the floor, pull the bar toward the lower part of your chest and then slowly lower it back down. You also can do this exercise with an underhand grip or with your hands a bit closer together.

Dumbbell Pullover

The Dumbbell Pullover is mainly a back exercise, but it also works a heckuva lot of other muscles, including your chest, shoulders, biceps, and abdominals. You may want to try the modified version if you have **shoulder** or **lower back** problems.

Getting Set

Holding a single dumbbell with both hands, lie on the bench with your feet flat on the floor and your arms directly over your shoulders. Turn your palms up so that one end of the dumbbell is resting in the gap between your palms and the other end is hanging down over your face. Pull your abdominals in but make sure your back is relaxed and arched naturally. See photo A in Figure 8-3.

The Exercise

Keeping your elbows slightly bent, lower the weight behind your head until the bottom end of the dumbbell is directly behind your head. Pull the dumbbell back up overhead, keeping the same slight bend in your elbows throughout the motion. See photo B in Figure 8-3.

A)

B)

Figure 8-3:
Don't let
your back
arch off the
bench.

Do's and Don'ts

- ✔ DO make sure you grip the dumbbell securely.

- ✔ DO concentrate on initiating the movement from the outer wings of your upper back rather than simply bending and straightening your arms.

- ✔ DON'T arch your back up off the bench, especially as you lower the weight.

- ✔ DON'T lower the weight too far behind you.

Other Options

Barbell Pullover: Do this same exercise with a bar, holding the bar in the center with your palms facing up. Another variation on the same theme: Hold a dumbbell in each hand with your palms facing in.

Machine Pullover: Many gyms have a machine that mimics the action of a dumbbell pullover while you're in a seated position.

Cross Bench Pullover (Harder): You can do this exercise squatting in front of the bench and resting your shoulders on the top. Because your body isn't supported by the bench, you have to work extra hard to maintain good form; this kicks in all of the deep muscles in the back and abs.

Dumbbell Shrug

The Dumbbell Shrug is a small movement with a big payoff: It strengthens your shoulders and the trapezius muscles of your upper back. Be careful if you're prone to **neck** problems.

Getting Set

Stand tall and hold a dumbbell in each hand, arms straight down, palms in front of your thighs and facing in. Pull your abdominals in, tuck your chin toward your chest, and keep your knees relaxed. See photo A of Figure 8-4.

The Exercise

Shrug your shoulders straight up toward your ears the same way you do if you don't know the answer to the $500 geography question on *Jeopardy!* Slowly lower your shoulders to the starting position. See photo B of Figure 8-4.

Figure 8-4:
Shrug your
shoulders
straight up
rather than
rolling them
in a circle.

A)

B)

Do's and Don'ts

✔ DO keep your neck and shoulders relaxed.

✔ DON'T roll your shoulders in a complete circle, a common exercise mistake that places too much stress on your shoulder joint.

✔ DON'T move body parts other than your shoulders.

Other Options

Barbell Shrug: Hold a bar with your hands shoulder-width apart and in front of your thighs, palms facing in. Do the exact same movement as in the basic version.

Shrug Roll (Harder): Shrug upward as in the basic version, squeeze your shoulder blades together, and then lower them back down. This version brings the trapezius and rhomboids (two back muscles) more into play.

Modified Upright Row: Stand tall with your feet hip-width apart while holding a barbell in front of you at waist level. Place your hands about six inches apart. Bend your elbows to raise the bar upward until it is just above the level of your bellybutton. Slowly return to the start. *Note:* We don't recommend the full Upright Row, which involves pulling your arms up until the bar is directly underneath your chin. This movement can be hard on your shoulder joints, rotator cuff, tendons, and ligaments.

Machine Row

The Machine Row focuses on your back, with additional emphasis on your shoulders and biceps. Take special care if you've had **lower back** or **shoulder** injuries.

Getting Set

Sit facing the weight stack of the machine with your chest against the chest pad. Adjust the seat so that your arms are level with the machine's handles and you must stretch your arms fully to reach them. This is an important adjustment — one that many people forget to make. If you can't fully straighten your arms when you grasp the handles, you'll end up using your arm muscles a lot more than your back muscles. Grasp a handle in each hand and sit up very tall. See photo A in Figure 8-5.

The Exercise

Pull the handles toward you until your hands are alongside your chest. As you bend your arms, your elbows should travel directly behind you, not out to the side. At the same time, squeeze your shoulder blades together. Slowly straighten your arms, feeling a stretch through your shoulder blades as you return the handles to their original position. See photo B of Figure 8-5.

A)

B)

Figure 8-5:
Sit up tall as
you perform
the Machine
Row.

Do's and Don'ts

- ✔ DO sit up even taller as you pull the weight.
- ✔ DON'T lean back so far that your chest comes off the pad as you bend your arms.
- ✔ DON'T round your back or lean forward as you return the handles to the starting position.
- ✔ DON'T stick your neck forward as you pull the weight.

Other Options

Other machines: Although each manufacturer has its own version of the Machine Row, the same basic rules apply. Depending on the brand, the handles may be parallel, perpendicular, or diagonal; some machines have all three grips. Experiment with different grips to get a different feel from this exercise.

Advanced Machine Row (Harder): Do this exercise without keeping your chest on the chest pad. Without the support, you have to work harder to sit up straight.

Lat Pulldown

The Lat Pulldown is primarily a back exercise, although your shoulders and biceps also see some action. Try switching grips and attachments to give this exercise a different feel. Be careful if you have **shoulder** or **lower back** problems.

Getting Set

Before you start, sit in the seat and adjust the thigh pads so that your legs are firmly wedged underneath the pads with your knees bent and your feet flat on the floor. Then stand up and grasp the bar with an overhand grip and your hands about six inches wider than shoulder-width apart. Still grasping the bar, sit back down and wedge the tops of your thighs (just above your knee) underneath the thigh pads. Stretch your arms straight up, keep your chest lifted, and lean back slightly from your hips. See photo A in Figure 8-6.

The Exercise

In a smooth, fluid motion, pull the bar down to the top of your chest. Hold the position for a moment, then slowly raise the bar back up. When you've completed the set, stand up in order to return the weights to the stack. Don't just let go of the bar while you're seated — this causes the weight stack to come crashing down. See photo B in Figure 8-6.

A)

B)

Figure 8-6:
Don't lean
more than
an inch or
two back as
you pull the
bar down.

Do's and Don'ts

- ✔ DON'T rock back and forth in an effort to pull down the weight.

- ✔ DON'T lean way back as you pull the weight down. Keep that inch-or-two lean that you had at the beginning of the movement.

- ✔ DON'T move so quickly that you jerk your elbows or shoulders.

- ✔ DON'T bend your wrists.

Other Options

Changing your grip: You can experiment with the width of your grip and the orientation of your palms to give this exercise a different feel. For example, you can use the triangle attachment for a **Triangle-grip Lat Pulldown.** Or you can use an underhand grip (**Reverse-grip Lat Pulldown**) and hold near the center of the bar for a pulldown that feels similar to a chin-up. For reasons we explain earlier in this chapter, avoid pulling the bar behind your neck. Experiment with other attachments of varying lengths and curves, such as the short straight bar and rope.

Cable Row

The Cable Row strengthens your back, along with your biceps and shoulders. Be especially careful if you've had **lower back** or **shoulder** problems.

Getting Set

Hook the short straight bar attachment onto a low pulley. Place a riser from a step bench (or box of similar length) directly against the base of the cable tower. (Some machines come with a foot bar so you don't need to add a box.) Sit facing the tower with your legs slightly bent and hip-width apart, and your feet firmly planted against the riser. Grasp the handle and straighten your arms out in front of your chest. Sit up as tall as you can, pulling your abdominals in and lifting your chest. See photo A in Figure 8-7.

The Exercise

Sitting up tall, pull the handle toward the lower part of your chest, squeezing your shoulder blades together as you pull. Your elbows should travel straight back, arms brushing lightly against your sides as you go. Without stretching forward, straighten your arms slowly back to the start. See photo B in Figure 8-7.

Figure 8-7:
Feel this
exercise in
your back,
not just
your arms.

A)

B)

Keep your knees slightly bent.

Do's and Don'ts

- ✔ DO feel this exercise in your back, not just your arms. Concentrate on starting the pull with the outer edges of your back.

- ✔ DON'T round your back.

- ✔ DON'T rock back and forth to help you lift and lower the weight.

Other Options

Extended Row: The basic version of this exercise is excellent for targeting the upper back muscles. However, you can strengthen your lower back at the same time by leaning forward a few inches at your hips as you stretch your arms out and by leaning back slightly as you pull the handle toward you. Some exercise purists scorn this version because it doesn't "isolate" your upper back, but we think it's great for people who do a lot of rowing or activities in which the upper and lower back work together: weeding, dancing, or climbing. However, skip this version if you have a history of low back pain.

One-arm Cable Row: Attach a horseshoe handle and perform this row one arm at a time.

Assisted Pull-up

The Assisted Pull-up targets your back, with additional emphasis on your shoulders and biceps. Be careful if you have **lower back** or **shoulder** problems.

Getting Set

Step up on the platform of an Assisted Pull-up machine (sometimes called a Gravitron) and carefully kneel onto the knee pads. (Some versions require you to stand.) Grab the handles that place your palms facing forward and straighten your arms. Pull your abdominals in and keep your body tall. See photo A in Figure 8-8.

The Exercise

Pull yourself up until your elbows are pointing down and then slowly lower your body back down. See photo B in Figure 8-8.

A)

B)

Figure 8-8:
Don't cheat
by rocking
your body.

Do's and Don'ts

- ✔ DO relax your shoulders so they don't hunch up by your ears.
- ✔ DON'T rock your body to help move you up and down.
- ✔ DON'T arch your back or round forward.
- ✔ DON'T dawdle at the bottom of the exercise. Move steadily until you finish your reps.

Other Options

Different grips: Some Assisted Pull-up machines have a choice of grips. Experiment to see which ones you like best.

Bar Pull-up (Harder): Using a Smith machine or power cage, set the bar so that it is securely resting against the stops set in the center of the frame. Grasp the center of the bar with your hands a few inches apart and palms facing you. Kick your legs out in front of you so that your torso forms a 45-degree angle with the floor. Bend your arms and pull yourself upward until the top of your chest touches, or nearly touches, the bar. Slowly lower to the start position. This version of the pull-up is a good precursor to learning the full-fledged Chin-up described in Chapter 14.

Lower Back Muscle Basics

Your lower back muscles have two main jobs: bending your spine backward and bracing your torso when you move some other part of your body. (Your lower back muscles perform this stabilizing job in tandem with your abdominal muscles, located directly in front of them.) The main lower back muscles you need to know about are the *erector spinae*. Feel along either side of your spine just above your hips and you have a handle on your lower erector spinae. Figure 8-9 points out your lower back muscles.

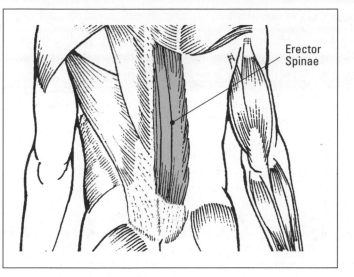

Erector Spinae

Figure 8-9: A look at the lower back.

Why You Need to Strengthen Your Lower Back

Most lower back exercises — especially those appropriate for beginners — don't involve free weights or machines. Usually, it's just you and the floor. Here's what you can accomplish without any equipment at all:

✔ **Real-life benefits:** Sitting puts your spine under a lot of pressure, much more pressure than if you stood all day. That's why your lower back can feel so sore after a day in front of the computer. When your back muscles are weak, you tend to slouch or sit at a funny angle, which places the spine under even more stress. (In addition to strengthening and stretching your lower back on a regular basis, you should take frequent breaks from the sitting position throughout the day.)

✔ **Injury prevention:** Ironically, even people with chronic lower back pain tend to neglect lower back exercises, often because they're afraid of inflicting even more damage. Also, while people have gotten the message that abdominal exercises can help alleviate back pain, many don't realize that lower back exercises are equally important in this pursuit. When one of these sets of muscles is stronger or more flexible than the other, your posture is thrown off kilter and you're more prone to back pain. This is a pretty common scenario.

✔ **The babe/hunk factor:** Strengthening your lower back will help you stand up straight, which, in turn, can make you look slimmer and give you a more confident, commanding presence.

Keys to a Great Lower Back Workout

We often take for granted the role that our lower back muscles play in our everyday mobility. So, while your lower back muscles need to be strong, they also need to be flexible.

This balance between strength and flexibility is perhaps more important with your lower back than with any other muscle group in your body. That's why we include the Pelvic Tilt, which both strengthens and lengthens out the muscles attached to your spine. This exercise won't score you any points in the macho department, but it's one that everyone should do. The same goes for back extension exercises. However, if you're experiencing back pain right now or have a history of back trouble, check with your doctor before performing extension exercises.

When you do a lower back exercise, you should feel a mild pull or pressure build within the muscle, *not* a sharp pain. If you do feel a piercing pain, back off. Review the exercise description to make sure that you haven't pushed your body too far and then try it again. If you still feel pain, seek medical advice before proceeding any further.

You may feel a dull ache in your back a day or two after you've worked your lower back. This is normal. But if the pain is sharp and so debilitating that your most upright posture looks like you're trying to duck under a fence, you've either pushed yourself too far or you have a back problem.

Mistakes to Avoid When Training Your Lower Back

Few people make mistakes when they do lower back exercises. That's because few people actually take the time to do these exercises, which is a pretty big mistake in itself. Here are a few other common errors:

- ✔ **Don't bend too far back.** On back extensions, raise your body just a few inches, and lengthen out as much as you can. With pelvic tilts, the point is to isolate your lower back muscles while keeping your back planted on the floor.

- ✔ **Always do back exercises slowly and carefully.** If you race through them, you may cause the very back problems you're trying to prevent.

Lower Back Exercises

Coming up in the chapter, we show you the following two lower back exercises, along with several variations:

- ✔ Pelvic Tilt
- ✔ Back Extension

Pelvic Tilt

The Pelvic Tilt is a subtle move that focuses on your lower back, but also emphasizes your abdominals and hamstrings. This is a good exercise to do if you have a history of lower back problems.

Getting Set

Lie on your back with your knees bent and feet flat on the floor about hip-width apart. Rest your arms wherever they're most comfortable. Gently press your back down and pull your abdominals in toward your spine. Don't tilt your head up and back. See photo A in Figure 8-10.

The Exercise

Keeping your entire back against the floor, gently squeeze your butt and tilt your hips up until your rear end curls an inch or two off the floor. Hold this position for a moment and then slowly lower your butt back down. See photo B in Figure 8-10.

Do's and Don'ts

✔ DO keep your head, neck, and shoulders relaxed.

✔ DON'T lift your lower back off the floor as you tilt your pelvis up.

✔ DON'T arch your back off the floor when you lower your hips back down.

Other Options

Chair Tilt (Easier): Lie on your back and place your heels up on the seat of a chair with your knees bent at a right angle and thighs perpendicular to the floor. Then perform the exercise exactly as you would in the basic version.

Focused Pelvic Tilt: While performing the Pelvic Tilt, place one hand on your stomach and one hand, palm down, directly underneath the small of your back. The top hand reminds you to keep your abdominals pulled in, and the bottom hand reminds you to keep your lower back on the floor.

Hip Lift (Harder): At the top of the Pelvic Tilt continue peeling your spine off the floor until only your shoulder blades and shoulders remain on the floor. Work hard to keep your abdominals pulled inward to prevent your back from sagging. Hold a moment and slowly lower your body downward.

A)

Figure 8-10:
Don't lift
your lower
back off the
floor as you
tilt your
pelvis up.

B)

Curl your butt a few inches off the floor.

Back Extension

The Back Extension strengthens your lower back muscles. Performing this exercise on a regular basis can help reduce lower back pain, but use caution if you have a history of back problems or if your **lower back** is bothering you right now.

Getting Set

Lie on your stomach with your forehead on the floor, arms straight out in front of you, palms down, and legs straight out behind you. Pull your abs in, as if you're trying to create a small space between your stomach and the floor.

The Exercise

Lift your right arm and left leg a couple of inches off the floor and stretch out as much as you can. Hold this position for five slow counts, lower back down, and then repeat the same move with your left arm and right leg. Continue alternating sides until you've completed the set. See Figure 8-11.

Do's and Don'ts

- ✔ DO exhale as you lift and inhale as you lower.

- ✔ DO pretend as if you're trying to touch something with your toes and fingertips that's just out of reach.

- ✔ DO pay special attention to how your lower back feels. This exercise may aggravate lower back pain more than other exercises do.

- ✔ DON'T lift up higher than a few inches.

Other Options

Sequential Back Extension (Easier): If the basic version of the Back Extension bothers your lower back, lift and lower your right arm, and then lift and lower your left leg.

Kneeling Opposite Extension (Easier): Kneeling on your hands and knees, extend your right arm out in front of you and your left leg out behind you. This version places less stress on the lower back and is an excellent modification for those new to lower back training and those who feel lower back discomfort when doing back extension exercises.

Same-side Back Extension (Harder): Do the same exercise lifting your right arm and right leg at the same time.

Figure 8-11:
Don't lift
your arms or
legs more
than a few
inches.

Chapter 9

Working Your Chest

· ·

In This Chapter

▶ Introducing your pecs

▶ Strategies for a great chest workout

▶ Mistakes to avoid when working your chest

▶ Chest exercises

· ·

Some people are so obsessed with their chests that they work this muscle group virtually to the exclusion of all others. In fact, there is an entire subset of the male species who resemble an inflated hot-air balloon from the front and a deflated tire from the back. Then there are those among us, mostly women, who fear that doing chest exercises may make them look like an East German shot-putter from the Iron Curtain days. These people won't walk anywhere *near* a chest machine.

When it comes to chest exercises, you need to find a happy medium. In this chapter, we explain why chest exercises are important — and why they won't transform you into Pamela Anderson Lee or Arnold Schwarzenegger. We offer tips on choosing the order in which you perform your chest exercises, and we caution you against using one of the most popular chest machines. We also run down the most common mistakes people make when working their chest muscles.

Chest Muscle Basics

The technical name for your chest muscles is the *pectorals,* but gym regulars shorten the term to *pecs.* You have two pec muscles: the *pectoralis major* and the *pectoralis minor.* Whenever you pledge allegiance, your hand is covering the meat of the pectoralis major; the pec minor resides underneath. Figure 9-1 shows the location of your pectorals. With the help of other muscles, such as your shoulder muscles and triceps, your pecs are in charge of a variety of pushing and hugging movements.

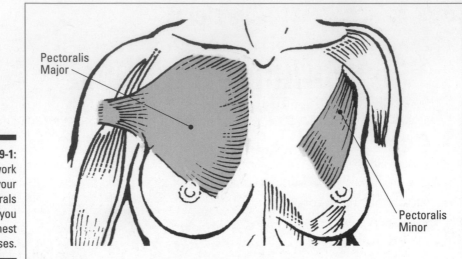

Pectoralis
Major

Pectoralis
Minor

Figure 9-1:
You work
your
pectorals
when you
do chest
exercises.

Why Strong Pecs Matter

This may be the first time you've given your chest muscles any thought, but you've been depending on them your whole life to push things around. Now that you'll be performing chest exercises, you can be pushier than ever. (However, you can never be as pushy as the perfume salespeople who assault us upon entering department stores.) Here's how you can profit from training your pecs:

- **Real-life benefits:** You'll have more oomph when you push a lawn mower or a full shopping cart with two kids hanging off the end — or when you wrap your arms around Uncle Leo at Thanksgiving after he's eaten an entire pumpkin pie.

- **Injury prevention:** Your chest muscles are attached to your shoulder joint. So with strong pecs, you're less likely to injure your shoulders while rearranging your furniture or pushing your car out of a snowbank.

- **The babe/hunk factor:** Chest exercises can make a woman's breasts appear firmer, although keep in mind that these exercises won't transform anyone from an AA cup to a C cup or vice versa. As for men: Pec training can make your chest fuller. However, both sexes should maintain realistic expectations about chest exercises.

Keys to a Great Chest Workout

You can change the feel and focus of many chest exercises by adjusting the angle of the bench you use. (See Chapter 1 for descriptions of various benches.) Performing chest exercises on a flat bench emphasizes those fibers in the center of your chest. When you adjust the bench a few degrees to an incline position, you shift the focus of the exercise to the fibers in your upper chest and shoulder muscles. Doing the opposite — adjusting the bench to a decline position — concentrates the work on the lower fibers of the chest. By the way, decline exercises are probably the least important category of chest exercises because they work a relatively small portion of the pecs.

We won't be showing you how to operate one popular chest machine: the *Pec Deck.* You sit with your arms spread apart, each arm bent and placed on a pad. You push the pads toward each other, as if you're clapping in slow motion. We think the Pec Deck should be renamed the *Pec Wreck,* or more accurately, the *Shoulder Wreck.* These machines place an enormous amount of pressure on the shoulder joint and rotator cuff and frequently lead to injury. What's more, they don't actually do much for your pec muscles. A safer and more effective alternative to the Pec Deck is the Dumbbell Chest Fly (shown in this chapter).

Because your chest muscles are among the largest in your upper body, we suggest that you perform more sets of exercises with these muscles than with the smaller muscle groups of your arms. In general, we recommend doing 3 to 12 sets of chest exercises per workout, although true beginners should start with one set. By the way, when we say 12 sets, we don't mean a dozen sets of the same exercise; you may want to do 3 or 4 (or more) different exercises. Also, remember to begin each exercise with an easy warm-up set. Even power-lifters who can bench press 500 pounds often warm up with a 45-pound bar.

Which chest exercises should you do first? Experts argue this point, but we suggest that you let personal preference be your guide. We like to perform free-weight exercises when we're fresh because they tend to require more strength and control. Also, we perform flat-bench exercises before incline or decline exercises. Experiment with the order of exercises for a couple of weeks until you come up with a sequence that works for you. You may even want to change the sequence from time to time. If you always do the Chest Fly before the Dumbbell Chest Press, for example, you may never realize your true Dumbbell Press potential because your chest muscles will always be tired by the time you get to that exercise.

As for the number of repetitions to perform per set, the general rule — 8 to 15 reps — certainly applies to chest work. However, determining your *one-rep max* — that is, the maximum amount of weight you can lift once — is somewhat of an ancient gym tradition with the Bench Press. Don't try this until you've been lifting weights for a month or two, and don't attempt to *max out* more often than once a week. In fact, some experts believe that maxing out once a month brings better results. When you do attempt a maximum weight, make sure that you have a *spotter,* a buddy ready to grab the weight in case you overestimated your strength. (See Chapter 2 for tips on how to be spotted.) If you're going for your one-rep max, do a few warm-up sets, gradually increasing the weight.

Mistakes to Avoid When Pumping Your Pecs

One morning Liz was working at a gym when a member came up and casually mentioned that another member needed help on the Bench Press. Liz strolled over to find this man trapped underneath a bar that apparently had been too heavy for his chest muscles to handle. "Caesar," she asked, "how long have you been there?" "About twenty minutes," he replied. Why hadn't he yelled for help? He was too embarrassed. Moral of the story: Safety is more important than lifting heavy weights. In addition to lifting the proper amount of weight, take the following precautions when working your chest:

- **Don't *lock* your elbows.** In other words, don't straighten your arms to the point that your elbows snap. This puts too much pressure on the elbows and can lead to *tendinitis* or inflammation of the elbow joint itself. When you straighten your arms, keep your elbows slightly relaxed.

- **Don't arch your back.** In an effort to hoist more poundage, some people arch their backs so severely that there's enough room between their back and the bench for a Range Rover to drive through. Sooner or later, this position causes a back injury. Plus, you're doing nothing to strengthen your chest muscles. Instead, you're overstraining your lower back.

- **Don't flatten your back.** In a sincere effort not to cheat, many people do the exact opposite of overarching their backs: They force their lower backs into the bench. This posture is equally bad for your back. When you lie down, there should be a slight gap between your lower back and the bench, reflecting the natural arch of your back.

- ✔ **Don't lift your shoulder blades off the bench or back rest.** Otherwise, your shoulders will bear too much weight — without any support from the bench. This is a subtle error but one that may be costly for your shoulder joint.

- ✔ **Don't stretch too far.** When you lie on your back and perform the Bench Press, you may be tempted to lower the bar all the way to your chest. Similarly, when you perform a Push-up, you may want to lower your body all the way to the floor. Don't. Instead, follow the instructions we provide for these and similar chest exercises.

Exercises in This Chapter

Here's a glance at the chest exercises featured in this chapter:

- ✔ Modified Push-up
- ✔ Bench Press
- ✔ Dumbbell Chest Press
- ✔ Incline Chest Fly
- ✔ Vertical Chest Press Machine
- ✔ Cable Crossover
- ✔ Assisted Dip

Modified Push-up

The Modified Push-up strengthens your chest muscles, with additional emphasis on your shoulders and triceps. Be extra careful if you have **lower back, shoulder, elbow,** or **wrist** problems.

Getting Set

Lie on your stomach, bend your knees, and cross your ankles. Bend your elbows and place your palms on the floor a bit to the side and in front of your shoulders. Straighten your arms and lift your body so that you're balanced on your palms and the part of your thighs just above your knees. Tuck your chin a few inches toward your chest so that your forehead faces the floor. Tighten your abdominals. See photo A in Figure 9-2.

The Exercise

Bend your elbows and lower your entire body at once. Rather than try to touch your chest to the floor, lower only until your upper arms are parallel to the floor. Push back up. See photo B in Figure 9-2.

Do's and Don'ts

- ✔ DO keep your abdominal muscles pulled in tight throughout the exercise so that your back doesn't arch like a swayback horse; otherwise you're begging for a lower back injury.

- ✔ DON'T lock your elbows at the top of the movement.

- ✔ DON'T do the dreaded *head bob*. That's when you dip your head toward the floor without moving any other part of your body. Talk about a giant pain in the neck!

Other Options

Wall Push-up (Easier): Stand a few feet away from a wall and place your palms flat on the wall slightly wider than your shoulders. Bend your elbows and lean into the wall. Then press yourself away from the wall by straightening your arms.

Incline Push-up: This version is easier than the Modified Push-up but harder than the Wall Push-up. Follow the same set-up as the basic version of this exercise, but place your hands on top of a step bench that has two or three sets of risers underneath.

Military Push-up (Harder): See Chapter 14 for a description.

A)

Figure 9-2:
Tighten your
abs so that
your back
doesn't sag.

B)

Lower your body
in a straight line.

Bench Press

The Bench Press, crowned the king of all chest exercises by bodybuilders, primarily works your chest muscles, with plenty of emphasis on your shoulders and triceps, too. You may want to try a modified version of this exercise — or avoid it altogether — if you have **lower back, shoulder,** or **elbow** problems.

Getting Set

Lie on the bench with your feet flat on the floor or up on the bench if the bench is too tall. Grip the bar so that your arms are evenly spaced a few inches wider than shoulder-width apart. Your upper arms should be slightly above parallel to the floor. Tuck your chin toward your chest and pull your abdominals in tight, but don't force your back into the pad, or overarch it, either. Lift the bar off the rack and push it directly up over your shoulders, straightening your arms without locking your elbows. See photo A in Figure 9-3.

The Exercise

Lower the bar until your elbows are slightly below your shoulders. The bar may or may not touch your chest — this will depend on how long your arms are and how big your chest is. Press the bar back up. See photo B in Figure 9-3.

Do's and Don'ts

- ✔ DO remember to breathe. Exhale as you press the bar up, and inhale as you lower it.

- ✔ DON'T cheat. In other words, if you have to wiggle around or arch your back in order to hoist the bar, you're not doing much for your chest, but you are asking for lower back injuries.

- ✔ DON'T press the bar up too high; your elbows should stay relaxed and your shoulder blades should remain on the backrest throughout the exercise.

Other Options

Towel Chest Press (Easier): Roll up a large bath towel and place it across your chest. Lower the bar until it touches the towel and then press back up. This is a good one if you have shoulder problems.

Incline Bench Press: Incline the bench a few inches and then do the exercise as described above. This version emphasizes the upper fibers of your pecs and shoulders.

Decline Bench Press: Do this exercise on a decline bench, with your head lower than your feet. This requires a special decline version of the bench press station. Some bench press stations can be set flat, incline, or decline whereas others are permanently fixed in the decline position.

A)

Figure 9-3:
Don't squirm
around or
arch your
back in
order to
hoist
the bar.

B)

Don't lower your elbows much below shoulder level.

Dumbbell Chest Press

The Dumbbell Chest Press closely mimics the Bench Press. It works your chest muscles, along with your shoulders and triceps. You may want to modify or avoid this exercise if you have **shoulder, elbow,** or **lower back** problems.

Getting Set

Lie on the bench with a dumbbell in each hand and your feet flat on the floor (or up on the bench if it's more comfortable). Push the dumbbells up so that your arms are directly over your shoulders and your palms face forward. Pull your abdominals in, but don't jam your back into the bench; don't let it arch way up, either. Tilt your chin toward your chest. See photo A in Figure 9-4.

The Exercise

Lower the dumbbells down and a little to the side until your elbows are slightly below your shoulders. Push the weights back up, taking care not to lock your elbows or allow your shoulder blades to rise off the bench. See photo B in Figure 9-4.

Do's and Don'ts

✔ DO allow your back to keep a natural arch so that you have a slight gap between your lower back and the bench.

✔ DON'T contort your body in an effort to lift the weight; lift only as much weight as you can handle while maintaining good form.

Other Options

Partial Dumbbell Press (Easier): Lower the weights only about three quarters the distance of the basic version of this exercise. Try this version if you have elbow, shoulder, or rotator cuff problems.

Incline Chest Press: Perform this exercise on an incline bench. You'll use less weight than when you perform a flat-bench press.

Decline Chest Press: Do this exercise on a decline bench, with your head lower than your feet. The hardest part of this version is picking up and releasing the weights. Grab the weights while you're sitting up, hold them against your chest, and ease yourself into the decline position. When you're done with the exercise, gently ease the dumbbells off to either side to the floor. (Don't just drop them.) Better yet, ask someone to hand the weights to you at the start of the exercise and take them away when you're done.

A)

B)

Figure 9-4:
Don't lock
your elbows
at the top
of the
movement.

Incline Chest Fly

The Incline Chest Fly primarily works your chest muscles, with lots of emphasis on your shoulder muscles. The exercise also places some emphasis on your triceps, although less so than many other chest exercises. Pay special attention to your form if you've had **shoulder** (rotator cuff especially), **elbow,** or **lower back** injuries.

Getting Set

Incline the bench a few inches. The incline should be 1-5 inches on the bench, depending on the bench. Holding a dumbbell in each hand, lie on the bench with your feet flat on the floor or on the bench, whichever feels more comfortable to you. Press the weights directly above your chest, palms facing each other. Tuck your chin to your chest to align your neck with the rest of your spine and maintain your natural back posture, neither arched nor flattened. See photo A of Figure 9-5.

The Exercise

Spreading your arms apart so that your elbows travel down and to the sides, lower the weights until your elbows are just below your shoulders. Maintain a constant bend in your elbows, as you lift the dumbbells back up. Imagine that you have a barrel lying on your chest, and you have to keep your arms wide to reach around it. See photo B in Figure 9-5.

Do's and Don'ts

- ✔ DO feel a stretch in the outer edges of your chest. Hold a moment in the lowered position to feel it even more.

- ✔ DON'T forget to keep the bend in your elbows as you lower the weights. If your arms are too straight, you place excessive pressure on your elbows and shoulder joints.

- ✔ DON'T move your elbows any lower than specified or you risk damaging your shoulder and rotator cuff muscles.

Other Options

Flat Chest Fly: Do the same exercise on a flat bench. The incline version emphasizes upper chest fibers, while the flat version calls in the middle and lower fibers as well.

Decline Chest Fly: Do this exercise on a decline bench, with your head lower than your feet. The hardest thing about this version is picking up and releasing the weights. Grab the weights while you're sitting up, hold them against your chest, and ease yourself into the decline position. When you're done with the exercise, gently ease the dumbbells off to either side to the floor. (Don't just drop them.) Better yet, ask someone to hand the weights to you at the start of the exercise and take them away when you're done.

A)

B)

Figure 9-5:
Maintain the
bend in your
elbows as
you lower
the weights.

Vertical Chest Press Machine

The Vertical Chest Press Machine focuses on your chest muscles, with additional emphasis on your triceps and shoulders. Most vertical chest machines have more than one grip so that you can work your chest muscles in different ways. Use caution if you have **shoulder** or **elbow** problems.

Getting Set

Sit in the machine so that the center of your chest lines up with the set of horizontal handle bars. Press down on the foot bar so that the handles move forward. Grip the horizontal handles. Straighten your arms, pushing the handles forward. Keep your abdominals tight so that your upper back remains on the pad. See photo A in Figure 9-6.

The Exercise

Remove your feet from the foot bar — you'll feel the weight of the stack transfer into your hands. Slowly bend your arms until your hands are just in front of your chest, and then push the handles forward until your arms are straight. When you have completed your set, put your feet back on the foot bar and let go of the handle bars *before* you lower the weight stack all the way down. See photo B in Figure 9-6.

Do's and Don'ts

✔ DO keep your neck against the backrest.

✔ DON'T press so quickly that your elbows snap shut and your shoulders come up off the backrest.

Other Options

Different angles: You may find chest machines that position you horizontally and at many angles between horizontal and vertical. Other machines are designed so that the left and right sides work independently of each other; in other words the left and right levers of the machine are not connected to one another so when you raise the weight, both sides of your body have to fend for themselves. Machines with independent action are a good alternative for those with left-right muscle imbalances or those who wish to combine the safety of using a machine with the feel of using free weights. Try 'em all and decide which ones you like best.

Vertical Grip (Harder): Use the vertical handle of your chest machine. This grip factors out a lot of the help you get from your shoulders when using the horizontal grip.

Don't lock your elbows.

A)

B)

Figure 9-6:
Don't press
so quickly
that your
elbows snap
shut.

Cable Crossover

The Cable Crossover strengthens your chest muscles, with emphasis on the shoulders as well. Be careful if you have **shoulder, elbow,** or **lower back** problems.

Getting Set

Set the pulleys on both towers of a cable machine to the top position. Clip a horseshoe handle (see Chapter 1 for description of all the different cable pulley handles) to each pulley. Stand between the towers with your legs comfortably apart and with one foot slightly in front of the other. Grasp a handle in each hand, palms facing down and slightly forward. Tighten your abdominals, lean slightly forward from your hips, and relax your knees. See photo A in Figure 9-7.

The Exercise

Keeping a slight bend in your elbows, pull the handles down so that one wrist crosses slightly in front of the other. Then slowly raise your arms up and out to the sides until your hands are level with your shoulders. See photo B in Figure 9-7.

Do's and Don'ts

- ✔ DO exhale deeply before bringing your hands together.

- ✔ DO initiate the move from your chest; in other words, keep your shoulders, elbows, and wrists in the same position throughout.

- ✔ DON'T forget that slight forward lean: It takes the pressure off your lower back.

Other Options

Flat Bench Cable Fly: Set the cables to the lowest point on the towers, and place a flat bench in the center of the towers. Grasp a handle in each hand and lie on your back. Straighten your arms up directly over your shoulders and then spread your arms down and to the side until your elbows are just below shoulder level. This is the same motion used in the Flat Bench Dumbbell Chest Fly.

One-hand Crossover: Do the basic cable crossover one arm at a time. Place the unused hand on your hip or hold onto the cable tower.

A)

B)

Figure 9-7:
Lean slightly
forward to
take the
pressure off
your lower
back.

Assisted Dip

The Assisted Dip primarily works your chest muscles, with a lot of emphasis on your shoulders and triceps, too. Use caution if you have **elbow, shoulder,** or **lower back** problems.

Getting Set

For this exercise, deciding which plate to put the pin in can be confusing because you follow the exact opposite rule of every other exercise. In this case, you choose *more* plates if you want the exercise to be *easier* and fewer plates if you want the exercise to be harder. The more plates you select, the more your weight is counterbalanced during the exercise. For example, if you weigh 150 pounds and you place the pin in the plate marked *100,* you have to lift only 50 pounds of your body weight. But if you put the pin into the plate marked *50,* you have to lift 100 pounds.

Once you've set your weight, step onto the platform of the Assisted Dip machine, and then carefully kneel onto the knee pad. Grip the lower bars with your palms facing inward, and straighten your arms. Pull your abdominals in and keep your body tall. See photo A in Figure 9-8.

The Exercise

Lower your body until your upper arms are parallel to the floor and then push back up. See photo B in Figure 9-8.

Do's and Don'ts

- ✔ DO relax your shoulders so they don't hunch up by your ears.
- ✔ DON'T explode back to the start and snap your elbows.
- ✔ DON'T lower your body further than the point at which your upper arms are parallel to the floor.

Other Options

Negative-only Dip (Easier): If you find a traditional dip (shown in Chapter 14) too difficult, perform only the *negative* phase: Use your muscle power to lower yourself and then jump up to the start after every repetition. However, when you jump up, take it easy on your elbows.

Check out Chapter 14 for more advanced versions of this exercise.

A)

B)

Figure 9-8:
Don't
explode
back to the
start and
snap your
elbows.

Chapter 10

Working Your Shoulders

*N*ext time the power goes out in your neighborhood, watch a police officer stand in the middle of a four-way intersection and direct traffic. Or next time you're at the video store, rent *Saturday Night Fever* and watch John Travolta do the Hustle. Either way, you'll get a good idea of what the human shoulder muscle can do. When you move your arms in virtually any direction — up, down, backward, forward, sideways, diagonally — your shoulders are in charge, or at least involved. The ingenious design of your shoulder joint makes the shoulders one of the most mobile, versatile muscle groups in your body.

Unfortunately, their amazing capacity for movement also makes the shoulders, along with a nearby muscle group called the *rotator cuff,* particularly vulnerable to injury. In this chapter, we show you how to protect your shoulders by performing a variety of exercises. And if disco ever makes a comeback, you'll be duly prepared.

Shoulder Muscle Basics

Your shoulder muscles are officially called the *deltoids,* or *delts,* but fitness types usually refer to them simply as your shoulders. These muscles run from the top down to the center of your upper arms. They're able to move in so many directions because your shoulder joint is a *ball-and-socket joint:* The round head of your arm bone snaps neatly into your shoulder socket. Your hip is another ball-and-socket joint, but even that joint doesn't have the mobility that your shoulder does.

The *rotator cuff* is a group of four muscles that keep your arm from slipping out of its socket. They reside underneath your delts, performing their job in complete anonymity. Unfortunately, they're so anonymous that many people don't even know that they exist and, therefore, don't bother to train them. The only time they seem to get any recognition is when a professional baseball pitcher is sidelined for the season by a rotator cuff injury. Your rotator cuff muscles enable you to twist your arm while your elbow is straight, such as when you turn your palm to face forward and then backward. They also get into the act during throwing and catching motions and when you raise your arms above your head. Figure 10-1 illustrates the shoulder muscles.

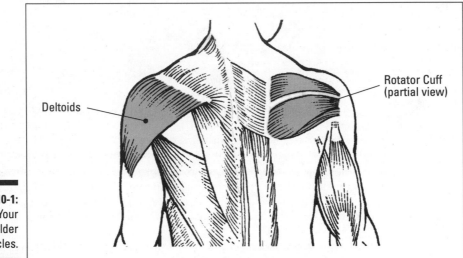

Deltoids

Rotator Cuff
(partial view)

Figure 10-1:
Your
shoulder
muscles.

Why You Need to Strengthen Your Shoulders

Your shoulders do a fair amount of work whenever you perform back and chest exercises, but performing exercises that single out your delts is also important for the following reasons:

✔ **Real-life benefits:** Strong shoulders make most arm movements easier, whether you're beaning your brother with a snowball, passing the potatoes across the table, or lifting your hands to do the "wave" at sporting events. Virtually every upper body exercise involves your shoulder muscles to some extent, so strengthening your shoulders enables you to lift heavier weights on chest and back exercises.

✔ **Injury prevention:** If your shoulders are weak, they're going to take a beating even if you perform chest and back exercises perfectly. Shoulder exercises also can prevent weekend-warrior type injuries, such as shoulder tears from throwing a softball or slapping a puck into the garbage can that serves as your hockey goal. If your shoulders are weak, you can even injure yourself while opening a dresser drawer.

✔ **Babe/hunk factor:** Open up any bodybuilding magazine and you see headlines such as, "Grow those big caps even bigger" or "Delts to die for." Bodybuilders take their shoulder training very seriously because they know that these muscles play a big part in their appearance, which, after all, is what bodybuilding is all about. Even if you don't want to develop delts to die for, you can still develop toned, shapely shoulders that look pretty darned good.

Keys to a Great Shoulder Workout

There are literally dozens of ways to strengthen these muscles, so if you're sitting there with a dumbbell in your hand saying to yourself, "I need to work my shoulders today, and I can't think of anything to do," you certainly can't blame us for your quandary. Here are the four main types of shoulder movements. (Later in this chapter, we offer several variations of each, as well as a few other shoulder movements that don't fall into these categories.)

✔ **Press:** You straighten your arms up over your head. Shoulder-press exercises work the entire shoulder muscle.

✔ **Lateral raise:** You raise your arms out to the sides. Lateral raises focus on the top and outside portions of the muscle.

✔ **Front raise:** You raise your arms directly in front of you. Front raises work the front and top of the deltoid.

✔ **Back fly:** In a bent-over position, you raise your arms out to the sides, working the rear and outside portions of the muscle.

We suggest performing these exercises in the order that they're listed. In general, you lift the heaviest weights while pressing and the lightest weights while doing back fly movements. You needn't include all four types of exercises in each shoulder workout, but you should aim to perform each type on a regular basis so that you develop evenly balanced shoulder muscles.

In general, we recommend performing shoulder exercises with free weights instead of machines. We've never met a shoulder machine we really loved, except maybe certain versions of the Shoulder Press Machine. Often, the motion feels unnatural and places excess strain on the neck.

As for your rotator cuff muscles: These are mighty susceptible to injury. You can protect them to some degree by using stellar weight lifting form for all upper body exercises. However, you also need to strengthen them with special exercises. In this chapter, we show you two rotator cuff exercises that you can do with dumbbells: internal and external rotation, which are just fancy terms for twisting your shoulder inward and outward. See Chapter 25 for nifty rotator cuff exercises that you can do with a rubber exercise band.

Mistakes to Avoid when Training Your Shoulders

For many avid weight lifters, shoulder injuries don't happen overnight. We know countless people who have lifted for years, sometimes ignoring minor shoulder pain, and then — pop! — they're finished. Kaput. But what they perceive as a sudden injury is really the result of years of overuse and poor form. Here are some tips to keep your shoulders strong and healthy:

- **Don't exaggerate the movement.** If we tell you to lift the dumbbell "to shoulder height," don't lift the weight up to the ceiling.

- **Don't arch your back.** When you perform shoulder exercises while sitting on a vertical bench, you shouldn't have more than a slight gap between the small of your back and the backrest. Arching your back gives you more leverage to lift heavier weights, but it also puts your lower back in a mighty vulnerable position.

- **Don't rock back and forth.** When you perform shoulder exercises while standing, relax your knees and maintain a tall posture. Many people lock their knees and lean back, a posture that your lower back muscles don't appreciate. If you're moving any body parts other than your arms, you're using too much weight.

- **Don't perform behind-the-neck shoulder exercises.** You're likely to see lifters press a barbell overhead and then lower it behind the neck rather than in front. Some shoulder machines also involve behind-the-neck movements. Stay away from these exercises! They require you to severely rotate your arm backward, placing your shoulder and rotator cuff muscles in a weakened and precarious position. This is not a good time for these muscles to be carrying the burden of added weight. The movement also compresses the top of your arm bone into your shoulder socket, which tends to grind the bones and place your rotators under a great deal of additional stress.

Suzanne, who knows better than to perform these exercises, nevertheless did a set of behind-the-neck shoulder presses while training for a weight lifting competition. The next day she could not reach her left arm backward without wincing in agony. Nor could she press a measly 5-pound dumbbell overhead without severe pain. Only after *seven* months of rest and rehab exercises did her rotator cuff injury begin to heal. Suzanne learned her lesson the hard way and now cringes when she sees people at her gym performing the very exercise that ruined her workouts for months on end.

Exercises in This Chapter

Here's a preview of the shoulder exercises coming up:

- ✔ Dumbbell Shoulder Press
- ✔ Lateral Raise
- ✔ Front Raise
- ✔ Back Delt Fly
- ✔ Internal and External Rotation
- ✔ Shoulder Press Machine
- ✔ Cable Lateral Raise

Dumbbell Shoulder Press

The Dumbbell Shoulder Press targets the top and center of your shoulder muscles. This exercise also works your upper back and triceps. Use caution if you have **lower back, neck,** or **elbow** problems.

Getting Set

Hold a dumbbell in each hand and sit on a bench with back support. Plant your feet firmly on the floor about hip-width apart. Bend your elbows and raise your upper arms to shoulder height so that the dumbbells are at ear level. Pull your abdominals in so that there's a slight gap between the small of your back and the bench. Place the back of your head against the pad. See photo A in Figure 10-2.

The Exercise

Push the dumbbells up and in until the ends of the dumbbells are nearly touching directly over your head and then lower the dumbbells back to ear level. See photo B in Figure 10-2.

Do's and Don'ts

- ✔ DO keep your elbows relaxed at the top rather than locking them.
- ✔ DO stop lowering the dumbbells when your elbows are at or slightly below shoulder level.
- ✔ DON'T let your back arch way off the back support.
- ✔ DON'T wiggle or squirm around in an effort to press the weights up.

Other Options

Palms-in Dumbbell Press (Easier): Do this exercise with your palms facing each other. This position allows your wrists and biceps muscles to help execute the movement.

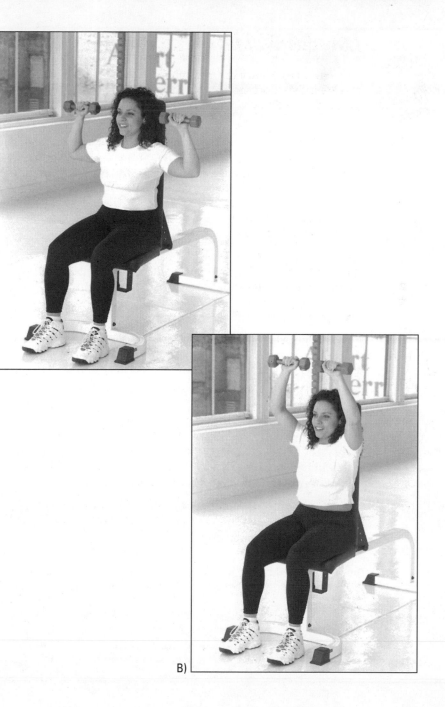

A)

B)

Figure 10-2:
Don't lock
your elbows
at the top
of the
movement.

Lateral Raise

The Lateral Raise works the center of your shoulder muscles. Make sure that you use stellar technique if you have **neck** or **lower back** problems.

Getting Set

Hold a dumbbell in each hand and stand up tall with your feet as wide as your hips. Bend your elbows a little, turn your palms toward each other, and bring the dumbbells together in front of the tops of your thighs. Pull your abdominals in. See photo A in Figure 10-3.

The Exercise

Lift your arms up and out to the side until the dumbbells are just below shoulder height. Slowly lower the weights back down. It may help to imagine that you're pouring two pitchers of lemonade onto the floor in front of you. See photo B in Figure 10-3.

Do's and Don'ts

- ✔ DO lift from the shoulders; in other words, keep your elbows stationary.
- ✔ DON'T arch your back, lean backward, or rock back and forth to lift the weights.
- ✔ DON'T raise the weights above shoulder height.

Other Options

Bent-Arm Lateral Raise (Easier): If you have weak shoulders or a history of shoulder problems, you can do this exercise with your arms bent at a 90-degree angle. Start with your arms bent, palms facing each other, and the dumbbells in front of your body. Keeping your elbows bent at 90 degrees throughout the motion, lift the weights until your elbows are at shoulder height. This exercise doesn't give your shoulders quite as good a workout as the basic version.

Seated Lateral Raise: For a change of pace, do this same exercise sitting on a bench, starting with your arms hanging straight down at your sides, elbows slightly bent.

Thumbs Up Lateral Raise (Easier): Do this movement with your palms facing forward and your thumbs pointing upward. This version places the least stress on your rotator cuff muscles and is often used in physical therapy.

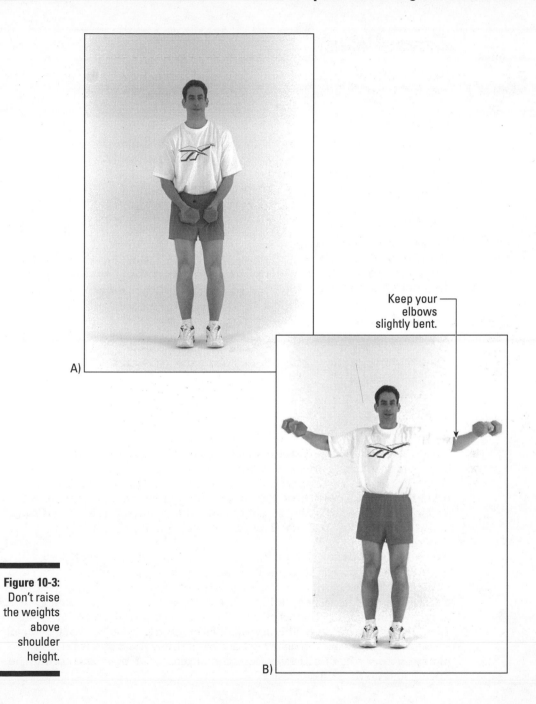

A)

Keep your
elbows
slightly bent.

B)

Figure 10-3:
Don't raise
the weights
above
shoulder
height.

Front Raise

The Front Raise isolates the front portion of your shoulder muscles. Use caution if you have a history of **lower back** or **neck** discomfort.

Getting Set

Hold a dumbbell in each hand and stand up tall with your feet as wide as your hips. Let your arms hang down at your sides, elbows relaxed and palms facing back. Stand up tall, pull your abdominals in, and relax your knees. See photo A in Figure 10-4.

The Exercise

Raise your right arm up to shoulder height and then lower it back down. Then do the same with your left arm. Continue alternating until you complete the set. Or, for more of a challenge, do all your reps with one arm and then the other. See photo B in Figure 10-4.

Do's and Don'ts

✔ DO keep your elbows slightly bent as you perform the exercise.

✔ DON'T arch, lean back, or wiggle around in an effort to lift the weight.

✔ DON'T lift your arm above shoulder height.

Other Options

Palms-up Front Raise: Turn your palm up and do the exercise exactly as it's described in the basic Front Raise. Try this version if you're prone to shoulder or rotator cuff injuries.

Diagonal Front Raise (Harder): When the dumbbell is at shoulder height, move your arm a few inches in until the weight is in front of the top of your chest. Skip this version if you have chronic shoulder problems.

Seated Front Raise (Harder): Do the same exercise sitting on a bench with a back support; this removes *any* possibility of cheating!

Lying Front Raises (Harder): Lie on your stomach on a bench holding a dumbbell in each hand, arms straight in front of you (or slightly out to the side), palms facing in and thumbs up. Raise the dumbbells as high as you comfortably can but no higher than shoulder level. You will have to use a much lighter weight for this version of the exercise. You can also incline the bench and do the same exercise.

A)

B)

Figure 10-4:
Don't lift
your arm
above
shoulder
height.

Back Delt Fly

The Back Delt Fly is an excellent move for strengthening the back of the shoulders and upper back and for improving your posture. If you have a history of **neck** pain, try the Cable Back Delt Fly version or skip the exercise altogether.

Getting Set

Hold a dumbbell in each hand and sit on the edge of a bench. Lean forward from your hips so that your upper back is flat and above parallel to the floor (if you can, support your chest against your knees). Let your arms hang down so that your palms are facing each other with the weights behind your calves and directly under your knees. Tuck your chin toward your chest and pull your abdominals inward. See photo A in Figure 10-5.

The Exercise

Raise your arms up and out to the sides, bending your elbows a few inches as you go until your elbows are level with your shoulders. Squeeze your shoulder blades together as you lift. Slowly lower your arms back down. See photo B in Figure 10-5.

Do's and Don'ts

- ✔ DO keep your chin tilted toward your chest throughout the motion so that your head and neck don't drop forward.

- ✔ DO lean forward from your hips rather than rounding your back.

- ✔ DON'T allow the rest of your body to move as you do the exercise.

Other Options

Back Delt Row: Use the same starting position except orient your palms backward. As you lift the weights, you need to bend your elbows more than in the basic version.

Cable Back Delt Fly: Set the cable on the setting closest to the floor; hook up a horseshoe handle. Kneel alongside the cable tower and grasp the handle in the hand that's farthest away from the tower. (The cable passes underneath your body.) Squeeze your shoulder blade and lift your arm up to the side, as in the basic version. Do the same number of reps with each arm.

Standing Back Delt Fly: Do the same exercise while standing with your feet placed as wide as your hips. Lean forward so that your torso forms a 45-degree angle with the floor. Keep your abs pulled in to protect your lower back and resist any rocking movement.

A)

B)

Figure 10-5:
Keep the
rest of your
body still
as you
perform the
exercise.

External and Internal Rotation

Internal and External Rotation focus on your rotator cuff muscles, but these exercises also work your shoulder muscles. If these movements bother your **neck,** try resting your head on your outstretched arm.

External Rotation

Holding a dumbbell in your right hand, lie on the floor on your left side. Bend your right elbow to a 90-degree angle and tuck it firmly against your side so that your palm is facing downward. Pull your abdominals in. Bend your left elbow and rest the side of your head in your left hand or lie on your outstretched left arm. Keeping your right elbow glued to your side, raise your right hand as far as you comfortably can (the distance depends on your flexibility). Slowly lower the weight back toward the floor. Figure 10-6 shows the External Rotation.

Internal Rotation

After you've completed all the External Rotation repetitions, switch the weight to your left hand and lie on your back. Bend your elbow so that your forearm is perpendicular to the floor and your palm is facing forward. Lower your hand down to the floor as much as your flexibility permits, and then lift back up. For both exercises, complete an equal number of repetitions with each arm. Figure 10-7 illustrates the Internal Rotation.

Do's and Don'ts

- ✔ DO imagine that your shoulder is the hinge of a door that's opening and closing.

- ✔ DON'T tighten up your neck and face.

- ✔ DON'T throw the weight up. Do both exercises gently and don't force the weight farther than your natural flexibility allows.

Other Options

Band Internal/External Rotation: See Chapter 25 for a version of these exercises that you can do with exercise bands.

Traffic Cop (Harder): Hold a weight in both hands and stand with your feet as wide as your hips. Bend your elbows and raise your arms up to shoulder height (in the classic stick-em-up position). Keeping your elbows still, rotate your forearms down until your palms are facing behind you and then rotate back up to the start.

Figure 10-6:
External Rotation. Imagine that your shoulder is the hinge of a door that's opening and closing.

Figure 10-7:
Internal Rotation. Perform this exercise gently, without throwing the weight up.

Shoulder Press Machine

The Shoulder Press Machine is a good overall shoulder exercise. It also works your triceps and upper back. Take extra caution if you're prone to **neck, elbow,** or **lower back** problems.

Getting Set

Set your seat height so that the machine's pulley is even with the middle of your shoulder. Hold onto each of the front handles. (Your palms are facing each other.) Pull your abdominals in tight but leave a slight, natural gap between the small of your back and the seat pad. See photo A of Figure 10-8.

The Exercise

Press the handles up without locking your elbows. Lower your arms until your elbows are slightly lower than your shoulders. See photo B in Figure 10-8.

Do's and Don'ts

✔ DO relax your shoulders and keep them well below your ears, especially while your arms are fully straightened.

✔ DON'T arch your back or wiggle around in an effort to lift the weight.

✔ DON'T thrust upward with more force than necessary; this puts a lot of stress on your elbows.

Other Options

Many shoulder machines have arms that work "independently" of each other. That is, the left and right sides aren't connected so that each arm is responsible for handling its own share of the load. If your gym has this option, we recommend that you give it a try. You'll get the structure and support that a machine has to offer but also develop balance and uniform strength as you would with free weights.

A)

B)

Figure 10-8:
Don't arch
your back
or wiggle
around in an
effort to lift
the weight.

Chapter 11

Working Your Arms

True story: Liz once met a woman from New York City who was forced to join a gym because of her new hairstyle. She explained that her "personal hair manager" had changed her blow-drying method to one that required more bending and straightening of the arms. "I couldn't believe how weak my arms were," she told Liz. "I had to start lifting weights so my hair would look good." Even if your hairstyle doesn't depend on your arm strength, plenty of other aspects of your life do. In this chapter, we explain how you can develop strong, firm arms.

Arm Muscle Basics

Your *biceps* muscle spans the front of your upper arm. Hang out in any gym and you'll see people flexing these muscles in the mirror, usually when they think that nobody's watching. The main job of your biceps (nicknamed your *bis* or your *guns*) is to bend your arm; in gymspeak, this motion is called *curling* or *flexing.*

Your *triceps,* located directly opposite your biceps, span the rear of your upper arm. Think of the biceps and triceps as the Hatfields and the McCoys. The biceps are always trying to bend the arm, while the triceps want to straighten it. This may be a contentious relationship, but it's a pretty good deal for you. If you had a choice of only one of these actions, you could scratch your head but not your knee, or vice versa.

Another group of arm muscles allow your wrists to move in a variety of ways. To spare you some jargon, we're going to refer to these as your *wrist muscles*. These muscles let you bend your wrist up, arch it down, twirl it in a circle, tilt it left and right, and turn your palm up or down. One of the most important jobs of the wrist muscles is not to move at all. If your wrists are weak, they can bend at inopportune times, like when you're holding a 100-pound barbell over your chest. Weak wrists also mean that you can't get a grip — on a baseball bat, a stubborn weed, or a can of mushroom soup. Figure 11-1 helps you locate your arm muscles.

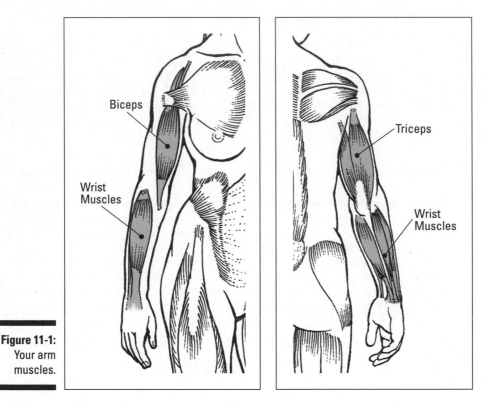

Figure 11-1: Your arm muscles.

Why You Need Strong Arms

Because we use our arms so often in daily life, we tend to take our arm muscles for granted. However, giving these muscles extra attention in the weight room really does pay off.

✔ **Real-life benefits:** Your arms are the link between your upper body and the rest of the world. If your arms are wimpy, your larger, upper body muscles can't work to full capacity. For example, the Lat Pulldown, a back exercise described in Chapter 8, mainly requires back strength, but weak biceps would sorely limit your ability to do this exercise. With stronger triceps, you can perform better on chest exercises such as the Push-up or the Bench Press. Strong wrists are crucial for many weight lifting exercises and for gripping a golf club, shelling peanuts, shuffling cards, or waving to your adoring public.

✔ **Injury prevention:** Strong arms help protect your elbows from harm. Carry around a heavy briefcase with a straight arm long enough and eventually your elbow starts to ache. With stronger arm muscles, you can haul that briefcase around longer without pain, and you're less likely to get tennis elbow. Powerful arms also minimize your chances of getting sore or injured when you perform weight lifting exercises or when you lift a dumbbell, barbell, or weight plate off of a rack. Strong wrists, in particular, help you avoid *carpal tunnel syndrome,* an inflammation of your wrist nerves. This painful and sometimes debilitating condition is caused by repetitive movements such as typing, scanning items at the grocery checkstand, or operating the mouse of your computer.

✔ **The babe/hunk factor:** Would our nation love Arnold Schwarzenegger if his biceps were not threatening to burst the seams of his shirt at any moment? Would we swoon over Sylvester Stallone if he sported skinny sticks in place of his great guns? We think not. And lately, the arms of many female stars have been getting equal billing. All three of TV's female *Friends* sport defined arms, which they seem to show off at every opportunity. Shania Twain and Madonna have some impressive triceps and biceps, too. If you want to go sleeveless in Seattle, or anywhere else for that matter, having toned arms can impress your friends and intimidate your touch football opponents.

Keys to a Great Arm Workout

Your arm muscles are smaller than your chest, back, and shoulder muscles, so you can spend less time training them and still get great results. If your goal is to increase your arm strength and develop some tone, one to three sets per arm muscle will suffice. You need to do five to eight sets per arm muscle if you want to develop maximum strength and significant size.

Give your biceps and triceps equal time. If one of these muscle groups is disproportionately stronger than the other, you're more prone to elbow injuries. Chances are, you'll enjoy training one of these muscle groups better than the other. For example, both of us tend to get bored training our biceps. No matter how you slice 'em, these exercises involve bending and then straightening your arms. On the other hand, we have lots of fun training our triceps. Of course, this is kind of odd, considering that working your triceps involves a movement that, on paper, is no more thrilling: straightening and then bending. Oh well, the psychology of weight training cannot always be explained. If you do prefer training one of these muscle groups over the other, work your least favorite group first so that you're not tempted to blow it off. If you do some of the split routines we describe in Chapter 16, you can work these muscle groups on different days.

Always work your arm muscles last in your upper body workouts. Otherwise, they may be too tired to help out when you do the big-money exercises for your much larger chest and back muscles. Your wrists should be the last upper body muscle you work before hitting the showers.

Mistakes to Avoid when Training Your Arms

Some people use such herky-jerky form when they perform arm exercises that they look like people dancing under a strobe light. Keep the following tips in mind when training your arms:

- ✔ **Don't cheat.** If you contort your whole body to lift the weight, you'll be working your whole body, not your arms. Rocking back and forth is also a great way to throw out your lower back. Think about how you'll feel explaining to your friends that you wrenched your back while exercising your arms.

- ✔ **Go easy on the elbows.** In exercise captions throughout this chapter, we tell you to straighten your arms, but this doesn't mean snapping your elbows into a fully straightened position.

- ✔ **Keep your elbows still.** When your elbows veer out to the side during many biceps and triceps exercises, you're able to lift more weight. However, this is only because you have more leverage; your arms won't get any stronger. When you're doing biceps exercises such as the Dumbbell Biceps Curl, you may also have a tendency to pull your arms and elbows forward to lift the weight. You can't avoid this extra movement completely, but keep it to a minimum.

- ✔ **Don't skip your wrists.** Few people pine away for forearms the size of Popeye's. However, as we explain in the "Why You Need Strong Arms" section of this chapter, you will go far in life with well-developed wrist muscles.

Exercises in This Chapter

Here's a list of the exercises for strengthening your arms:

- ✔ **Biceps Exercises:** Barbell Biceps Curl, Dumbbell Biceps Curl, Concentration Curl, and Arm Curl Machine
- ✔ **Triceps Exercises:** Triceps Pushdown, Triceps Kickback, Bench Dip, and Triceps Dip Machine
- ✔ **Wrist Exercises:** Wrist Curl and Reverse Wrist Curl

Barbell Biceps Curl

The Barbell Biceps Curl targets your biceps. Be especially careful if you have **elbow** problems. If you have **lower back** problems, you may want to choose a seated biceps exercise instead.

Getting Set

Hold a barbell with an underhand grip and your hands about shoulder-width apart. Stand with your feet as wide as your hips and let your arms hang down so that the bar is in front of your thighs. Stand up tall with your abdominals pulled in and knees relaxed. See photo A of Figure 11-2.

The Exercise

Bend your arms to curl the bar *almost* up to your shoulders, and then slowly lower the bar *almost* to the starting position. See photo B of Figure 11-2.

Do's and Don'ts

- ✔ DO keep your knees relaxed. This will protect your lower back.

- ✔ DON'T rock back and forth or lean way back to lift the weight. If you need to do that, you should be arrested for using too much weight.

- ✔ DON'T just straighten your arms and let the bar drop down to your thighs like a sack of rocks. Instead, lower the bar slowly to get the most muscle power from the exercise and to protect your elbows. And don't lower the bar all the way back down because you'll lose tension on the muscle.

Other Options

Reverse-grip Biceps Curl (Harder): Do the basic version holding the bar with an overhand grip. You feel this exercise more in your wrists. (**Hint:** Use a lighter weight for this version.)

Cable Biceps Curl: Place the cable on the setting closest to the floor and attach a short or long straight bar. Hold the bar with an underhand grip and stand about a foot away from the cable tower. Curl the weight up and down exactly as in the basic version.

Double Biceps Curl: Hold a dumbbell in each hand with your palms facing up, elbows resting lightly against your sides, arms hanging down. Curl the dumbbells up and down together as if they were a barbell.

Don't curl all
the way to
your shoulders.

A)

B)

Figure 11-2:
Don't rock
back and
forth to lift
the weight.

Dumbbell Biceps Curl

The Dumbbell Biceps Curl focuses on your biceps. Use caution if you have **lower back** or **elbow** problems.

Getting Set

Hold a dumbbell in each hand and stand with your feet as wide as your hips. Let your arms hang down at your sides with your palms facing in. Pull your abdominals in, stand tall, and keep your knees relaxed. See photo A of Figure 11-3.

The Exercise

Curl your right arm close to your shoulder, twisting your palm as you go so that it faces the front of your shoulder at the top of the movement. Slowly lower the dumbbell back down, and then repeat with your left arm. Continue alternating until you've completed the set. See photo B of Figure 11-3.

Do's and Don'ts

- ✔ DO keep your knees relaxed and your posture tall. This will prevent you from swinging your body forward and back to help move the weight.

- ✔ DON'T swing your elbows out wide as you bend your arm to raise the weight. Keep your elbows close to your body *without* supporting them on the sides of your stomach for leverage.

- ✔ DON'T just let the weight fall back to the starting position. Lower it slowly and with control.

Other Options

Hammer Curl: Instead of twisting the dumbbell as you curl your arm, keep your palms facing in throughout the motion. Imagine that you're pounding nails into a board with two large hammers. This version of the exercise puts more emphasis on your forearm muscles, as well as some of the muscles that reside underneath the biceps.

Zottman Curl: As you curl your arm upward, rotate your palm in toward your body and bring it up and across to the opposite shoulder. This version of the dumbbell curl is slightly harder than the basic version.

Seated Biceps Curl: If you find yourself cheating too much even with light weights, try sitting on a bench or a chair.

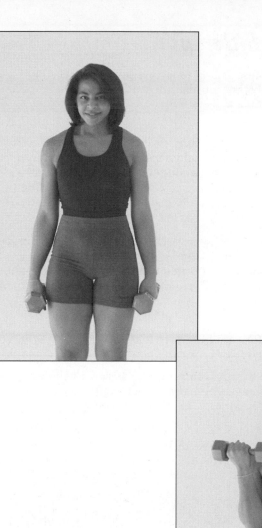

A)

B)

Figure 11-3:
Keep your
elbows
close to
your body
throughout
the
exercise.

Concentration Curl

The Concentration Curl is especially good for targeting your biceps to the exclusion of all other muscles. Be careful if you've had **elbow** injuries or are prone to **lower back** discomfort.

Getting Set

Hold a dumbbell in your right hand and sit on the edge of a bench or a chair with your feet a few inches wider than your hips. Lean forward from your hips and place your right elbow against the inside of your right thigh, just behind your knee. The weight should hang down near the inside of your ankle. Place your left palm on top of your left thigh. See photo A of Figure 11-4.

The Exercise

Bend your arm and curl the dumbbell almost up to your shoulder, and then straighten your arm to lower the weight back down. See photo B of Figure 11-4.

Do's and Don'ts

- ✔ DO bend forward from your hips rather than rounding your lower back to lean forward.

- ✔ DON'T lean away from your arm as you lift the weight up to help get better leverage. (Hey, that's cheating!)

Other Options

Slant Biceps Curl: Sit on a bench with the back inclined a few inches. Lean back and curl the weight up. You can do this one hand at a time or with both hands together, and with a twist as you curl upward or without a twist.

Standing Concentration Curl: Hold a dumbbell in one hand. Stand alongside a flat bench, lean over, and place your other hand on top of bench. Let the arm holding the weight hang straight down to the floor. Bend your elbow so that the weight moves up and in toward your armpit, and then slowly lower it back down.

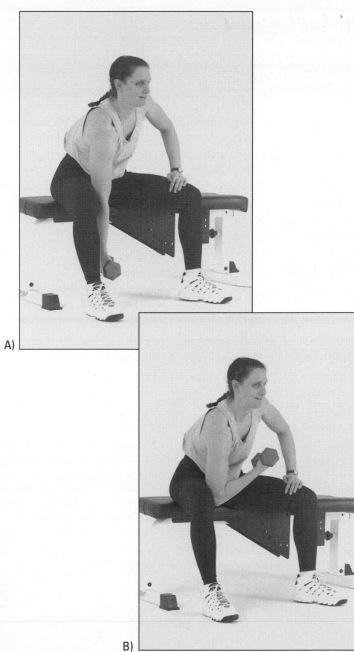

Figure 11-4:
Bend
forward
from your
hips rather
than round
your lower
back.

A)

B)

Arm Curl Machine

The Arm Curl Machine focuses on your biceps. Be careful if you've had **elbow** injuries.

Getting Set

Adjust the seat so that when you sit down and extend your arms straight out, they are level with your shoulders and your elbows are lined up with the moving hinge or pulley of the machine. Sit down and grasp a handle in each hand with an underhand grip. See photo A in Figure 11-5.

The Exercise

Bend your elbows and pull the handles until they are just above your shoulders, and then slowly lower the handles back down. See photo B of Figure 11-5.

Do's and Don'ts

- ✔ DO make sure you set the seat height correctly. If you set the seat too low, you'll have trouble bending your arms and may place too much strain on your elbows.

- ✔ DO sit up tall and make an effort to pull exclusively with your arms as opposed to hunching up your shoulders or leaning back.

- ✔ DON'T use a chest pad, if there is one, to help haul the weight. Use it for a light support only.

Other Options

Some gyms have arm curl machines that do a fair job of mimicking dumbbell work: the two sides are not connected so each arm has to do the work of lifting the weight. This type of machine is a good substitute or supplement for free weight work.

A)

B)

Figure 11-5:
Don't hunch
your
shoulders
as you pull
the machine
handles.

Triceps Pushdown

The Triceps Pushdown targets your triceps. Pay special attention to your form if you have **elbow** problems. Standing up straight with your abdominal muscles pulled in will help you avoid **lower back** problems.

Getting Set

Set the pulley of the cable at the topmost setting and attach a straight or U-shaped bar. Grasp the bar with your palms facing down and your hands about a thumb's distance from the center of the bar. You can stand either with your feet parallel or with one foot slightly in front of the other. Bend your elbows so that your forearms are parallel to the floor and your elbows are alongside your waist. You can lean *slightly* forward at the hips, but keep your abdominals pulled in and your knees relaxed. See photo A of Figure 11-6.

The Exercise

Push the bar straight down, keeping your elbows close to your sides. Then bend your arms to allow the bar to slowly rise until your arms are slightly above parallel to the ground. See photo B of Figure 11-6.

Do's and Don'ts

- ✔ DO push down smoothly, exerting the same amount of pressure with both hands so that both sides of the bar travel down evenly.
- ✔ DON'T lean too far forward or too heavily on the bar.
- ✔ DON'T allow your elbows to splay out to the sides, especially as you push down.
- ✔ DON'T let your arms fly back up as you return the bar to the starting position. Do concentrate on controlling the bar.

Other Options

Reverse Grip Pushdown (Easier): Turn your hands around and use an underhanded grip. Since this version allows your biceps to assist your triceps a great deal, it is less challenging than the basic version.

One-hand Triceps Pushdown: Attach the horseshoe and grasp it with one hand in an underhand grip. (You can also use an overhand grip, although it's tougher.) Place your other hand on your hip. Straighten your arm, pushing the handle until it is alongside your hip. Then slowly raise the handle back up.

Rope Attachment (Harder): Use the rope attachment, and move your hands a few inches apart as you press the rope down. You may need to use less weight with the rope than you do with a bar.

Figure 11-6:
Don't let
your elbows
splay out to
the sides as
you push
down.

A)

Keep your knees relaxed.

B)

Triceps Kickback

The Triceps Kickback works your triceps. Use caution if you have **elbow** or **lower back** problems.

Getting Set

Hold a dumbbell in your right hand and stand next to the long side of your bench. Lean forward at the hips until your upper body is at a 45-degree angle to the floor, and place your free hand on top of the bench for support. Bend your right elbow so that your upper arm is parallel to the floor, your forearm is perpendicular to it, and your palm faces in. Keep your elbow close to your waist. Pull your abdominals in and relax your knees. See photo A of Figure 11-7.

The Exercise

Keeping your upper arm still, straighten your arm behind you until the end of the dumbbell is pointing down. Slowly bend your arm to lower the weight. When you've completed the set, repeat with your left arm. See photo B of Figure 11-7.

Do's and Don'ts

- ✔ DO keep your abdominals pulled in and your knees relaxed to protect your lower back.

- ✔ DON'T lock your elbow at the top of the movement; do straighten your arm but keep your elbow relaxed.

- ✔ DON'T allow your upper arm to move or your shoulder to drop below waist level.

Other Options

Cable Triceps Kickback: Put the pulley on the topmost setting and attach a horseshoe handle. Grasping the handle in one hand, position yourself in the same way described in the basic kickback, and perform the same exercise. You may have to step a foot or two away from the cable tower to prevent the cable from going slack.

Triceps Kickback with a Twist (Harder): As you straighten your arm, twist it so that at the top of the movement, your palm faces up.

A)

Figure 11-7:
Don't let
your upper
arm move
or your
shoulder
drop below
waist level.

B)

Bench Dip

The Bench Dip is one of the few triceps exercises that strengthens other muscles, too — in this case, the shoulders and chest. Be careful if you have **wrist**, **elbow**, or **shoulder** problems.

Getting Set

Sit on the edge of a bench with your legs together and straight in front of you, toes pointing up. Keeping your elbows relaxed, straighten your arms, place your hands so that you can grip the underside of the bench on either side of your hips and slide your butt just off the front of the bench so that your upper body is pointing straight down. Keep your abdominals pulled in and your head centered between your shoulders. See photo A of Figure 11-8.

The Exercise

Bend your elbows and lower your body in a straight line. When your upper arms are parallel to the floor, push yourself back up. See photo B of Figure 11-8.

Do's and Don'ts

- ✔ DO try to keep your wrists straight rather than bent backwards.

- ✔ DO keep hips and back (as you lower) as close to the bench throughout the motion.

- ✔ DON'T simply thrust your hips up and down, a common mistake among beginners. Make sure your elbows are moving.

- ✔ DON'T lower yourself past the point at which your upper arms are parallel to the floor.

Other Options

Bent-leg Bench Dip (Easier): Rather than extending your legs out in front of you, bend your knees at a right angle so you're positioned as if you're sitting in a chair.

Feet-up Bench Dip (Harder): Place your feet on another chair of equal height. Or, for an even tougher version, place a weight plate or dumbbell on your lap.

A)

B)

Figure 11-8: Don't lower yourself past the point at which your upper arms are parallel to the floor.

Your upper arms should be no lower than parallel to the floor.

Triceps Dip Machine

The Triceps Dip Machine targets your triceps and, to some extent, your shoulder and chest muscles. Take special care if you have **shoulder, elbow,** or **neck** problems.

Getting Set

Set the seat height so that when your arms are fully bent, your elbows are at or below chest level. Sit in the seat with your feet flat on the floor. If the machine has a seat belt, wear it to prevent you from popping up out of the seat while you do the exercise. Grasp a handle in each hand so that your elbows are bent and your palms are facing in. Pull your abdominals in and sit with your back, buttocks, and shoulder blades against the back support. See photo A of Figure 11-9.

The Exercise

Press the handles down until your arms are straight but your elbows remain relaxed. Slowly bend your arms until your elbows are up near chest height. See photo B of Figure 11-9.

Do's and Don'ts

- ✔ DO keep your shoulders relaxed rather than hunching them up near your ears.

- ✔ DO keep your wrists in line with your forearm rather than bending them outward.

- ✔ DON'T slam your arms or lock your elbows.

Other Options

Different Grips: Most triceps dip machines have the option of a narrow or a wide grip. Start with the wide grip because you'll be more likely to use correct form. However, when you become more proficient with this machine, the inside grip does an excellent job of isolating the triceps muscles.

Modified Triceps Dip Machine: You can raise the seat higher to restrict the distance your arms travel. This is an excellent option for those with neck and shoulder problems.

Triceps Extension Machine: Some gyms have a Triceps Extension Machine rather than a Triceps Dip Machine. The extension machine works the muscles the same way except that you start with your arms at shoulder height with your elbows resting on a pad; then you press the handles, straightening your arms out in front of you rather than downward.

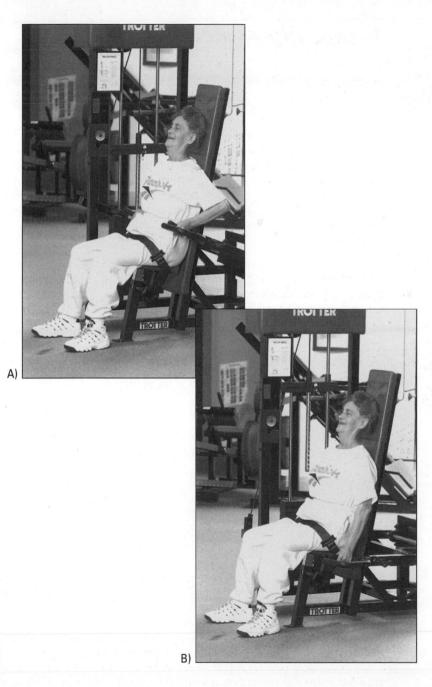

A)

B)

Figure 11-9:
Don't slam
your arms
or lock your
elbows.

Wrist Curl and Reverse Wrist Curl

The Wrist Curl and Reverse Wrist Curl are great for strengthening your wrist muscles. But be careful if you've had **wrist** or **elbow** problems.

Wrist Curl

Hold a weight in your right hand with an underhand grip and sit on the edge of your bench with your knees as wide as your hips. Lean slightly forward and place your entire forearm on top of your thigh so that your hand hangs over the edge of your knee. Clasp your left palm over your wrist to hold it steady. Curl your wrist up so that the dumbbell moves toward your forearm, and then lower the weight back down. See photo A of Figure 11-10.

Reverse Wrist Curl

Turn your palm down, and, again, secure your wrist in place with your other hand. Bend your wrist up to raise the dumbbell to thigh height, and then lower the weight back down. *Hint:* You may need slightly less weight to do the Reverse Wrist Curl. See photo B of Figure 11-10.

Do's and Don'ts

- ✔ DO curl straight up; try to avoid moving the weight to the side.
- ✔ DON'T let your forearm lift off your thigh.

Other Options

Modified Wrist Curl: If you have very weak wrists and find this exercise difficult, simply move the weight up and down a shorter distance.

Wrist-and-finger Curl (Harder): At the bottom of the wrist curl, roll the weight down to the tips of your fingers and then roll it back before curling the weight up. This is an excellent exercise for typists or others who use their hands a lot.

A)

B)

Chapter 12

Working Your Abdominals

....

In This Chapter

▶ Introducing your abs

▶ Why you need strong abdominals

▶ Debunking myths about abdominal training

▶ Mistakes to avoid when training your abs

....

*W*e were pretty darned happy a few years back when the market for abdominal gizmos went flabby. After spending more than a half billion dollars on the AbFlex, AbTrainer, and their two dozen inbred cousins, the public finally seemed to have tired of these gizmos (although, remarkably, a few new ones are on the market). We thought this was great news — that the public finally saw through the misleading slogans like "Go from flab to abs!" and "Get a flat stomach before you know it!"

But it seems we were wrong. America may have stopped buying these products like crazy, but many people are still buying into the notion that abdominal exercises can melt the fat off of your midsection. Suzanne writes *Shape* magazine's Weight Loss Q&A column, and every month she receives a dozen or so letters from readers who won't let go of this idea. "I have been doing 100 abdominal crunches a day for two months and my belly isn't dropping any inches," one reader recently wrote. Another reader wrote: "Help! My lower abdomen pooches out and no amount of crunching seems to slim down this area."

In this chapter, we explain why abdominal exercises — with or without machinery — are *not* an effective way to shrink your midsection. We also explain why it's important to train your abdominals anyway.

Abdominal Muscle Basics

You have four abdominal muscles. At this point, every household in America probably knows that these muscles are collectively referred to as the abs. Your largest abdominal muscle is the *rectus abdominis*. This is a wide, flat sheet of muscle that runs down your middle, from your lower chest to a few inches below your belly button. The rectus abdominis curls your spine forward, like when you do the Crunch or when you double over with laughter from watching *Sex and the City*. This muscle also keeps your spine still when you move other parts of your body, such as when you lift a heavy box off the floor.

Your internal and external *obliques* run diagonally up and down your sides. In addition to helping your rectus abdominis curl your spine forward, your obliques enable you to twist and bend to the side. Because the fibers of your oblique muscles are interwoven and wrap all the way around the sides of your middle, they provide a lot of lower back support.

The *transversus abdominis*, which sits directly beneath the rectus abdominis, is the deepest of all your abdominal muscles. This muscle isn't responsible for any type of movement per se, but you use it whenever you exhale force-fully, cough, or sneeze. This chapter features exercises that emphasize the rectus abdominis and the obliques. You don't need to specifically target your transversus abdominis, but you can strengthen this muscle by pulling your abs inward and exhaling strongly as you perform exercises for your rectus and obliques. Figure 12-1 gives you a view of your abdominal muscles.

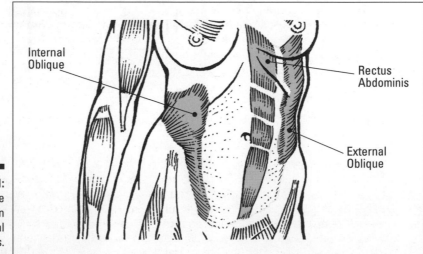

Figure 12-1: These are your main abdominal muscles.

Why You Need Strong Abdominals

Abdominal exercises won't zap the fat around your midsection, but these exercises can serve you in many other important ways.

✔ **Real-life benefits:** Your abs play a crucial behind-the-scenes role in your daily life, supporting your spine in all sorts of movements. For instance, as you're sitting here reading this book, you probably think your abs have very little to do. In fact, they're the reason you can sit up reasonably straight in your chair, as opposed to oozing off the edge like a blob of Jell-O. Your abs are even more important when your movements are more complicated. Strong abs also enable you to stand in line or shovel dirt in your garden for a lot longer without getting a backache.

✔ **Injury prevention:** Most back pain could be reduced — perhaps even eliminated — by strengthening the abdominal muscles along with the lower back muscles. All of your abdominals, but especially your obliques, support and move your spine. When your abs are weak, they sag forward, throwing your lower back off kilter.

✔ **The babe/hunk factor:** You'll be happy to know that ab exercises can improve your appearance by improving your posture. When you have weak abs, your back arches and your stomach area pooches out. By strengthening your abs, you can reduce this arch; when you stand up straighter, your abdominal area appears flatter — although how flat depends on how much fat is obstructing the view.

Strategies for a Great Abdominal Workout

To design an effective abdominal program, you need to separate the hype from the truth. So forget everything you may have learned from TV infomercials. Here we debunk the remarkably persistent myths about abdominal training.

Myth #1: Doing abdominal exercises will get rid of the blubber around your middle.

Reality: Ab exercises cannot help you "go from flab to abs," as the infomercials claim, because flab and abs are separate entities. Abdominal exercises strengthen and tone your abs, but you won't notice the results until you reduce the layer of flab on top. Abdominal exercises contribute nothing toward this goal: Spot reducing is a fantasy. The only way to lose your gut is to eat less and exercise more, a strategy that reduces your overall body fat. However, even then you have no guarantee that you will lose the fat from your middle.

Myth #2: Everyone can develop washboard abs if they try hard enough.

Reality: Even if you make it your life's mission to eat a low-fat diet, spend hours a day on the StairMaster, and perform abdominal exercises to utter perfection, you *still* may not develop that rippled look unless your body is genetically programmed to carry almost no fat in the abdominal area. And very few of us are built that way.

Myth #3: For best results, you should do several hundred repetitions of abdominal exercises.

Reality: Treat your abs like any other muscle group; in other words, perform 8 to 15 repetitions per set. If you can do more than this, you are either doing the exercise incorrectly or you are performing an exercise that's too easy for you. Either way, you're not doing your abs much good.

Myth #4: You need to work your abs every day.

Reality: Again, your abdominals are like every other muscle group. They respond best to hard work followed by a day or two of rest. Overtraining your abs simply invites neck and lower back problems, not to mention boredom.

Myth #5: The front of your stomach has two separate muscles: the upper abs and one called the lower abs.

Reality: The rectus abdominis is one long, flat, continuous sheet of muscle. Any abdominal crunch exercise works the entire muscle, although lifting your upper body off the floor emphasizes the upper portion of the rectus, and lifting your hips off the floor emphasizes the lower portion. When you do ab exercises slowly and with perfect form, you feel the entire muscle working no matter what exercise you do.

Myth #6: You need a gadget to train your abs.

Reality: Although ab roller-type contraptions can help novices learn the crunch movement, the floor works as well as or better than any gizmo, and last time we checked, it was free. Besides, exercises such as the ones shown in this chapter are more challenging and versatile than those performed with a gadget. We're not fond of health club abdominal machines, either. Most of them strengthen your back and hips more than they do your abs.

Myth #7: Sit-ups are better than crunches.

Reality: With any sit-up-type movement, your abdominals are involved only in the first part of the motion. After your shoulders clear the floor, your hip and lower back muscles take over. So there's no point in sitting all the way up to your knees.

Mistakes to Avoid when Training Your Abdominals

Mistakes are so common with abdominal exercises that the Crunch has the dubious honor of qualifying for a spot in Chapter 24 as one of the exercises most often performed incorrectly. Here's a close look at abdominal training no-nos:

- **Avoid doing neck-ups.** In other words, lift from your abs, not your neck; otherwise you're asking for neck pain. Your head and neck shouldn't be involved in abdominal exercises at all — they're just along for the ride. Place your hands behind your head without lacing your fingers together, and tilt your chin slightly upward so that there's about a fist's worth of space between your chin and your chest. Your head and neck should stay in this position throughout the exercise.

- **Don't move your elbows.** Your elbows have nothing to do with abdominal exercises. Once you position your elbows out and slightly rounded inward, leave them there. If you pull your elbows up and in, you'll end up pulling on your neck.

- **Don't arch or flatten your back.** We frequently remind you to pull your abs in, but always keep a slight gap, the width of a finger or two, between the small of your back and the floor.

- **After the lift, don't forget the curl.** The Crunch involves more than simply lifting your head, neck, and shoulder blades off the floor; you also need to curl forward, as if you are doubling over. Imagine how you'd move if you were lying there and someone dropped a weight on your stomach. That's the movement you're aiming for here.

Exercises in This Chapter

Here's a list of the abdominal exercises that we present in this chapter:

- Basic Abdominal Crunch
- Reverse Crunch
- Abdominal Crunch with a Twist
- The Slide
- The Rolling Ball
- Wall Roll-up
- Ball Crunch

Basic Abdominal Crunch

The Basic Abdominal Crunch is the fundamental abdominal exercise, working all of your ab muscles. Pay special attention to your form if you have **lower back** or **neck** problems.

Getting Set

Lie on your back with your knees bent and feet flat on the floor hip-width apart. Place your hands behind your head so that your thumbs are behind your ears. Don't lace your fingers together. Hold your elbows out to the sides and rounded slightly in. Tilt your chin slightly so that there's a few inches of space between your chin and your chest. Gently pull your abdominals inward. See photo A of Figure 12-2.

The Exercise

Curl up and forward so that your head, neck, and shoulder blades lift off the floor. Hold for a moment at the top of the movement, and then lower slowly back down. See photo B of Figure 12-2.

Figure 12-2:
Gently pull your abdominals inward.

Curl up and forward.

A)

B)

Do's and Don'ts

- ✔ DO keep your abdominals pulled in so that you feel more tension in your abs and so you don't overarch your lower back.

- ✔ DO curl as well as lift. For an explanation of curling, refer to the introduction to this chapter and to Chapter 24, in which we describe common crunch mistakes.

- ✔ DON'T pull on your neck with your hands or draw your elbows in.

Other Options

Cross-arm Crunch (Easier): Fold your arms across your chest, palms down, and tuck your chin so that it rests on your hands. This will save you the effort of having to lift the weight of your arms.

Legs-up Crunch: Keeping your knees bent, pick your legs off the floor and cross your ankles.

Weighted Crunch (Harder): Hold a *light* weight plate on your chest, or for an even greater challenge, hold a weight on top of or behind your head. Just don't press the plate down too hard.

Reverse Crunch

The Reverse Crunch emphasizes the lower portion of your main abdominal muscles (the rectus abdominis). Use caution if you're prone to **lower back** discomfort.

Getting Set

Lie on your back with your legs up, knees slightly bent, and ankles crossed. Rest your arms on the floor beside you or behind your head. Rest your head on the floor, relax your shoulders, and pull in your abdominals. See photo A of Figure 12-3.

The Exercise

Lift your butt one or two inches off the floor so that your legs lift up and a few inches backward. Hold the position for a moment, and then lower slowly. See photo B of Figure 12-3.

Do's and Don'ts

✔ DO keep your shoulders relaxed and down. Don't involve your upper body at all.

✔ DO keep this movement small and precise; you don't have to lift very high to feel this exercise working.

✔ DO use a minimum of leg movement; don't thrust or jerk your hips.

✔ DON'T roll your hips so that your buttocks and back come way off the floor. This type of movement involves your front hip muscles more than your abdominals.

Other Options

Modified Reverse Crunch (Easier): Hold onto the back edges of an exercise mat or stable object such as the underside of a couch or stuffed chair to help stabilize your upper body.

One-leg Reverse Crunch (Easier): Lift one leg at a time. Bend your other knee so that your foot is flat on the floor.

Incline Reverse Crunch (Harder): Place three risers underneath one end of a step bench and one riser underneath the other end. Lie on the step with your head at the higher end of it. Stretch your arms out behind you and hold on to the undercling of the step directly behind your head. Perform a reverse crunch by lifting your hips up. This version of the Reverse Crunch is more difficult because you are working against gravity.

A)

B)

Figure 12-3:
Lift your butt
one or two
inches off
the floor.

Crunch with a Twist

The Abdominal Crunch with a Twist works all your abdominal muscles with an emphasis on your obliques. Pay special attention to form if you have a history of **lower back** or **neck** discomfort.

Getting Set

Lie on your back with your knees bent and your feet hip-width apart and flat on the floor. Place your left hand behind your head so that your thumb is behind your left ear. Place your right arm along the floor beside you. Bring your elbow out to the side and round it slightly inward. Tilt your chin so that your chin and your chest are a few inches apart. Pull your abdominals in. See photo A of Figure 12-4.

The Exercise

As you curl your head, neck, and shoulder blades off the floor, twist your torso to the right, bringing your left shoulder toward your right knee. (Your elbow will not actually touch your knee.) Lower back down. Do all of the repetitions on one side and then switch to the other side. See photo B of Figure 12-4.

Do's and Don'ts

- ✔ DO concentrate on rotating from your middle rather than simply moving your elbows toward your knees.

- ✔ DO keep both hips squarely on the ground as you twist to protect your lower back.

Other Options

Legs-up Crunch with a Twist (Harder): Lift your bent knees off the floor and cross one ankle over the other.

Straight-arm Crunch with a Twist (Harder): Reach for your opposite knee with your arm straight rather than your elbow bent. Reach past the outside edge of your knee.

Drop-knee Cross Crunch: Drop both of your knees to one side and crunch straight upward. This will force the obliques to work along with the other abdominal muscles.

Figure 12-4:
Your elbow
doesn't
have to
touch
your knee

Twist from your middle; don't pull from your elbow.

The Slide

The Slide is the perfect abdominal exercise for people who are prone to lower back or neck pain. Performing the Slide is a good way to get your abs in shape for more challenging abdominal exercises.

Getting Set

Remove your shoes. Lie on your back with your knees bent comfortably, feet hip-width apart, toes up, and heels digging into the floor. Rest your arms at your sides. Pull your abdominals in and gently push — but don't force — your back into the floor so that, to some extent, you flatten out the natural curve of the small of your back. See photo A of Figure 12-5.

The Exercise

Slowly slide your heels forward as you gradually straighten your legs; don't allow your abs to push upward or your back to pop up off the floor, even a little. Continue straightening your legs until you can't keep your abs tight or your back on the floor, or until your legs are fully extended. Then slowly slide your heels back to the starting position, again taking care not to relax your middle muscles. See photo B of Figure 12-5.

Do's and Don'ts

✔ DO slide your legs out only as far as you can while keeping your back in contact with the floor. As you get stronger, you'll be able to straighten your legs all the way while keeping your abs pulled in and your back flat.

✔ DO keep your head, neck, and shoulders relaxed.

✔ DO move slowly and take the time to feel your abs working.

Other Options

Single-leg Slide (Easier): Slide out one heel at a time. Do an equal number of reps with each leg.

Slide with Paper Plates (Harder): Place your heels on two paper plates or in plastic bags. You have to work even harder to slide slowly and with control.

Short Slide (Harder): Slide your heels out to the point where you need to work the hardest to maintain your back placement on the floor. Slide your heels a few inches back and forth several times so that you are constantly working.

Figure 12-5:
Don't allow
your lower
back to
pop up.

A)

B)

The Rolling Ball

Rolling like a ball strengthens all your abdominal muscles as well as the muscles of your lower back. This exercise is also a great massage for your spine.

Getting Set

Sit up tall and hug your knees into your chest by loosely clasping a hand around each ankle. Drop your chin to your chest, pull your abs in, and round your back a bit. Point your toes and lift your feet an inch or so off the floor so that you are balanced evenly on the center of your tailbone. See photo A of Figure 12-6.

The Exercise

Pull your abs in even more to gently shift your weight backward so that you roll back as far as your shoulder blades. Pull your abs in once again to shift your weight forward, and then roll back up into the balanced position. Hold the position for a moment before rolling back again. See photo B of Figure 12-6.

Do's and Don'ts

✔ DO control the movement with your abdominals, *not* with momentum. You're doing this move correctly if you roll easily up into the balanced position and are able to hold it without a lot of additional body movement.

✔ DO try to roll up and down evenly on the center of your spine.

✔ DON'T roll back onto your neck and head.

Other Options

Modified Rolling Ball (Easier): Hold on to your lower legs just underneath your knees so that you don't form quite as tight a ball.

Advanced Rolling Ball (Harder): Rather than grab your ankles, hold your hands out in front of them. In this position, you can't use your hands to help you maintain your ball shape.

Figure 12-6:
Roll back
into a
balanced
position.

A)

B)

Don't roll onto your neck.

Wall Roll-up

The Wall Roll-up strengthens all your abdominal muscles as well as your lower back muscles. If you have a history of **lower back** problems, you may want to limit the distance that you roll.

Getting Set

Stand with your back against a wall and your feet a comfortable distance from the wall, heels together, and toes apart. Pull your abs in, and gently press your entire back, including your neck and shoulders, into the wall. Let your arms hang down at your sides, loose and relaxed. See photo A of Figure 12-7.

The Exercise

Drop your chin to your chest, and then peel your neck off the wall, followed by your shoulders, then your upper back, then your middle back, and then your lower back. Keep your tailbone and your butt against the wall. Hang forward a moment and then slowly reverse the movement, pasting your entire spine back onto the wall until you have returned to the starting position. See photo B of Figure 12-7.

Do's and Don'ts

✔ DO try to move one vertebrae at a time so you feel as if you're curling down and then up.

✔ DO keep your abdominals pulled in the entire time, and use them to control the speed and degree of movement.

Other Options

Modified Wall Roll-up (Easier): If this exercise bothers your lower back or you don't have the strength to lower all the way down, move only to the last point at which you can still maintain good form. Then curl back up again. You'll gradually build enough strength to perform the complete exercise.

Floor Roll-up (Harder): Do the Roll-up lying on your back with your knees bent and feet flat on the floor. You can place your hands underneath your thighs to assist you upward on the hard parts. Don't do this version if you're prone to lower back trouble. And don't just sit up by lifting your back straight up off the floor. Instead, curl up and down one vertebra at a time.

Figure 12-7:
Keep your
tailbone
against
the wall.

Ball Crunch

The Ball Crunch strengthens the abs by keeping your balance and reducing movement except for the crunch.

Getting Set

Sit on top of the center of your ball with your feet flat on the floor and placed as wide as your hips. Place your hands behind your head so that your thumbs are behind your ears. Don't lace your fingers together. Hold your elbows out to the sides and round them slightly in. Tilt your chin slightly so that there's a few inches of space between your chin and your chest. Gently pull your abdominals inward as you lean back on to the ball so that your entire back, from your tailbone to your shoulders, is resting on the ball. Your head and arms will be suspended above the ball. See photo A of Figure 12-8.

The Exercise

Curl up and forward so that your shoulder blades lift up off the ball. Move slowly and carefully to help maintain your balance and reduce any movement other than the crunch. Hold for a moment at the top of the movement, and then lower slowly back down. See photo B of Figure 12-8.

Do's and Don'ts

- ✔ DO keep your abdominals pulled in so that you feel more tension in your abs and so you don't overarch your lower back.

- ✔ DO keep your feet firmly planted on the floor for support and balance.

- ✔ DON'T pull on your neck with your hands or draw your elbows in.

Other Options

One-Legger (Harder): Perform the same exercise with one foot lifted a few inches off the floor. Your abdominals will have to work harder to keep you still and in balance.

Modified Ball Crunch (Easier): Prop the ball against a wall or other sturdy object. Squat low and prop your back against the ball so that your upper body is at a slight angle to the floor. This version of the exercise requires less balance.

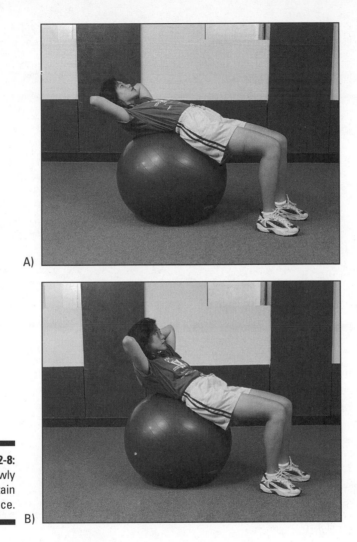

Figure 12-8:
Move slowly
to maintain
balance.

Chapter 13

Working Your Butt and Legs

Your butt and legs are home to the largest muscle groups in your body, and these muscles carry you everywhere you go — unless, of course, you live in Los Angeles, in which case your car carries you everywhere you go, even if you're going only one block. At any rate, your lower body muscles deserve plenty of attention. If you give them their proper due in your strength training routine, they will carry you even further and faster. In this chapter, we introduce you to terms such as *glutes* and *quads,* and we explain how best to strengthen and tone these and other lower body muscles.

Butt and Leg Muscle Basics

Your largest lower body muscle, as if we have to tell you, is your *gluteus maximus,* emphasis on the maximus. This is the granddaddy of all muscles, and it covers your entire butt, both cheeks. The main job of the gluteus maximus, also known as the *glutes,* is to straighten your legs from your hips, such as when you stand up from a chair. The muscles opposite your gluteus maximus, located at the front of your hips, are collectively known as the *hip flexors*. These muscles help you lift your leg up high so you can march in a parade or step up onto a ladder. You don't need to spend much time working your hip flexors; they tend to be strong to begin with. When they become disproportionately strong and tight compared to other muscles, they throw your hip and lower spine out of whack. This strength imbalance may contribute to poor posture and lower back pain.

The sides, or meat, of your hips are called your *abductors* or outer thighs. Your outer hips move your leg away from your body, like when you push off while ice skating. The main outer hip muscle is called the *gluteus medius.* The muscles that span the inside of your upper leg are known as your *adductors,* or inner thighs. They pull your leg back in toward your body or, when they're feeling really ambitious, they sweep one leg in front of and past the other, like when you kick a soccer ball off to the side. The *quadriceps,* or *quads* for short, are located at the front of your thighs. Together these four muscles that create the quads have one purpose: to straighten your leg from the knee. The hamstrings, also known as the *hams,* reside directly behind your thigh bone. These muscles bend your knee and help the glutes do their thing.

You have two calf muscles: the *gastrocnemius* (*gastroc* for short) and the *soleus.* The gastroc is shaped like a diamond. Check out the calves of any competitive bicyclist and you'll see precisely what this muscle looks like. The gastroc allows you to raise up on tip toe to see over your neighbor's fence. Your soleus sits directly underneath the gastroc and helps out the gastroc when your knee is bent and you need to raise your heels up, like when you're sitting at the movies and you realize that you just stepped in gum. Your shin muscle, covering the front of your lower leg, is the *tibialis anterior.* Whenever you're feeling stubborn and want to dig your heels in, you can thank this muscle for allowing you to literally make this gesture happen. Check out Figures 13-1 and 13-2 for a look at the muscles you'll be working on when you do the exercises in this chapter.

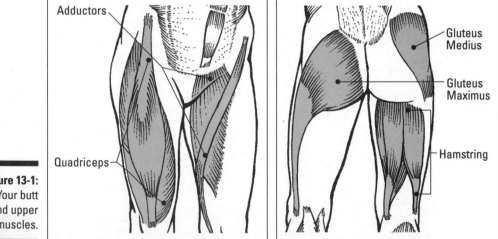

Figure 13-1:
Your butt and upper leg muscles.

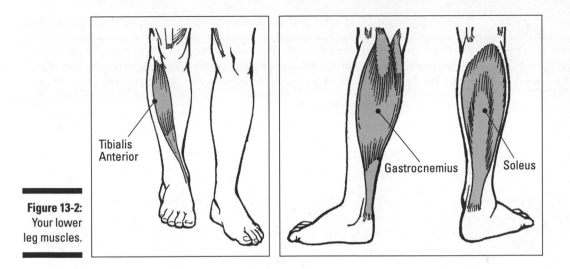

Figure 13-2:
Your lower
leg muscles.

Why You Need Strong Legs

Many men are too busy attempting to inflate their upper body muscles to epic proportions, while many women are afraid of developing tree trunks where their legs once were. Here's why you should get to work on those glutes, quads, hams, and calves:

- **Real-life benefits:** When you take the time to strengthen your legs, you have more stamina for waiting in line at the ballpark hot-dog stand, racing through the mall to find a last-minute birthday gift, climbing the office stairs when the elevator is broken, and standing on tip-toe to paint the corner of your ceiling.

  If you're on an aerobic mission like training for a 10K or a bike-a-thon, strong legs are even more essential. Many runners and cyclists are afraid to lift weights, figuring that they'll develop bulky legs that'll slow them down. But the reality, according to mounds of research, is that leg and butt exercises will help you go farther and faster.

One guy we know couldn't break the 4-hour barrier in the marathon until he started doing lower body weight training exercises. His hips used to tire out at around mile 16, so he wasn't able to stretch his legs out to their full stride, and he'd shuffle through the last ten miles. At age 49, thanks to a regular leg routine, he was finally able to cruise through the finish line in 3 hours and 50 minutes. Even if your athletic goals aren't as ambitious as running 26.2 miles, leg workouts are important. Say you simply want to ride your stationary bike for 30 minutes three times a week. Stronger legs help you pedal faster and harder, so that you can burn more calories during that half hour.

✔ **Injury prevention:** Strengthening your lower body muscles is a good way to preserve your hip, knee, and ankle joints — three joints that put in a lot of overtime and are particularly susceptible to injury. It's true that many joint injuries result from torn ligaments or tendons (the connective tissue that holds your bones in place), but many of these injuries won't occur in the first place if you have a strong army of muscles surrounding and protecting your joints. Often, lower body injuries result from a life-time of repetitive motions such as walking up and down stairs.

By strengthening the muscles that surround the joints, you give them the competitive edge they need to do their job day after day. With strong lower body muscles you're less likely to sprain your ankle by stepping off a curb because your joints have the strength to hold up even when they're wrenched into positions they'd prefer to avoid. If you're already at the point where you have bad knees or a "trick ankle," it's not too late to pump some iron with your lower body muscles.

✔ **The babe/hunk factor:** People look strange when they have a fabulously built upper body and little bitty, microscopic legs — or a toned upper body and shapeless legs.

Keys to a Great Leg Workout

You should work your large muscles before moving on to your small ones. So, perform your lower body workouts in the following order: glutes, quads, hamstrings, inner and outer thighs, calves, and shins.

In general, you should do at least four or five lower body exercises on a regular basis. Your workouts should include two types of exercises: *compound* exercises, which involve several muscle groups at once, and *isolation* exercises, which hone in on a single muscle group. If you're starting out with bad knees or hips, you may want to take a few weeks to simply focus on the muscles surrounding those joints. If your knees are the problem, for example, you could start with exercises that isolate your quads (the Thigh Squeeze and the Leg Extension Machine) and your hams (the Leg Curl Machine) and wait a few weeks before graduating to compound exercises (the Squat and the Lunge). Here are some tips for working specific lower body muscle groups:

✔ **Glutes:** It's tough to isolate your butt muscles because nearly every butt exercise also involves the front and/or rear thigh muscles. However, you can maximize the emphasis on your maximus with a few simple technique tricks. For instance, when you're doing the Leg Press or the Squat, keep your weight shifted slightly back onto your heels, especially as you press back up into the straight-leg position. The more weight you shift onto your toes, the more your quadriceps become involved. Also, when you stand up, squeeze your cheeks to make sure your glutes are really working and are not just going along for the ride.

✔ **Quadriceps:** The Leg Extension — an exercise in which you straighten your legs from a bent position — may give you a twinge of pain in your kneecap as you near the fully extended position. In this case, stop just before your legs are straight. Many leg extension machines have a device that stops the lever of the machine from going past the point you set. The machine may also let you start from a higher position than normal if you feel pain when you're initiating the movement.

✔ **Hamstrings:** The most popular way to work the hamstrings is with a leg curl machine; you start with your legs straight and curl your heels toward your butt. You typically find this machine in three varieties: lying, seated, and standing. In this chapter we show you how to use the lying leg curl because it's the one you see most often and the one we generally like best, although our opinions vary from brand to brand. With some leg curl machines, you lie flat on your stomach; others have a severe bend in the support pad. Our favorite variety has you lying at an angle with your hips above your head. Try all the hamstring machines available to you, and use any of the machines that feel comfortable.

✔ **Calves:** When you perform the Standing Calf Raise, experiment with the angle of your toes to find the position that's most comfortable. But don't angle your toes too much outward or inward or you'll place too much stress on your knees and ankles. And perform calf exercises slowly. Bouncing your heels up and down can cause your calf muscles to tighten.

Expect to feel sore and walk a little stiffly for a day or two after your first few lower body workouts. Of course, any muscle that's new to weight training is likely to be sore after the first few sessions, but leg muscles seem particularly prone to this phenomenon. Start out with very light weights; otherwise, you may find yourself walking like Herman Munster or wincing in agony when you get up from the breakfast table.

Mistakes to Avoid When Working Your Lower Body

Here are the most common pitfalls to watch out for when training your butt and legs:

✔ **Don't play favorites.** In other words, don't work your butt muscles and neglect your thighs just because you want to fill out the back of your jeans. Strive for balance. If one lower body muscle group is monstrously strong compared to the others, you may end up with an injury.

✔ **Don't put your knees in jeopardy.** Avoid locking your knees when you're lifting a weight, and don't allow your knees to shoot out past your toes in the Squat, Lunge, or Leg Press. If you feel knee pain during an exercise, stop immediately. Try another exercise and return to the one that gave you trouble after you've been training for a few weeks. Or do a simpler version of the exercise, restricting the distance you move the weight.

✔ **Don't perform more than 15 repetitions for any leg exercise.** Some people, afraid of developing bulky legs, use extremely light weights and perform 40 repetitions. You're not going to build much strength this way, and you'll probably fall asleep in the middle of a set. You also increase your chance of injury.

Exercises in This Chapter

Here's a preview of the exercises we show you in this chapter:

- ✔ **Butt and Leg Exercises:** Squat, Lunge, Leg Press, and Kneeling Butt Blaster

- ✔ **Quadriceps (Front Thigh) Exercises:** Quad Press and Leg Extension Machine

- ✔ **Hamstring (Rear Thigh) Exercises:** Kneeling Leg Curl and Leg Curl Machine

- ✔ **Inner and Outer Thigh Exercises:** Inner and Outer Thigh Machine, Side-lying Leg Lift, and Inner Thigh Lift

- ✔ **Calf and Shin Exercises:** Standing Calf Raise and Toe Lift

Squat

In addition to strengthening your butt muscles, the Squat also does a good job of working your quadriceps and hamstrings. If you have **hip, knee,** or **lower back** problems, you may want to try the modified version.

Getting Set

Hold a dumbbell in each hand or place your hands on your hips or on the tops of your thighs, or allow them to hang comfortably down at your sides. Stand with your feet as wide as your hips and with your weight slightly back on your heels. Pull your abdominals in and stand up tall with square shoulders. See photo A of Figure 13-3.

The Exercise

Sit back and down, as if you're sitting into a chair. Lower as far as you can without leaning your upper body more than a few inches forward. Don't lower any further than the point at which your thighs are parallel to the floor, and don't allow your knees to shoot out in front of your toes. Once you feel your upper body fold forward over your thighs, straighten your legs and stand back up. Take care not to lock your knees at the top of the movement. See photo B of Figure 13-3.

Do's and Don'ts

- ✔ DON'T allow your knees to travel beyond your toes. We know we said this before, but it bears repeating.

- ✔ DON'T look down. Your body tends to follow your eyes. So if you're staring at the ground, you're more likely to fall forward. Instead, keep your head up and your eyes focused on an object directly in front of you.

- ✔ DON'T shift your body weight forward so that your heels lift up off the floor. When you push back up the standing position, concentrate on pushing through your heels.

- ✔ DON'T arch your back as you stand back up

Other Options

Weightless Squat (Easier): If you have trouble balancing or completing at least 8 repetitions of the Squat with good form, skip the weights. Instead place your hands on your hips or the tops of your thighs as you do the exercise.

Bench Squat (Easier): Place the end of a bench behind you and allow your buttocks to lightly touch the top of it as you sit downward. This helps you guide your movement and perfect your form.

Plié Squat: To add emphasis to the inner and outer thighs, place your feet out a little wider apart and angle your toes outward. Most people can lower further in this position because they feel more stable. Still, don't travel any lower than the point at which your thighs are parallel to the floor, and don't let your knees shoot out past your toes.

Don't arch your back.

Figure 13-3:
Don't shift your body weight forward so that your heels lift up off the floor.

Lunge

The Lunge is a great overall lower body exercise: It strengthens your butt, quadriceps, hamstrings, and calves. If you feel pain in your **hips, knees,** or **lower back** when you do this exercise, try the Split Lunge version.

Getting Set

Stand with your feet as wide as your hips and your weight back a little on your heels, and place your hands on your hips. Pull your abdominals in and stand up tall with square shoulders. See photo A of Figure 13-4.

The Exercise

Lift your right toe slightly and, leading with your heel, step your right foot forward an elongated stride's length, as if you're trying to step over a crack on the sidewalk. As your foot touches the floor, bend both knees until your right thigh is parallel to the floor and your left thigh is perpendicular to it. Your left heel will lift off the floor. Press off the ball of your foot and step back to the standing position. See photo B of Figure 13-4.

Do's and Don'ts

- ✔ DO keep your eyes focused ahead; when you look down, you have a tendency to fall forward.

- ✔ DON'T step too far forward or you'll have trouble balancing.

- ✔ DON'T lean forward or allow your front knee to travel past your toes.

Other Options

Split Lunge (Easier): Start with one leg a stride's length in front of the other. Bend both knees, and lower your body so that your ending position is the same as in the basic lunge. You may want to lightly grasp the back of an upright bench or a chair for support.

Lunge with Weights (Harder): Hold a dumbbell in each hand with your arms down at your sides, or place a barbell behind your neck and across your shoulders. You also can do the Split Lunge while holding a dumbbell in each hand or using the Smith Machine.

Backward Lunge (Harder): Step your right leg back about a stride's length behind you, and bend both knees until your left thigh is parallel to the floor and your right thigh is perpendicular to it. You'll feel this version a bit more in your hamstrings.

Traveling Lunge (Harder): Perform the basic lunge, alternating legs so that you travel forward with each repetition. You need a good 10 yards of space to do this. Bend your arms to 90 degrees and swing them purposefully. This is a great variation for skiers, hikers, and climbers.

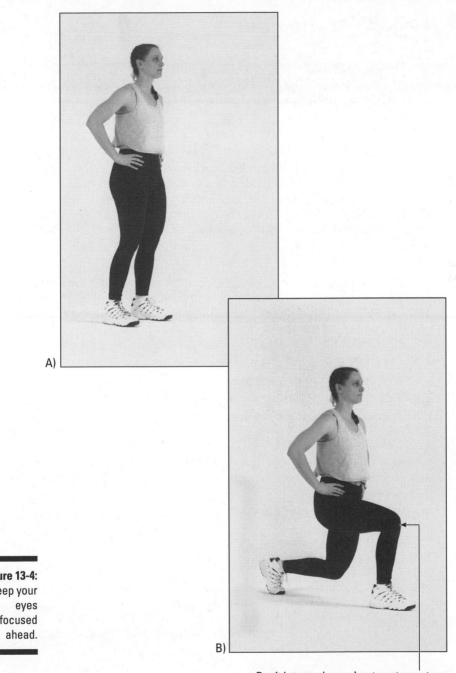

A)

B)

Figure 13-4:
Keep your
eyes
focused
ahead.

Don't let your knee shoot past your toes.

Leg Press Machine

The Leg Press Machine covers a lot of ground, strengthening your butt, quadriceps, and hamstrings. It's a good alternative if the Squat or Lunge bothers your lower back. You may want to try the modified version if you experience pain in your **hips** or **knees**.

Getting Set

Set the machine so that when you lie on your back with your knees bent and feet flat on the foot plate, your shoulders fit snugly under the shoulder pads and your knees are bent to an inch or so below parallel to the foot plate. Place your feet as wide as your hips with your toes pointing forward and your heels directly behind your toes. Grasp the handles. Pull your abdominals in and keep your head and neck on the back pad. See photo A of Figure 13-5.

The Exercise

Pressing through your heels, push against the platform until your legs are straight. Then bend your knees until your thighs are parallel with the platform and the weight plates you are lifting are hovering just above the weight stack. See photo B of Figure 13-5.

Do's and Don'ts

- ✔ DO press your heels into the foot plate rather than allowing them to lift up.
- ✔ DON'T lower your thighs past parallel with the foot plate or allow your knees to shoot in front of your toes.
- ✔ DON'T arch your back off the pad to help move the weight.
- ✔ DON'T lock your knees when your legs are straight.

Other Options

Different types of machines: You may run across several types of leg press machines. One has you sitting in an upright position, pressing your legs out straight. Another is called a 45-degree leg press: You lie in a reclining position and press up and out diagonally. Yet another version has you lie on your back and press your legs straight up. All these variations are acceptable. Just remember: Don't bend your legs so far that your thighs are smooshed against your chest and your knees are hanging out there in Never Never Land. Keep in mind that your foot position can change the emphasis of the exercise. The higher you place your feet on the foot platform, the more you emphasize your butt muscles.

Modified Leg Press (Easier): If you have chronic knee problems, you can still do this exercise. Set the seat height so that your thighs are a few inches above parallel — this position limits the distance you can bend your knees. However, this version focuses more on your front thigh muscles and less on your butt.

A)

B)

Figure 13-5:
Don't lower
your thighs
past parallel
with the
foot plate.

Don't lock your knees.

One-leg Leg Press (Harder): Use the same form as with the basic version of this exercise with one foot lifted up and off the foot plate. After you complete your reps, switch legs.

Kneeling Butt Blaster

The Kneeling Butt Blaster works your butt with some emphasis on your hamstrings, too. Make sure that you keep your abdominals pulled in on this exercise, especially if you're prone to **lower back** discomfort.

Getting Set

Kneel on your elbows and knees on top of a thick towel, with your knees directly under your hips and your elbows under your shoulders. Clasp your hands together or turn your palms toward the floor. Flex your right foot so that it is perpendicular to the floor. Tilt your chin slightly toward your chest, and pull your abdominals in so that your back doesn't sag toward the floor. See photo A of Figure 13-6.

The Exercise

Keeping your knee bent, lift your right leg and raise your knee to hip level. Then slowly lower your leg back down. Between repetitions, your knee should almost, but not quite, touch the floor. Complete all the repetitions with one leg before switching sides. See photo B of Figure 13-6.

Do's and Don'ts

✔ DO keep your neck still and your shoulders relaxed.

✔ DON'T throw your leg up in the air; do move slowly.

✔ DON'T raise your knee above hip height or arch your back as you lift your leg.

Other Options

Kneeling Butt Blaster with Weight (Harder): Add an ankle weight to this exercise or squeeze a small dumbbell in the well of your knee. We love this last option because your muscles have to work even harder to hold the weight in place.

Butt Blaster Machine: This machine mimics the Kneeling Butt Blaster. You kneel with one knee on a platform, place your other foot onto a foot plate, and then press back and up. This is a fine machine as long as you remember to keep your abdominals pulled in and resist arching your lower back.

A)

Figure 13-6:
Don't arch
your back
as you lift
your leg.

B)

└─Raise your knee to hip.

Quad Press

The Quad Press is a particularly good quadriceps exercise for people who feel pain when they bend and straighten their knees.

Getting Set

Roll up a bath towel. Sit on the floor and lean against a wall with your legs straight out in front of you. (Or, bend the non-working knee into your chest if that's more comfortable.) Place the towel underneath the well of your right knee. See photo A of Figure 13-7.

The Exercise

Squeeze your quadriceps tightly and press down on the towel. Hold for five slow counts, relax, and repeat until you complete the set. Then switch legs. See photo B of Figure 13-7.

Do's and Don'ts

- ✔ DO bend your non-working knee into your chest if that makes the exercise more comfortable.

- ✔ DON'T tighten your face, hunch your shoulders, or round your back.

Other Options

Modified Quad Press (Easier): If you experience pain in your knee when you do this exercise, try squeezing your muscle for a shorter period of time. Start with one second and build up. You can also try squeezing without the towel underneath your knee. Or to make the exercise tougher, replace the towel with a firmer object such as a tennis ball or filled water bottle. This allows you to squeeze harder.

Straight Leg Raise (Harder): Sit in the same position, but instead of pressing your thigh downward, lift your entire leg up and off the floor a few inches. Hold a moment and slowly lower to the start. You can also do this version of the exercise with an ankle weight wrapped around your ankle or draped across your thigh.

A)

B)

Figure 13-7:
Don't
hunch your
shoulders
or round
your back.

When you squeeze your quadriceps, your heel will lift slightly off the floor.

Leg Extension Machine

The Leg Extension Machine zeroes in on your quadriceps muscles. If this exercise bothers your **knees,** try the modified version or choose a different exercise.

Getting Set

Set the machine so that your back sits comfortably against the back rest, the center of your knee is lined up with the machine's pulley, and your shins are flush against the ankle pads. (On most machines you can move the back rest forward and back and the ankle pads up and down.) Sit down and swing your legs around so that your knees are bent and the tops of your shins are resting against the underside of the ankle pads. Hold on to the handles. Sit up tall and pull your abdominals in. See photo A of Figure 13-8.

The Exercise

Straighten your legs to lift the ankle bar until your knees are straight. Hold for a second at the top position, and then slowly bend your knees. See photo B of Figure 13-8.

Do's and Don'ts

✔ DO make sure you take the time to set the machine properly.

✔ DO move slowly; don't ram your knees at the top of the movement.

✔ DON'T arch your back in an effort to help you lift the weight.

Other Options

Modified Leg Extension (Easier): If one leg is noticeably stronger than the other, slide one leg out of the way and do this exercise one leg at a time. You probably will need less than half the weight you use when lifting both legs together.

Single-leg Extension: Many leg extension machines have a mechanism you can set to limit the distance that you can bend and straighten your legs. Use this device if your knees give you trouble at any point of the exercise.

Ball Squeeze Leg Extension (Harder): Place a soccer ball, weighted ball, or rolled up towel between your knees. As you extend your leg, concentrate on squeezing the ball so it does not slip out of place. This version of the exercise forces your Quads to work harder in order to hold onto the ball.

A)

B)

Figure 13-8:
Don't arch
your back in
an effort to
help you lift
the weight.

Kneeling Leg Curl

The Kneeling Leg Curl targets your hamstring muscles. Pay extra attention to good form if you have **lower back** or **knee** troubles.

Getting Set

Kneel on your elbows and knees on a mat or thick towel, with your knees directly under your hips and your elbows directly under your shoulders. Clasp your hands together or turn your palms toward the floor. Flex your right foot so that it is perpendicular to the floor. Keeping your knee bent, lift your right leg and raise your knee up to hip level. Tilt your chin slightly toward your chest and pull your abdominals in so your back doesn't sag. See photo A of Figure 13-9.

The Exercise

Straighten your leg and then bend your knee. Complete all of the repetitions with one leg before switching sides. See photo B of Figure 13-9.

Do's and Don'ts

- ✔ DO keep your neck still and your shoulders relaxed.

- ✔ DON'T use an ankle weight for this exercise: It places too much pressure on your knee.

- ✔ DON'T just throw your leg out straight and snap it back again; do move slowly so that you feel the tension in the back of your thigh.

- ✔ DON'T raise your leg above hip height or arch your back as you curl and uncurl your leg.

Other Options

Variations (Easier): To make this exercise easier, lie on the floor with your forehead resting on your forearms. Lift your thigh slightly off the floor, and then curl and uncurl. Or do this exercise while standing and holding onto the back of a chair or the back of an upright bench with your hands.

Weighted Leg Curl: You can add weight to this exercise by wrapping an ankle weight around your ankle or thigh. Or, do a kneeling or standing version of the exercise with the low pulley of a cable machine that has a padded ankle strap.

Keep your neck in line with the rest of your spine.

A)

B)

Figure 13-9:
Don't arch
your back
as you curl
and uncurl
your leg.

Leg Curl Machine

The Leg Curl Machine does a great job of strengthening your hamstring muscles. Use caution if you have a history of **lower back** discomfort.

Getting Set

Set the ankle pads of the machine so that when you lie on your stomach, the underside of the pads are flush with the tops of your heels. Lie down, rest the side of your face on the support pad, and grasp the handles. Gently flex your feet. Pull your abdominals in and tuck your hips down so that your hip bones press into the pad. See photo A of Figure 13-10.

The Exercise

Bend your knees to lift the ankle bar until your calves are perpendicular to the floor. Then slowly straighten your legs. See photo B of Figure 13-10.

Do's and Don'ts

- ✔ DO keep your hip bones pressed against the machine and your abdominals pulled in. You may want to lift your thighs just a hair upward before you bend your knees.

- ✔ DO lower your legs back down slowly so the weights you are lifting don't slam down against the rest of the stack.

- ✔ DON'T — and this is a *big* don't — allow your butt to pop off the pad. This puts stress on your lower back and minimizes the work being done by your hamstrings.

- ✔ DON'T kick your heels all the way to your butt.

Other Options

Other Curl Machines: Some machines work your hamstrings from a standing or seated position. Others have independent left and right sides so that each leg has to carry its own share of the weight. Still others have a "range limiting" device that allows you to cut off the movement at the top or bottom — a good variation if you are experiencing any pain while doing this exercise.

Single-leg Curl: Lift with both legs, straighten one out of the way, and lower the weight down with one leg only.

A)

B)

Figure 13-10:
Don't let
your butt
pop off
the pad.

Don't let your hips pop up.

Inner/Outer Thigh Machine

The Inner/Outer Thigh Machine can be set to strengthen either your inner thigh muscles or your outer thigh muscles. Skaters, skiers, basketball players — anyone involved in side-to-side movements — can help prevent injury by using this machine.

Getting Set

Set the machine so that the leg mechanisms are together and the knee and ankle pads are rotated to the outside. Sit up tall in the seat, and bend your knees so that they rest against the thigh pads and the outside of your ankles rest against the ankle pads. If there's a seat belt, wear it to help keep you from popping out of the machine. Pull your abdominals in and sit up tall. See photo A of Figure 13-11.

The Exercise

Press your knees outward until you feel tension in your outer thighs. Hold the position for a moment, and then slowly allow your legs to move back together. This is the outer thigh, or *abduction,* exercise. To set the machine for the inner thigh, or *adduction,* exercise, shift the leg mechanisms so they're comfortably spread apart, and turn the knee and ankle pads toward the inside. Position your legs so that the inside of your knees rest against the thigh pads, and the inside of your ankles rest against the ankle pads. Pull your legs together, and then slowly move them back out to a point at which you feel a comfortable stretch through your inner thighs. See photo B of Figure 13-11.

Do's and Don'ts

✔ DO control the movement in both directions. If you hear the weight stack come crashing down, slow down.

✔ DO change the weight between exercises if you need to. Most people use approximately the same weight for both inner and outer thigh exercises, but don't take that for granted.

✔ DON'T arch your back or wiggle around in the seat in an effort to assist your legs.

Other Options

Vary seat position: Some machines allow you to decline the seat back a few degrees or even all the way down so you can lie flat. Experiment with different back positions to see what's most comfortable for you and to give the exercise a different feel.

A)

B)

Figure 13-11:
Control the
movement
in both
directions.

Side-lying Leg Lift

The Side-lying Leg Lift strengthens your outer thigh muscles. Pay attention to the instructions marked by the Posture Patrol icon, particularly if you have a history of **lower back** pain.

Getting Set

Lie on the floor on your left side with your legs a few inches in front of you, knees bent slightly, and head resting on your outstretched arm. Bend your right arm and place your palm on the floor in front of your chest for support. Align your right hip directly over your left hip and pull your abdominals in so your back isn't arched. See photo A of Figure 13-12.

The Exercise

Keeping your knee slightly bent, raise your right leg until your foot reaches shoulder height. Then slowly lower your leg back down. Switch sides and do the same number of repetitions with your left leg. See photo B of Figure 13-12.

Do's and Don'ts

✔ DO keep your top hip stacked directly over your bottom hip; don't roll backward.

✔ DO keep your head down and your neck and shoulders relaxed.

✔ DO keep your abdominals pulled in to help your body remain still so that you work only your outer thigh.

✔ DON'T raise your foot any higher than shoulder height.

Other Options

Modified Leg Lift (Easier): Bend your top knee even more when performing the Side-lying Leg Lift.

Leg Lift with Rotation (Harder): When you reach the top of the movement, rotate your thigh outward by turning your knee up to the ceiling; then rotate back to the original position and lower your leg back down.

Leg Lift with a Weight (Harder): Place an ankle weight on your ankle or, if you have knee problems, on top of your thigh.

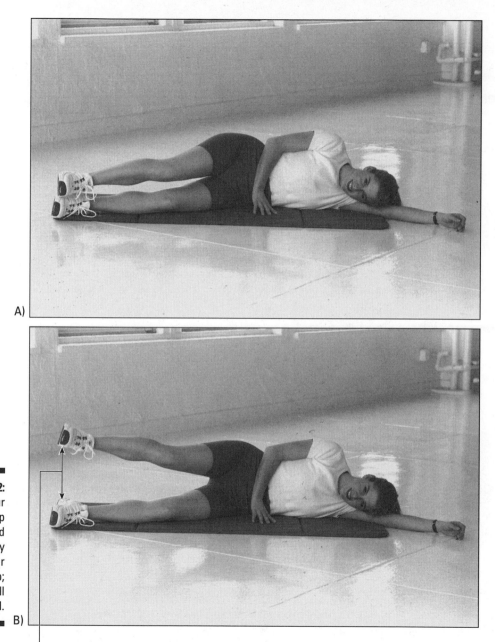

A)

Figure 13-12:
Keep your
top hip
stacked
directly
over your
bottom hip;
don't roll
backward.

B)

└Lift your foot to shoulder height.

Inner Thigh Lift

The Inner Thigh Lift strengthens your inner thigh muscles. Use caution if you have **lower back** problems.

Getting Set

Roll up a bath towel (or use a step aerobics platform). Lie on your right side with your head resting on your outstretched arm. Bend your left leg and rest your knee on top of the rolled towel so that your knee is level with your hip and your top hip is directly over your bottom hip. Place your left hand on the floor in front of your chest for support. Pull your abdominals in. See photo A of Figure 13-13.

The Exercise

Lift your bottom (right) leg a few inches off the floor. Pause briefly at the top of the movement, and slowly lower your leg back down. Switch sides and do the same number of repetitions with your left leg. See photo B of Figure 13-13.

Do's and Don'ts

✔ DON'T lift your leg more than a few inches. Stop when you feel tension in your inner thigh. How high you need to lift depends on your flexibility, your strength, and your build.

✔ DON'T arch your back as you lift your leg.

Other Options

Modified Inner Thigh Lift (Easier): Instead of placing your top knee on the towel, bend your knee and place your foot behind your bottom leg.

Inner Thigh Lift with a Weight (Harder): Wear an ankle weight while performing the Inner Thigh Lift. If you have bad knees, drape the weight on top of your inner thigh.

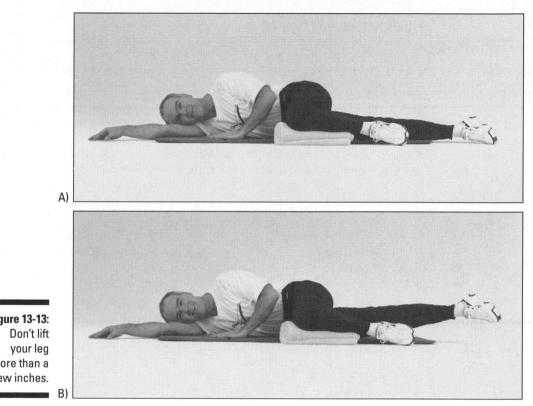

A)

B)

Figure 13-13:
Don't lift
your leg
more than a
few inches.

Standing Calf Raise

The Standing Calf Raise hones right in on your calf muscles.

Getting Set

Stand on the edge of a step. (Or, if you have a step aerobics platform, place two sets of risers underneath the platform.) Stand tall with the balls of your feet firmly planted on the step and your heels hanging over the edge. Rest your hands against a wall or a sturdy object for balance. Stand tall with your abdominals pulled in. See photo A of Figure 13-14.

The Exercise

Raise your heels a few inches above the edge of the step so that you're on your tiptoes. Hold the position for a moment, and then lower your heels back down. Lower your heels below the platform in order to stretch your calf muscles. See photo B of Figure 13-14.

Do's and Don'ts

  ✔ DO lift as high as you can onto your toes.

  ✔ DO lower your heels down as much as your ankle flexibility will allow.

Other Options

Standing Calf Machine: Stand with your shoulders snugly underneath two pads and your heels hanging off the edge of a platform. The standing calf machine isolates the gastrocnemius. If you want to get your soleus into the act (and you do if you do a lot of activities that involve walking, running, or jumping), look for a seated calf machine. Your knees fit underneath a platform and your heels again hang off the edge.

Add a Dumbbell (Harder): Holding a dumbbell in one hand adds resistance to this exercise and also forces you to balance more because you won't be able to hold onto something with both hands.

One-leg Calf Raise: To work one calf at a time, bend one knee behind you and raise the heel of your other foot up and down. Do the same number of repetitions with each leg.

Toe Lift

If you're prone to shin splints or ankle problems, adding the Toe Lift to your repertoire is a must.

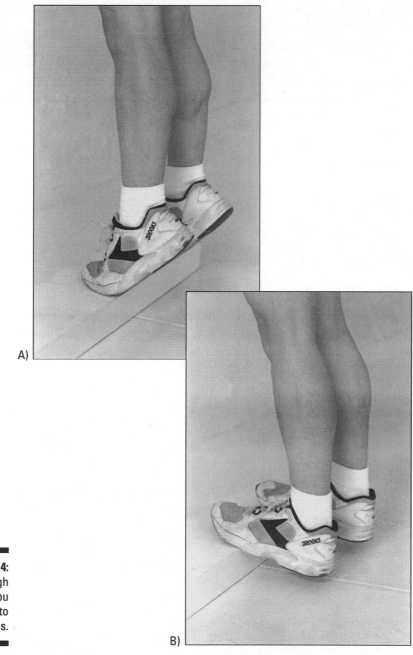

Figure 13-14:
Lift as high
as you
can onto
your toes.

A)

B)

Getting Set

Stand with your feet as wide as your hips and your legs straight but not locked. You may hold on to a sturdy object for support. See photo A of Figure 13-15.

The Exercise

Keeping your heels firmly planted into the floor, lift your toes as high as you can. You should feel a tightening though the lower part of your shins. Lower your toes. See photo B of Figure 13-15.

Do's and Don'ts

✔ DO lift only the part of your foot that's in front of the ball of your foot.

✔ DON'T rock back onto your heels.

Other Options

Seated Toe Lift (Easier): Do the Toe Lift while seated with your knees bent.

Exercise Sequence (Harder): Do the Toe Lift immediately following Calf Raises.

Band Toe Lift (Harder): Do the Toe Lift while seated, but wrap a band around the back edges of your toes. You'll feel resistance both when lifting your toes and lowering them. (Don't use the band to help lift though.)

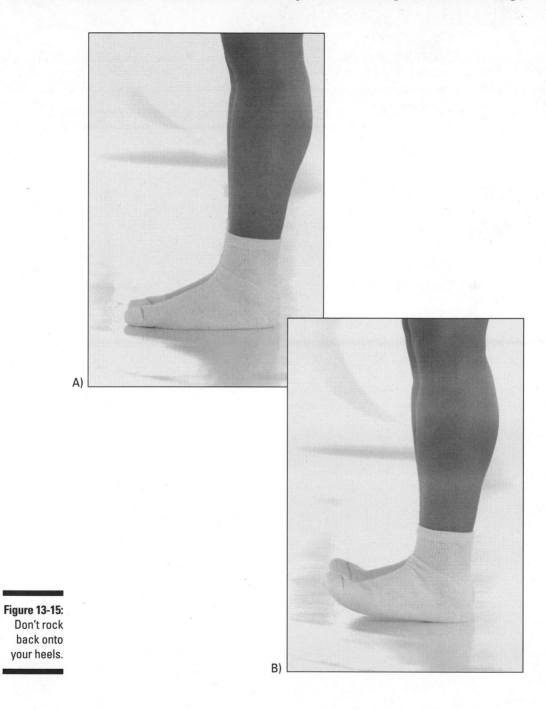

Figure 13-15:
Don't rock
back onto
your heels.

A)

B)

Chapter 14

Advanced Weight Training Exercises

*Y*ou may think that "advanced" weight training exercises require lifting barbells heavier than a Ford Expedition. And you may think that these exercises are appropriate only for hardcore bodybuilders who have been pumping iron practically since birth.

Not true on either count! Many of the exercises that experienced lifters perform at the gym are perfectly suitable for lifters with four to six months of consistent weight training experience. Sure, as a relative newcomer, you will be lifting a lot less weight than the monster-sized guys and gals. But you can perform the same motions and look almost as cool doing them.

These moves are impressive to perform, especially if you do them with textbook form, and they will earn you the respect of your friends, family, and coworkers. Okay, maybe not. But your street credibility is likely to go up among other gym members, especially those who haven't yet mastered these exercises. If you're not yet ready for these moves, consider them something to shoot for.

Of course, we're not recommending the exercises in this chapter simply because they have a high macho factor. They also happen to be exceptionally effective at developing strength and, in many cases, coordination. Most are *compound exercises,* which means that they work several muscle groups at once and build strength that translates well into everyday life tasks. For instance, the Military Push-up uses your chest, shoulders, and triceps the exact same way you'd use them if you were pushing a lawnmower or shopping cart. A few of the exercises in this chapter work only one muscle group, but we include them here because they're tougher than comparable moves shown in other chapters.

We've added these advanced exercises to the second edition to give you even more ways to vary your routine. Just make sure you heed the cautions below. The advanced moves are tougher to perform correctly than most of the exercises shown elsewhere in the book. They carry a greater risk of injury, so it's essential that you perform them correctly.

Important Safety Cautions

We strongly recommend that you get at least a few months of regular weight training under your belt before you attempt the exercises in this chapter. Even then, you may want to skip some — or all — of them. For instance, if you have even the slightest hint of lower back pain, avoid the Deadlift. If you're unsure whether other exercises are appropriate for you, consult a trainer. (Chapter 5 tells you how to determine whether a trainer is qualified to help you.)

Pay particular attention to the Joint Cautions listed in the beginning of each exercise description, and follow these important safety tips:

- **Add only one advanced exercise to your routine at a time.** If, after a week or two, you have mastered the move and don't feel any discomfort, go ahead and add another advanced exercise to your repertoire.

- **Start with a very light weight and focus on form, form, form.** Performing these exercises with the proper technique is far more important than attempting to push around heavy poundage.

- **Do only one set of each new exercise for the first two workouts.** Then, if you want to, gradually add another set or two. How many sets you add and how quickly you add them depends on your goals and abilities.

- **If the basic version of an exercise is too challenging at first, don't sweat it.** Try one of the easier modifications, which are designed to help you build up to the real thing. For instance, if you can't do the Chin-up on your own, start the modification that involves standing on a chair with one leg. After a few weeks, there's a good chance you'll have worked your way up to doing at least a few full-fledged Chin-ups.

- **Use a spotter, preferably a trainer or very experienced lifter**. Your spotter can help you get in and out of the starting position, offer technique tips, and, of course, save your muscles and joints from destruction if something goes wrong and you're not able to complete the exercise. (We tell you all about spotting in Chapter 2.) Even if you've already mastered the technique for an advanced move, enlist a spotter when you're moving to a significantly heavier weight. Some of these exercises, such as the Deadlift and Barbell Squat, should *never* be done without a spotter.

> ✔ **If something hurts, don't do it!** If you hear a ripping sound as you reach down to grab the bar for the Military Press, that's a pretty good indication that this exercise isn't for you.

The Exercises

Here's a look at the advanced exercises described in this chapter:

- ✔ Chin-up
- ✔ Push-up
- ✔ Dip
- ✔ Military Press
- ✔ Preacher Curl
- ✔ French Press
- ✔ Barbell Squat
- ✔ Stiff-legged Deadlift
- ✔ Hanging Abs

Chin-up

The Chin-up targets your upper back, with additional emphasis on your shoulders, biceps, and wrists. Be careful if you have **lower back** or **shoulder** problems.

Getting Set

You can do chin-ups with a pull-up bar, a chin/dip frame, or by placing a barbell in one of the upper positions of a power rack or Smith machine. Stand underneath the bar and grab it with your palms facing you and hands slightly closer than shoulder-width apart. Pull your abdominals in and keep your body tall. See photo A of Figure 14-1.

The Exercise

Hoist your chest up to the bar by bending your arms; don't contort or swing your body to help out. Slowly lower yourself until your arms are fully straightened before beginning the next rep. See photo B of Figure 14-1.

Do's and Don'ts

✔ DO keep your legs straight and together. (However, if the bar is too low, you may have to bend your knees.)

✔ DO relax your shoulders so they don't hunch up by your ears.

✔ DON'T rock your body to help move you up and down.

✔ DON'T arch your back or round forward.

Other Options:

Chin-up with a Chair (Easier): Stand on a chair with one leg hanging off to the side. As you lower your body, bend the knee of the leg that's on the chair. As you raise yourself, straighten your leg. Use only as much leg strength as you need to help you through the exercise.

Pull-up (Harder): Grasp the bar with your palms facing forward and your arms spread a few inches wider than shoulder-width apart. Always lift your chest — rather than the back of your neck — up to the bar. Behind-the-neck pull-ups are very hard on your shoulders and rotator cuff muscles.

A)

B)

Figure 14-1:
Don't rock
your body to
help move
you up and
down.

Push-up

The Push-up strengthens your chest muscles, with emphasis on your shoulders and triceps as well. Be extra careful if you have **lower back, shoulder, elbow,** or **wrist** problems.

Getting Set

Lie face-down with your legs straight out behind you. Bend your elbows and place your palms on the floor a bit to the side and in front of your shoulders. Straighten your arms and lift your body so that you're balanced on your palms and the underside of your toes. Tuck your chin a few inches toward your chest so that your forehead faces the floor. Tighten your abdominals. See photo A of Figure 14-2.

The Exercise

Bend your elbows and lower your entire body at once. Rather than try to touch your chest to the floor, lower only until your upper arms are parallel to the floor. Push back up. See photo B of Figure 14-2.

Do's and Don'ts

- ✔ DON'T lock your elbows at the top of the movement, but do bring your arms to a full extension.

- ✔ DON'T do the dreaded head bob. That's when you dip your head toward the floor without moving any other part of your body. Talk about a giant pain in the neck!

Other Options

Negative Push-up (Easier): Just do the lowering phase of this exercise. Slow the movement down and try to lower yourself in five counts. Or try the Modified Push-up, shown in Chapter 9.

A)

Figure 14-2:
Keep your
abs tight so
your back
doesn't arch
like a
swayback
horse.

B)

Dip

Dips work your chest muscles but also place a lot of emphasis on your shoulders and triceps. Take extra care with this exercise if you have **lower back** or **shoulder** issues.

Getting Set

Stand facing a dip station, and place your hands on the dip bars. Hop up so that your feet are off the floor. Straighten your arms and lift your body upward. Keep your legs straight, or bend your knees slightly and cross one ankle over the other. Remain tall and relaxed with your abdominals pulled inward. See photo A of Figure 14-3.

The Exercise

Bend your elbows and lower your body only until your upper arms are parallel to the floor. Straighten your arms to lift yourself back up. See photo B of Figure 14-3.

Do's and Don'ts

- ✔ DO keep your abdominals pulled in so that your back doesn't arch.
- ✔ DO keep your neck aligned with the rest of your spine rather than allow your chin to jut forward.
- ✔ DON'T bend your elbows too far. This places a great deal of strain on your elbows and shoulders.

Other Options

Assisted Dip (Easier): Have a partner hold your feet and assist you upward. Or, try the Assisted Dip, described in Chapter 9.

Negative Dip (Easier): If you can't push yourself back up, do only the downward part of this exercise. Lower yourself slowly, taking about five slow counts to complete the movement.

Weighted Dip (Harder): Do the basic version of the exercise with a special waist belt designed to hold a weight plate on the end of it.

A)

B)

Figure 14-3:
Lower your
body only
until your
upper arms
are parallel
to the floor.

Military Press

The Military Press targets the top and center of your shoulder muscles. This exercise also works your upper back and triceps. Use caution if you have **lower back, neck,** or **elbow** problems.

Getting Set

Sit on a bench with back support just behind a barbell that is set on stanchions higher than chest level. Place your hands on the bar with your palms facing forward, arms slightly wider than shoulder-width apart, and elbows slightly below your shoulders. Lift the bar off the safety rack and slowly straighten your arms to press the bar up. Pull your abdominals inward and keep your back against the support. See photo A of Figure 14-4.

The Exercise

Lower the bar toward the top of your chest until your elbows are just below shoulder height. Press the bar back up. See photo B of Figure 14-4.

Do's and Don'ts

- ✔ DO keep your head and back against the pad rather than let your head dip forward or your back arch off the support.

- ✔ DO keep your elbows relaxed at the top rather than locking them.

- ✔ DON'T lower the bar behind your neck. This puts a lot of stress on your shoulders and rotator cuff.

- ✔ DON'T wiggle or squirm around in an effort to press the weights up.

Other Options

Smith Machine Military Press (Easier): Do the same exercise using the bar of a Smith Machine or power cage. The frame will help guide the bar. You can also set the range-limiting device to ensure you don't lower the bar too far.

A)

B)

Figure 14-4: Don't lower the bar behind your neck.

Preacher Curl

The Preacher Curl targets your biceps. Use caution if you have **elbow** problems.

Getting Set

Place an EZ-curl bar in the cradle of the preacher bench. Set the seat of the bench so that your chest rests comfortably on the support pad and you can easily reach over the top of the bench to grasp the bar. Sit down on the seat of the preacher curl bench with your feet firmly planted on the floor. Grasp the bar on the outside curves with your palms facing up. Pull your abdominals in, and keep your shoulders down and relaxed. See photo A of Figure 14-5.

The Exercise

Bend your arms and lift the bar upward until your hands are level with your shoulders. Straighten your arms to lower the bar. See photo B of Figure 14-5.

Do's and Don'ts

- ✔ DO lower the bar slowly rather than letting it drop quickly downward.

- ✔ DO remain seated throughout the exercise; don't pop up as you lower the bar.

- ✔ DON'T lean back or wiggle around to lift the bar.

- ✔ DON'T lower the bar to a full arm extension as this may place undue stress on your joints. Do leave a small bend in your elbow at the end of the movement.

Other Options

Cable Preacher Curl: Attach a straight or curved bar to the low pulley of a cable column, and place the preacher bench so that it is facing the pulley. Perform the same exercise as the basic version using the cable instead of the EZ-Curl bar.

Scott Curl (Easier): This is a machine version of the Preacher Curl. It's a good option to help you build up enough strength to perform the Preacher Curl.

A)

B)

Figure 14-5:
Remain
seated
rather than
popping up
as you
lower the
bar.

French Press

The French Press targets your triceps. This exercise tends to aggravate **elbow** injuries if you use too much weight or don't use proper form.

Getting Set

Grasp an EZ-curl bar with an overhand grip and your hands about shoulder-width apart. (You can do the French Press using a straight bar, although you'll need to concentrate more on steadying the bar.) Lie face-up on the bench with your feet on the floor. Straighten your arms up to raise the bar directly over your shoulders. Pull your abdominals in and keep the back of your head firmly on the bench. See photo A of Figure 14-6.

The Exercise

Keeping your upper arms still and your elbows in, bend your elbows and lower the bar toward your forehead. Then straighten your arms to raise the bar back up overhead. See photo B of Figure 14-6.

Do's and Don'ts

- ✔ DO squeeze your elbows together.
- ✔ DO keep your upper arms in exactly the same position throughout the motion.
- ✔ DO lower the bar slowly and stop just short of touching your forehead so that you don't clunk yourself in the head with the weight!
- ✔ DON'T arch your back up off the bench to help move the weight.

Other Options

Dumbbell French Press: Lying on a bench, hold a dumbbell in each hand and straighten your arms directly over your shoulders with your palms facing each other. Keep your upper arms still, and bend your elbows to lower the weights until they are alongside either ear. Then press the weights back up to the starting position.

A)

Figure 14-6:
Keep your
upper arms
in the same
position
throughout
the motion.

B)

Barbell Squat

In addition to strengthening your butt muscles, the Barbell Squat also works your quadriceps and hamstrings. Take extra care if you have **hip, knee,** or **lower back** problems.

Getting Set

Place a weighted bar in a power cage so that when you stand underneath it, the bar rests gently across the top of your shoulders. Stand with your feet as wide as your hips, weight shifted slightly back on to your heels, and hold on to either side of the bar with your hands wider than shoulder-width apart. Pull your abdominals in and stand up tall with square shoulders. See photo A of Figure 14-7.

The Exercise

Sit back and down, as if you're sitting into a chair. Lower as far as you can without leaning your upper body more than a few inches forward. Don't lower any further than the point at which your thighs are parallel to the floor, and don't allow your knees to shoot out in front of your toes. Once you feel your upper body fold forward over your thighs, straighten your legs and stand back up. Take care not to lock your knees at the top of the movement. See photo B of Figure 14-7.

Do's and Don'ts

- ✔ DON'T allow your knees to travel beyond your toes.

- ✔ DON'T allow your body to fall forward. It helps to keep your eyes focused forward.

- ✔ DON'T shift your body weight forward so that your heels lift off the floor. When you push back up to the standing position, concentrate on pressing through your heels.

- ✔ DON'T arch your back as you stand back up.

Other Options

Smith Machine Squat (Easier): Do this exercise with a Smith Machine. The guides help you maintain balance and keep you in a fixed position.

Front Squat (Harder): Rather than placing the bar behind your neck, place it across the top of your chest. You can hold it there by crossing your arms and placing your hands on the bar to keep it resting gently across your shoulders. Because this version of the Squat requires a lot of balance and coordination, we strongly recommend you do this exercise with a spotter or with a Smith Machine.

A)

B)

Figure 14-7:
Don't let
your knees
travel
beyond
your toes.

Stiff-legged Deadlift

This exercise strengthens your hamstrings, buttocks, and lower back. Avoid this exercise if you have **lower back** problems.

Getting Set

Place a barbell just in front of your feet, and stand tall with your feet as wide as your hips. Bend from the hips and grasp the bar so that your palms are facing you and your hands are approximately shoulder-width apart. Pull in your abdominals. See photo A of Figure 14-8.

The Exercise

Keeping your arms and legs straight, stand and lift the bar until it is resting against the tops of your thighs. Carefully bend over to lower the bar. See photo B of Figure 14-8.

Do's and Don'ts

- DO be sure to pull your abdominals inward.

- DO move slowly and carefully. *Never* jerk the bar upward or plop it back down on the floor.

- DON'T arch or round your lower back.

Other Options

Bent-Knee Deadlift (Easier): Do this exercise with your knees slightly bent. This version will not emphasize your hamstrings as much but will be easier on your lower back.

Platform Deadlift (Harder): Do this exercise while standing on a step bench or low platform. If you have enough flexibility, you will be able to lower the bar beyond the level of your feet.

A)

B)

Figure 14-8:
Don't arch
or round
your lower
back.

Hanging Abs

This exercise is a real ab burner; it works the rectus abdominals, obliques, and transverse abdominals.

Getting Set

Slide your arms into two padded loops suspended on a bar or a frame. Keep your feet together and let your legs hang downward directly below your body. Pull your abdominals inward. See photo A of Figure 14-9.

The Exercise

Keeping your feet together, slowly bend your knees and lift them toward your chest. Slowly straighten your legs back down. See photo B of Figure 14-9.

Do's and Don'ts

- ✔ DO move slowly so that your abdominals do all the work and you don't rely on momentum.

- ✔ DO keep your torso still and stabilized against the back pad.

- ✔ DON'T hunch your shoulders upward or dip your chin forward.

Other Options

One-leg Hanging Abs (Easier): Lift one knee at a time.

Straight-leg Hanging Abs (Harder): This extremely difficult version of the exercise calls for you to straighten your legs up and outward until your legs are parallel to the floor. We don't recommend this version for anyone with lower back problems.

A)

B)

Figure 14-9:
Move slowly
so that your
abs do the
work and
you don't
rely on
momentum.

Part IV
Designing Your Workout Program

The 5th Wave   By Rich Tennant

Scottish Home Gym

You spend good money on a nice piece of equipment, and now it just sits in the corner of the room collecting dust.

In this part . . .

*P*art IV shows you how to custom-design your workout program — whether you lift weights twice a week or five times, whether you have 20 minutes or 2 hours, or whether your goal is to build strong bones or a biceps the diameter of a watermelon. In this part, we give you the basic recipe for effective weight workouts — a list of the ingredients essential to all routines. Then we help you tinker with the recipe to concoct routines that suit your personal needs, and we describe plenty of training techniques to give your workouts extra pizazz. We also show you how to structure your routines if you lift weights more than three times per week.

Chapter 15

Designing a Basic Workout

• •

In This Chapter

▶ Key weight training vocabulary

▶ Essential elements of a weight routine

▶ Custom-designing your routine

▶ How to liven up your workout

▶ Sample routines that strengthen your whole body

• •

*I*n Part III, we describe more than 160 exercises. Certainly we don't expect you to do all of these moves in one workout — your workouts would last longer than the Academy Awards. So how do you choose?

Consider that weight training is a lot like baking: part science, part art. Baking is governed by certain immutable rules — for instance, you can't bake oatmeal cookies without flour. However, there's no limit to what ingredients you can *add* to your oatmeal cookies, whether it's raisins, cinnamon, chocolate chips, cranberries, or nutmeg. The cookie recipe you choose on a given day depends on a lot of things, including your taste preferences, the ingredients you have in the house, and how much time you have.

The same principles apply to weight training routines. You've got your basic rules — you can't develop a well-toned body without chest exercises, for example. But you can pick from a whole variety of chest exercises. You can do them sitting, standing, or lying down. You can use dumbbells, barbells, machines, or no equipment at all. You can do one chest exercise or six.

In this chapter, we give you a basic recipe for effective weight workouts — a list of the ingredients essential to all routines. Then we help you fiddle with the recipe to create routines that are based on your own goals, preferences, time schedule, and available equipment. We also include a number of sample beginner routines. All the workouts in this chapter strengthen the entire body. In Chapter 16, we include more advanced routines that focus on specific body parts.

Jargon You Actually Need to Know

Weight training has its fair share of gobbledygook. You don't need to be fluent in the language spoken at bodybuilding competitions and physiology conferences, but to design an effective workout, you do need to know the basics. In this section, we explain key strength training terminology.

✓ **Repetition:** This term, often shortened to *rep,* refers to a single rendition of an exercise. For example, pressing two dumbbells straight above your head and then lowering them back down to your shoulders constitutes one complete repetition of the Dumbbell Shoulder Press, shown in Chapter 10.

Anyone who lifts weight for general fitness, should perform 4-second repetitions — 2 seconds to lift the weight and 2 seconds to lower it. Don't pause for more than a split second at the end of a repetition. Each rep should flow seamlessly into the next. Athletes and those who are lifting for extreme strength or bulk may do slower or faster reps depending on their goals.

✓ **Set:** A *set* is a group of consecutive repetitions that you perform without resting. When you've done 12 repetitions of the Dumbbell Shoulder Press and then put the weights down, you have completed one set. If you rest for a minute and then perform 12 more repetitions, you have done two sets.

✓ **Routine:** This is a broad term that encompasses virtually every aspect of what you do in one weight lifting session, including the type of equipment you use; the number of exercises, sets, and repetitions you perform; the order in which you do your exercises; and how much rest you take between sets. By varying the elements of your routine — say, decreasing the number of reps or adding new exercises — you can significantly change the results you get from weight training. Your routine (also referred to as your program or your workout) can change from one exercise session to the next, or it can stay the same over a period of weeks or months.

The Rap on Reps

The number of repetitions you perform matters a lot. In general, if your goal is to build the largest, strongest muscles that your genetic makeup allows, perform relatively few repetitions, about 4 to 6 (perhaps even fewer). If you're seeking a more moderate increase in strength and size — for example, if your goal is to improve your health or shape your muscles — aim for 8 to 15 repetitions.

Performing reps in the 8-to-15 range also gives you something that a low-rep routine doesn't: *muscular endurance,* in other words, the ability of that muscle to perform longer. Muscular endurance comes in handy for everyday tasks like carrying a heavy box from your house to the car. Don't confuse muscular endurance with *cardiovascular endurance,* which is the stamina of your heart and lungs. Muscular endurance affects only the muscle in question and lasts only a minute or two; you improve the staying power of one muscle rather than the stamina of your entire body.

Why does performing 6 reps result in more strength than doing 15 reps? Because the number of reps you perform is linked to the amount of weight you lift. Always use a weight that's heavy enough to make that last repetition a real challenge, if not an outright struggle. So when you perform 6 reps, use a much heavier weight than when you perform 15 reps of the same exercise. If you were to perform only 6 reps with a weight that you were capable of lifting 15 times, you wouldn't develop much strength.

Weight training isn't an exact science, so don't take these rep numbers too literally. It's not as if performing 6 repetitions will transform you into Xena: Warrior Princess whereas performing 10 reps will make you look like Julia Roberts. Everyone's body responds a bit differently to weight training.

Bodybuilders (who aim for massive size) and powerlifters (who aim to lift the heaviest weight possible) often train by hoisting so much poundage that they can perform only 1 or 2 reps. However, most of us have goals that are best served by doing between 6 and 15 repetitions. Performing fewer reps — and thus using ultra-heavy weights — carries a greater risk of injury. And doing more than 15 reps is generally not effective for building strength. To keep yourself motivated and your muscles challenged, you may want to vary the number of reps you perform. For example, you could do 6 to 8 repetitions one month and then 12 to 15 the next.

Finding the right weight for each exercise requires some trial and error. Don't be afraid to add or subtract weight after you start a set. We've seen people contort their bodies to finish a set just because they overestimated what they could lift but were too embarrassed to drop down a plate.

The Scoop on Sets

Beginners should start with one set for each of the major muscle groups listed below. That's roughly 11 sets per workout. After a month or two, you may want to increase the number of sets. But then again, you may not. If your goal is to gain moderate amounts of strength and improve your health, one set may be as much as you ever need to do.

However, if your goal is to become as strong as you can or reshape an area of your body, you need to perform more than three sets per muscle group. Some serious weight lifters perform as many as 20. (However, they don't do 20 sets of the same exercise; they may do five sets each of four different exercises that work the same muscle.) See Chapter 16 for more guidelines on how many sets to perform if you're an experienced lifter.

Beginners should take all the rest they need between sets. Most people find that 60 to 90 seconds is enough to feel fully recovered from the previous set. As you get more fit, you can gradually decrease your rest periods. *Circuit training* (described later in this chapter) involves taking little or no rest between sets.

Essential Elements of a Weight Routine

If an orchestra were to play Vivaldi's *Four Seasons* minus the string section, the piece would lack a certain vitality and depth. Likewise, if you leave out a key element of your weight workout, you may end up with disappointing results. So follow the guidelines below.

Work all of your major muscle groups

Be sure that your routines include at least one exercise for each of the following muscle groups. (In Part III, we show you precisely where each muscle is located.)

- Butt (glutes)
- Front thighs (quadriceps)
- Rear thighs (hamstrings)
- Calves
- Chest (pecs)
- Back
- Abdominals (abs)
- Shoulders (delts)
- Front of upper arm (biceps)
- Rear of upper arm (triceps)

In Part III, we include exercises for additional muscle groups, such as the wrist and shin muscles and inner and outer thighs. But for general fitness, the preceding muscles should be your highest priorities. If you neglect any of these muscle groups, you'll have a gap in your strength, and you may set yourself up for injury.

If you avoid training any particular muscle group, you also may end up with a body that looks out of proportion. You don't need to hit all your muscle groups on the same day — just make sure you work each group twice a week. In Chapter 16, we discuss several ways you can split up your workouts.

Do the exercises in the right order

In general, work your large muscles before your small muscles. This practice ensures that your larger muscles — such as your butt, back, and chest — are sufficiently challenged. Suppose that you're performing the Dumbbell Chest Press, shown in Chapter 9. This exercise primarily works your chest muscles, but your pecs do require assistance from your shoulders and triceps. If you were to work these smaller muscles first, they'd be too tired to help out the chest.

In order to perform your exercises in the right order, you need to understand which exercises work which muscle groups. Many people do their routines in the wrong sequence because they don't realize the purpose of a particular exercise (the purpose is not always obvious). When you pull a bar down to your chest, as in the Lat Pulldown (see Chapter 8), you may think that you're doing an arm exercise when, in fact, the exercise primarily strengthens your back. So, make a point of learning which muscles are involved in each move that you do.

When choosing the sequence of a workout, imagine that your body is divided into three zones: upper, middle, and lower. Within each zone, do your exercises in the following order. Feel free to mix exercises from different zones.

Upper body

1. Chest and back (It doesn't matter which comes first.)

2. Shoulders

3. Biceps and triceps (It doesn't matter which comes first.)

4. Wrists

Middle body

You can perform your abdominal and lower back muscle exercises in any order you want.

Lower body

1. Butt

2. Thighs

3. Calves and shins (It doesn't matter which comes first although we prefer to work our calves before our shins.)

Don't exercise the same muscle two days in a row

Always let a muscle rest at least one day between workouts. This doesn't preclude you from lifting weights two days in a row; you could work your chest and back one day and then your legs the next. But if you're doing a full-body routine, don't lift weights more than three times a week and don't cram your three workouts into one weekend.

How to Custom-design a Routine

You've probably read magazine articles that reveal an athlete or actor's weight training routine. Often, the stories imply that if you follow the routine to the letter, you too can become a sculpted celebrity — or at least look like one. Don't buy into this notion. Everyone has a unique genetic makeup — and a unique set of preferences and priorities. You certainly can pick up good ideas from reading about other peoples' workouts, but you're better off designing your own routines by taking the following elements into consideration.

Your goals

Too many people blindly go through the motions of a weight training program without stopping to ask themselves, "What the heck am I trying to accomplish?" So give this question some serious thought. Are you planning to scale the Grand Tetons, or do you just want to strengthen your back to add oomph to your golf swing?

Here's a rundown of some common goals and suggestions for how you can reach each of them. You may want to consult a trainer or medical doctor for advice that's even more specific to your needs.

✔ **Goal: Improve your health.** If you aspire to increase your strength, keep your bones strong, and avoid common injuries, you need not spend half your waking hours with hunks of steel in your hands. You can get by with one exercise for every major muscle group in your body. Simply do one set of 8 to 15 repetitions for each muscle listed earlier in this chapter. We recommend doing two or three workouts a week.

✔ **Goal: Alter your looks.** Weight training can be a powerful tool for changing your appearance, whether you're looking to do a major overhaul or simply aiming to tone your triceps. But don't get carried away with any fantasies. Keep in mind the old joke about the 75-year-old woman who walks into a hair salon with a picture of a 20-year-old model. "I want to look like *this*," she says. "Lady," the hairdresser replies, "I'm a hairdresser, not a magician." If you're large boned and muscular, weight training cannot make you lean and lithe — and vice versa. You need to work within your body's parameters.

Significantly changing your looks requires more of a time commitment than simply improving your health. (And keep in mind that your diet and cardiovascular workouts play a large role, too.) Instead of training your entire body in 20 minutes, you may need to spend 20 minutes simply on your upper body. To develop a noticeably firmer body, we suggest performing at least three sets per muscle group. To build some serious bulk, you may need to perform even more sets and use some of the advanced techniques we describe in Chapter 16.

By the way, don't expect to look like the sculpted, fat-free people who sell weight training products on TV infomercials. Many of these people have unusual genetics, have taken drugs, and/or have undergone surgery to achieve their looks.

✔ **Goal: Train for an athletic event.** Preparing for an athletic challenge at any level takes time and dedication (and weight training, of course, is just one aspect of your training). For best results, you need to tailor your weight routine precisely to the event. For example, if you're working toward a hilly 10K walk or run, you need to give extra attention to your leg and butt muscles. And your workout will be very different if you want to simply complete a 10K run rather than win it. Serious competitors should expect to spend a lot of serious time in the weight room at certain times of the year (primarily the off-season).

Your equipment

Naturally, the exercises you choose are limited to the equipment that's available to you. If you belong to a health club the size of Wal-Mart, you may be able to try every exercise in this book — and probably a few thousand more. One four-story club in New York City devotes an entire *floor* to leg machines.

If you work out at a smaller club or at home, your choices are more limited, but even with rudimentary equipment, you can get your body into great shape. In Part III, for example, we describe dozens of exercises that you can do at home with nothing more than dumbbells and a bench. If you're short on equipment, you may want to consult a trainer to find out how to make the most of the gizmos you have access to.

Your exercise preferences

When you first take up weight training, you may be overwhelmed by the challenge of learning the basics of each exercise — how to stand, where to grab the weight, how to adjust the machines. But you soon develop strong preferences for certain exercises and equipment. Before you know it, you'll be saying things like, "I love the Incline Chest Fly, but I'd much rather do the Dumbbell Chest Press on a flat bench." Pay attention to which exercises feel good to you and which equipment you enjoy using, and design your workout accordingly.

Your lifestyle

Ask yourself (and answer honestly): "How many times can I work out each week? How many hours can I spend at the gym, including time in the shower and the locker room?" If you're a busy parent who also works full time, chances are you have less time to work out than a college student or retired person.

Be realistic. Don't vow to do six sets per muscle group if the only time you can lift weights is during your 30-minute lunch break on Tuesdays and Thursdays. Otherwise, you can fall into that *why-bother?* trap. You're better off doing a 20-minute routine than skipping that 2-hour workout you planned but somehow never got around to.

Your current level of fitness

If you haven't lifted weights since high school 20 years ago, don't start with the routine your old football coach gave you. Otherwise, you can expect a lot of muscle soreness — and maybe an injury or two — in your immediate future. Don't let your enthusiasm, your flexible schedule or your access to fancy equipment cloud your judgment as you design your routine.

Sample Beginner Routines

Following are just a few of the countless ways you can combine exercises to create an effective weight routine. All these routines include one or two exercises per muscle group.

Machine circuit

Many gyms have a dozen or so machines arranged in a circle or row called a *circuit.* They're placed in a logical order (earlier in this chapter we discuss what's logical), so that you can move from machine to machine without having to use any brain power to decide which exercise to do next. For reasons we explain in Chapter 12, we suggest skipping the abdominal machines and doing the Basic Abdominal Crunch (or other ab floor exercises) instead.

Sample Weight Machine Circuit	
Butt and Legs	Leg Press Machine, Leg Extension Machine, Leg Curl Machine
Back	Lat Pulldown
Chest	Vertical Chest Press Machine
Shoulders	Shoulder Press Machine
Arms	Arm Curl Machine
Triceps	Triceps Dip Machine
Abdominals	Basic Abdominal Crunch

Dumbbells-and-a-bench routine

For this routine, you need several sets of dumbbells and a bench with an adjustable back rest. This is a typical workout for someone who works out at home, but many gym-goers like it, too.

Sample Dumbbells-and-a-Bench Routine	
Butt and Legs	Squat, Lunge, Standing Calf Raise
Back	One-arm Row, Back Extension

(continued)

Sample Dumbbells-and-a-Bench Routine *(continued)*	
Chest	Incline Chest Fly
Shoulders	Lateral Raise
Arms	Dumbbell Biceps Curl, Triceps Kickback
Abdominals	Abdominal Crunch with a Twist

The time-crunch routine

On some days you may not even have 15 minutes to lift weights. Rather than skip your workout altogether, we suggest plan B: the absolute bare minimum. The following workout is for emergency situations only — it's by no means a complete routine. But it can tide you over for a few sessions until you get back on track.

Time-crunch Machine Routine	
Butt and Legs	Leg Press Machine
Back	Machine Row
Chest	Vertical Chest Press Machine
Shoulders	Shoulder Press Machine
Abdominals	Basic Abdominal Crunch

Time-crunch Dumbbell Routine	
Butt and Legs	Squat
Back	One-arm Dumbbell Row
Chest	Dumbbell Chest Press
Shoulders	Dumbbell Shoulder Press
Abdominals	Basic Abdominal Crunch

The mix 'n' match routine

Most experienced weight lifters use a combination of machines and free weights. Over time you develop certain preferences — some exercises feel better with free weights, others are more fun with machines. We encourage you to try all the equipment at your disposal at least a few times.

Liz's Favorite Mix 'n' Match Routine	
Butt and Legs	Lunge, Leg Press, Inner/Outer Thigh Machine, Standing Calf Raise
Back	Cable Row
Chest	Push-up
Shoulders	Cable Lateral Raise
Arms	Dumbbell Biceps Curl, Triceps Pushdown, Wrist Curl
Abdominals	Abdominal Crunch

Suzanne's Favorite Mix 'n' Match Routine	
Butt and Legs	Squat, Seated Leg Curl, Standing Calf Raise
Back	Pull-up
Chest	Bench Press
Shoulders	Dumbbell Shoulder Press
Arms	Barbell Biceps Curl, Triceps Kickback
Abdominals	Reverse Crunch

How to liven up your weight workout

If "Weight training is boring" starts to become your daily mantra, revisit this page and remind yourself of the numerous ways you can jazz up your routine. Here's a recap of the main components — or variables — you can experiment with. You can change one or several of these variables from month to month, week to week, workout to workout.

✔ **Repetitions:** For variety, you could go heavy on Monday, performing 6 reps of each exercise. On Wednesday, you could use lighter weights and perform 12 to 15 repetitions. On Friday, you could use moderate weights and perform 8 to 10 reps. You also can vary your repetitions within a workout. You could do 12 reps on your first set of an exercise, then increase the weight and perform 9 reps on your second set, then increase the weight again, performing 6 reps on your third set.

✔ **Sets per muscle group:** Some days you may have the time or inclination to do three or more sets per muscle group; other days, one set may be your limit. If you do multiple sets, try different exercises. For example, if you're doing three sets of shoulder exercises, you could do one set each of the Shoulder Press, Lateral Raise, and Front Raise (all described in Chapter 10).

✔ **Rest:** Some days, you may want to rest a minute or two between sets so that you can challenge yourself with relatively heavy weights (or so you can schmooze with your friends). Other days, you may want to zoom through your workout, taking 30 seconds or less between sets. Just remember that the less rest you take, the less weight you'll be able to lift.

✔ **Equipment:** Tired of sticking those pins into the weight machines? March over to the free weight room and pick up some dumbbells. You can work almost any muscle group with dumbbells, barbells, machines, and rubber exercise bands.

✔ **Exercises:** Paul Simon counted 50 ways to leave your lover, but you can find even more ways to strengthen your leg muscles. So if you're getting stale, vary the moves in your repertoire.

✔ **Exercise sequence:** As we explain earlier in this chapter, the general rule is to work larger muscles before smaller ones (within each region of your body). But you can still mix up the order plenty. You can vary the order of, say, your three back exercises. You can alternate between upper body and lower body exercises. Or you can work your upper body and then your lower body, or vice versa.

Chapter 16

Expanding Your Repertoire

● ●

In This Chapter

▶ Periodization

▶ Split routines

▶ Super sets and giant sets

▶ Pyramids, breakdowns, and negatives

● ●

*Y*ou may come to a point in your weight training career when moving through the same 12 weight machines or performing the same old dumbbell exercises is not enough — not enough to keep you interested and not enough to keep giving you results. Out of boredom or disappointment, you may start skipping your workouts. This is a warning sign.

In this chapter, we show you how to move beyond the basics to create a more sophisticated, stimulating weight training program. The strategies we present fall into four basic categories: organizing your program from month to month, designing your weekly schedule, arranging your exercises during a particular workout, and structuring an individual set.

You can experiment with a couple of the strategies we discuss in this chapter, or you can use every one. Just don't try them all at once. You'll feel less overwhelmed if you incorporate changes one by one. Plus, you can pinpoint more precisely which strategies work for you and which don't. Beginners certainly can benefit from the techniques we discuss here and should read this chapter. But you'll find the strategies here more valuable if you've been lifting weights for at least a month.

The Big Picture: Organizing Your Program Month to Month

One excellent strategy for yanking yourself out of a rut is periodization (another bit of weight training jargon that we feel compelled to foist upon you). *Periodization* simply means organizing your program into different *periods,* each lasting about four to eight weeks. Each period has a different theme. For example, one month you may use weight machines, and the next month you may switch to dumbbells and barbells. Or you can change the number of sets, repetitions, and exercises you perform from one period to the next. Athletes use periodization to vary their weight lifting (and other types of training) from their off season to their competitive season.

Periodization is more than a fun diversion; this strategy may also give you better results. Consider a study of more than 30 women conducted at Penn State University. Half the women did a typical circuit of 12 weight machines (see Chapter 15 for a definition of circuit), performing one set of 8 to 10 repetitions per machine. They continued this workout three times a week for nine months. The second group engaged in *periodized* training, systematically changing the number of sets, reps, and exercises they performed. Initially, the groups showed comparable strength gains. But after four months, the circuit group hit a plateau. The periodization group continued to make steady progress throughout the nine months.

We recommend that an introductory periodization program include five distinct phases, each lasting about a month. (However, depending on your goals, each phase can be as short as two weeks or as long as eight weeks.) You can repeat this cycle over and over again. Here's a look at each phase:

- ✔ **The Prep Phase:** During this period, you prepare your body for the challenges ahead with a basic workout. Use light weights, perform 1 to 4 sets per muscle, do 12 to 15 repetitions per set, and rest 90 seconds between sets.

- ✔ **The Pump Phase:** In this phase, you step up your efforts a bit. You lift slightly heavier weight, perform 10 to 12 reps per set, do 3 to 8 sets per muscle group, and rest only 60 seconds between sets. The pump phase is a good time to introduce a few of the advanced training techniques we describe later in this chapter, such as super sets and giant sets.

- ✔ **The Push Phase:** In this period, you do 8 to 10 reps per set, resting 30 seconds between sets. You do only two or three different exercises per muscle group, but you do several sets of each so that you can use the advanced training techniques, such as pyramids, that we describe later.

✔ **The Peak Phase:** In this phase, you focus on building maximum strength. Do 6 to 8 reps per set, 15 to 20 sets per muscle group but fewer different exercises. For instance, you may only do 1 or 2 leg exercises, but you do multiple sets of each exercise and 6 to 8 repetitions per set. Rest a full two minutes between sets so that you can lift more weight. This phase is your last big effort before you take a break from heavy training.

✔ **The Rest Phase:** In this phase, you either drop back to the light workouts you did in the prep phase, or you take a break from weight training altogether. Yes, that's right, we're giving you permission to stop lifting weights — for as long as two weeks. Resting gives your body (and your mind) a chance to recover from all the hard work you've been putting in. After your break, you move back into your next periodization cycle with fresh muscles and a renewed enthusiasm for your training.

If you're hell-bent on toning or building up your body, you may be tempted to skip the rest phase. Don't. If you never rest, at some point your body will start to break down. You stop making progress, and you may get injured. If you want to get fit, resting is just as important as working out.

We present just one model of periodized training. The possibilities are endless. Depending on your goals, you may want to emphasize or play down a particular phase. For example, if your aim is to get as strong as possible, spend more time in the peak phase; if you've been lifting weights for years, you can shorten the prep phase or skip it altogether. An experienced and well-educated personal trainer can help you design a periodization program to meet your needs. We also recommend *Periodization Training for Sports,* by Tudor O. Bompa and *Periodization Breakthrough!: The Ultimate Training System,* by Steven J. Fleck, Ph.D. and William J. Kraemer, Ph.D.

Periodization in a nutshell

Here's a recap of the five-phase periodization program.

Phase	Weight	Number of Sets per Muscle Group	Reps per Set	Rest between Sets
Prep	Light	1–4	12–15	1½ min.
Pump	Moderately light	3–8	10–12	1 min.
Push	Moderately heavy	8–15	8–10	30 sec.
Peak	Heavy	15–20	6–8	2 min.
Rest	Complete rest or light weights	0–2	12–15	1½ min.

Weight Training Week by Week

Periodization gives you an overall sense of purpose. Now we're going to narrow the focus of our discussion and hone in on each week of exercise. Regardless of your goals, you need to hit each muscle group at least twice a week. The simplest way to accomplish this is to perform two *total-body* workouts per week; in other words, twice a week do a routine that works every major muscle group.

Total-body workouts are great if you're doing only one or two exercises per muscle group. But once you get serious about weight training — adding exercises and sets — a total-body workout can become tedious. If your schedule permits you to lift weights at least four days a week (the sessions can be as short as 15 minutes), consider doing a *split routine*. You split a total-body routine into two or three shorter routines. For example, you can train your upper body on one day and your lower body the next. You can even split your upper-body muscles into three different workouts. (We discuss these options in detail later in this section.)

Split routines are ideal for people who have the time to work out several days a week but may not have much time for each workout session. Split routines also work well for people who have a short attention span for weight training or who want to give each muscle group an extra-hard workout. Brief, focused workouts help you stay motivated. If you walk into the gym knowing that all you have to do today is work your back and biceps, you're more likely to give those muscle group exercises an all-out effort.

If you're looking to make some serious changes in your body, split routines are the way to go. As we explain in Chapter 15, transforming your body requires doing at least 3 sets per body part and perhaps as many as 20 sets. Depending on your goals, a total-body workout could take you four hours. By splitting up your routine, you can give all your muscles a good workout because they'll always be fresh.

When designing a split routine, you need to follow two basic rules: Hit each muscle group at least twice a week, and don't work the same muscle group on consecutive days. This second rule is a bit more complicated than it sounds. For example, you may think that it's okay to work your triceps and thighs on Monday and then your chest and butt on Tuesday. Actually, it's not. You see, most chest exercises *also* work the triceps, and most butt exercises *also* work the thighs. So, if you work your triceps on Monday, they will not have recovered sufficiently by Tuesday to help out on your chest exercises. These rules may sound confusing, but within a few weeks, they'll become second nature. Until then, here's a list of muscle pairs that you should not work on back-to-back days:

- ✔ Chest and triceps
- ✔ Back and biceps
- ✔ Butt and thighs

The split routines that we describe in the following sections heed the preceding two basic rules.

The upper body/lower body split

The upper body/lower body split is perhaps the simplest split, a good one for beginners to try. You don't have much to remember: It's pretty obvious which exercises work the muscles above the belt and which work your muscles down south. When you work your upper body one day and your lower body the next, each zone of your body gets more of a complete rest than for any other way you do your split.

People who do the upper/lower split generally train their abdominals with their lower body, but this isn't a hard-and-fast rule. Don't make the mistake of working your abs every workout. Remember, the abs are like any other muscle group: They need time to recover. Two or three abdominal workouts a week will suffice. Table 16-1 shows two sample weekly schedules based on the upper/lower split.

Table 16-1	Sample Weekly Schedules for Split Routines
Day of the Week	*Body Area or Rest Period*
Sample Upper/Lower Split #1	
Monday	Upper body
Tuesday	Lower body and abdominals
Wednesday	Rest
Thursday	Upper body
Friday	Lower body and abdominals
Saturday	Rest
Sunday	Rest
Sample Upper/Lower Split #2	
Monday	Upper body and abdominals
Tuesday	Rest
Wednesday	Lower body and abdominals
Thursday	Rest
Friday	Upper body and abdominals
Saturday	Rest
Sunday	Lower body

Tables 16-2 and 16-3 are two examples of the exercises you can include in your upper body/lower body split routine — one routine is for beginners and one is for more experienced lifters.

Table 16-2	Sample Exercises for Basic Upper Body/Lower Body Split Routine
Body Part	**Exercises**
Upper Body	
Back	Lat Pulldown, Machine Row, Pelvic Tilt
Chest	Dumbbell Chest Press, Incline Chest Fly
Shoulders	Dumbbell Shoulder Press, Lateral Raise
Biceps	Hammer Curl, Concentration Curl
Triceps	Triceps Pushdown, Triceps Kickback
Lower Body	
Butt and Legs	Squat, Lunge, Leg Extension Machine, Leg Curl Machine, Inner and Outer Thigh Machines, Standing Calf Raise Machine
Abdominals	Slide, Basic Abdominal Crunch

Table 16-3	Sample Exercises for Advanced Upper Body/Lower Body Split Routine
Body Part	**Exercises**
Upper Body	
Back	Chin-up, Lat Pulldown with Triangle Grip, Seated Cable Row, Back Extension, Machine Pullover
Chest	Bench Press, Incline Dumbbell Press, Assisted Dip, Decline Fly
Shoulders	Military Press, Lateral Raise, Back Delt Fly, Internal and External Rotation
Biceps	Barbell Biceps Curl, Preacher Curl, Alternating Dumbbell Biceps Curl
Triceps	Triceps Pushdown, French Press, Bench Dip

Body Part	Exercises
Lower Body	
Legs	Barbell Squat, Backward Lunge, Stiff-Legged Deadlift, Leg Extension Machine, Leg Curl Machine, Inner/Outer Thigh Machine, Single-leg Calf Raise
Abdominals	Hanging Abs, Reverse Crunch, Abdominal Crunch with a Twist

Push/pull split routine

This type of split separates your upper body *pushing* muscles (the chest and triceps) from the upper body muscles involved in *pulling* (your back and biceps). You can do your lower body and abdominal exercises on either day or on a separate day altogether. Or you can include your legs with your pushing muscles and your abdominals with your pulling muscles.

Savvy readers will notice that we have not mentioned where your shoulders fit into the push/pull split. There's no simple answer because shoulders don't fit neatly into either the push or the pull category; the shoulders are partially involved in both movements. Where you work in your shoulders is a matter of personal preference. Some people like to work their shoulders right after their chest muscles. Others like to do shoulder exercises after their back exercises. Still others prefer to divide their body into three workouts: back and biceps; chest and triceps; shoulders, leg, and abs.

Push/pull split routines are popular among experienced exercisers who really want to go to town with each muscle group. You may see people spend two hours just working their back and biceps. However, other people feel unbalanced after one of these routines because they worked only one side of their torso. Table 16-4 shows sample push/pull split routine schedules.

Table 16-4	Sample Push/Pull Split Routine Schedules
Day of the Week	*Body Area or Rest Period*
Sample Four-day Week	
Day 1	Chest, triceps, and shoulders
Day 2	Back, biceps, abdominals, and lower body
Day 3	Rest

(continued)

Table 16-4 (continued)

Day of the Week	Body Area or Rest Period
Day 4	Chest, triceps, and shoulders
Day 5	Rest
Day 6	Back, biceps, abdominals, and lower body
Day 7	Rest
Sample Five-day Week	
Day 1	Chest and triceps
Day 2	Back and biceps
Day 3	Shoulders, lower body, and abdominals
Day 4	Rest
Day 5	Chest, triceps, and shoulders
Day 6	Back, biceps, lower body, and abdominals
Day 7	Rest

Table 16-5 suggests exercises to include for each of the four main push/pull split combinations. You can mix and match these combinations to fit the workouts that we describe for the weekly schedules in Table 16-4.

Table 16-5	Sample Exercises for Push/Pull Split Routines
Body Parts	**Exercises**
Back and Biceps	
Back	Assisted Pull-up, Lat Pulldown, Seated Cable Row, Dumbbell Pullover, One-arm Row, Back Extension
Biceps	Barbell Biceps Curl, Concentration Curl, Arm Curl Machine
Chest and Triceps	
Chest	Bench Press, Incline Chest Fly, Vertical Chest Press Machine, Cable Crossover, Push-up
Triceps	Triceps Pushdown, Triceps Kickback, Triceps Dip Machine
Shoulders	
Shoulders	Dumbbell Shoulder Press, Cable Lateral Raise, Front Raise, Back Delt Fly, Internal/External Rotation

Body Parts	Exercises
Lower Body and Abdominals	
Legs	Lunge, Leg Press Machine, Leg Extension Machine, Leg Curl Machine, Inner/Outer Thigh Machine, Standing Calf Raise
Abdominals	Rolling Like a Ball, Reverse Crunch, Abdominal Crunch with a Twist

Ideas for Organizing Your Daily Workout

Now we're going to narrow our focus even further. Once you decide that you're going to work, say, your chest, triceps, and shoulders on Monday, you need to decide the order in which to do the exercises. In Chapter 15, we explain that you should work your large muscles before your smaller ones within each zone of your body. However, you still have plenty of options. Certain exercise sequences can save you time by reducing the amount of rest you need between sets; other sequences take longer but give your muscles a tougher challenge. Use the suggestions in the following sections to vary the order of your exercises.

Super sets

Doing a *super set* simply means performing two different exercises without resting between the sets. There are two types of super sets, each with a different purpose:

✔ **Same-muscle super sets:** You do consecutive sets of different exercises that work the same muscle group. For example, go immediately from the Dumbbell Chest Press to the Chest Fly, rest for a minute, and then do the Press + Fly sequence again. This type of super set really challenges the muscle in question. Just when your pecs think that they've completed a job well done — Bam! You blindside them with another exercise right away.

You can do super sets with just about any two exercises. Keep in mind that you'll probably use less weight than usual on the second exercise because your muscles are already fairly tired. You may want to enlist a spotter if you're doing super sets that involve lifting a weight directly over your face or head.

Table 16-6 shows some super set combinations. You can string them all together to form a whole super set workout. Or you can insert any number of these combinations into your workout.

✔ **Different-muscle super sets:** With this type of super set, you do back-to-back exercises that work different muscles. For example, go from a front thigh exercise directly to a rear thigh exercise. This type of super set is a great way to speed up your routine because it cuts back on the rest you need to take during a routine. Your front thighs rest while you perform the rear thigh exercise, and vice versa. Table 16-7 shows a sample different-muscle super set routine.

Table 16-6	Sample Same-muscle Super Set Routine
Body Parts	*Exercise Combinations*
Butt and Legs	Squat + Lunge
Back	Lat Pulldown + Machine Row
Chest	Bench Press + Push-up
Shoulders	Dumbbell Shoulder Press + Lateral Raise
Biceps	Barbell Biceps Curl + Dumbbell Biceps Curl
Triceps	French Press + Bench Dip
Abdominals	Basic Abdominal Crunch + Abdominal Crunch with a Twist

Table 16-7	Sample Different-muscle Super Set Routine
Body Parts	*Exercise Combinations*
Butt and Legs + Chest	Leg Press + Vertical Chest Press Machine
Back + Quadriceps	Dumbbell Pullover + Leg Extension Machine
Shoulders + Hamstrings	Shoulder Press + Leg Curl Machine
Biceps + Legs	Barbell Biceps Curl + Calf Raise
Triceps + Abdominals	Triceps Pushdown + Basic Abdominal Crunch
Wrists + Lower back	Wrist Curl + Back Extension

Giant sets

Giant sets take the super set idea one step further: Instead of doing two consecutive sets of different exercises without rest, you string *three* exercises together. For example, for a killer abdominal workout, you could link together three different abdominal exercises, rest, and then repeat the sequence. Or, to save time in your workout, you could move from a back exercise to a chest exercise to a butt exercise. Table 16-8 shows some of our favorite giant sets that you can work into your routines.

Table 16-8	Suggested Giant Exercise Sets
Body Parts	*Exercise Combinations*
Abdominals	Basic Abdominal Crunch + Reverse Crunch + Abdominal Crunch with a Twist
Butt and Legs	Leg Press Machine + Leg Extension Machine + Leg Curl Machine
Back	Lat Pulldown + Cable Row + Seated Back Machine
Chest	Dumbbell Chest Press + Chest Fly + Cable Crossover
Shoulders	Shoulder Press + Front Raise + Lateral Raise

Circuits

A *circuit* is a routine in which you do one set each of several exercises, taking little or no rest between sets. Then you repeat the whole shebang as many times as you want. The typical circuit uses weight machines because they save you time. (In Chapter 15, we list exercises for a typical weight machine circuit.) However, you can create your own circuit using free weights or a free weight/machine combination. Here are some basic rules to keep in mind when designing your circuit workout:

✔ Try to alternate upper, lower, and middle body (abdominal and lower back) muscles so that no single muscle group gets tired too quickly. However, you also can do opposing muscle groups in the same region of the body, such as chest and back or quadriceps and hamstrings.

✔ Switch between lying, standing, and seated exercises very carefully. Moving from one posture to another too quickly can cause sudden changes in blood pressure, which can cause you to feel dizzy or pass out.

✔ Even though you're moving quickly between exercises, don't speed up the repetitions within a set. Good form still applies.

✔ Expect to use about 20 percent less weight than usual for each exercise because you're moving so fast. Sure, your front thighs are resting while you work your rear thighs, but your whole body, including your heart and lungs, is still working at a pretty quick pace.

✔ Don't do circuits more than once a week. Circuit training is a good way to pull yourself up out of rut, but you won't gain as much strength from working out this way.

Advanced Training Techniques

After you choose which exercises to do and what order to do them in, you still have a few decisions to make. Suppose that you're going to perform three sets on the Leg Extension machine. Are you going to perform the same number of repetitions for each set? Or do you want to decrease the number of repetitions from one set to the next so that you can lift more weight?

Pyramids

If you have the time or inclination to perform at least five sets of an exercise, consider a pyramid. You start with a light weight and then gradually work your way up to the heaviest weight you can lift for 1 or 2 repetitions. Or you could do a modified pyramid. Instead of piling on the weight until you can do only one repetition, stop at the point where 5 or 6 reps is tough. This is a better approach for beginners and for people who don't have a buddy to spot them while lifting heavy weights.

You can also do a descending pyramid, starting with the heaviest weight you think you can lift once, and working down until you're lifting a weight that allows you to perform 12 to 15 reps. However, don't do your heaviest set without first doing at least one warm-up set.

A third option is to combine a regular pyramid with a descending pyramid. In other words, you could start with 10 reps and a light weight, work your way up to a heavy weight and 1 to 3 reps, and then work your way back down to a light weight and 10 reps again. This technique brings new meaning to the word *fatigue*. Expect to lift a lot less weight on the way down than you do on the way up. For example, if you can bench press 80 pounds ten times on the way up, you may be able to bench press 80 pounds only six times on the way down. For the 10-rep set, you may be lifting only 50 pounds.

Breakdowns

Breakdown training is just another way of tiring out the muscle. You do multiple sets of an exercise without resting between sets; meanwhile, you decrease the weight for each set. Suppose that you're doing the Lateral Raise. First line up four to six sets of dumbbells near you, from heaviest to lightest. After a light warm-up set, do 10 repetitions with the heavy set, put the weights down, do 8 reps with the next lightest dumbbells, put those down, and so on (until you either run out of gas or run out of dumbbells). Breakdowns also are fun to do with machines because, instead of putting down and picking up weights, all you have to do is move the pin.

Another option is to do modified breakdowns using just two different weights. For example, first choose a weight that enables you to do 10 repetitions, and then immediately put it down and pick up a lighter weight, squeezing out as many repetitions as possible until failure, usually about 4 or 5.

Negatives

Negatives is an advanced technique that can cause extreme muscle soreness, so beginners should not try it. Someone helps you lift a weight, and then you're on your own for the lowering, or *negative,* phase of the lift. The negative phase is also referred to as the *eccentric* phase, pronounced EE-sentric, as opposed to ECK-sentric. The positive, or lifting, phase is called the *concentric* phase.

Your muscles generally can handle more weight when you lower a weight than when you lift it, so this technique gives you a chance to really max out on the negative phase. This is a good technique to try on the Bench Press and also many lower body machines such as the Leg Extension and Leg Curl because it's easy for your buddy to help you lift up a handle or a machine's lever. Negative sets done with machines are safer than free weight negative sets because you're not in danger of dropping a dumbbell on your dental work if your arms or shoulders suddenly give out.

Part V
Beyond the Barbell

The 5th Wave   By Rich Tennant

©RICH TENNANT

MIKE'S GYM

"I heard it was good to cross-train, so I'm
mixing my weight training with scuba diving."

In this part . . .

Our mission in this book is to get you started on a weight training program and to get you feeling comfortable with hunks of steel in your hands. However, we would feel remiss if we did not give at least a nod to several related topics: yoga, Pilates, cardiovascular exercise, stretching, balance, and nutrition. In Part V, we compare the benefits of yoga and Pilates to those of weight training. We remind you why it's important to combine weight lifting with activities such as walking and stairclimbing. And we cover the often forgotten subject of stretching, which is sort of the Delaware of fitness topics. A new chapter in this part shows you how to improve your balance and coordination, important attributes even if you have no intention of joining the circus. Also in this part, we give you the lowdown on some of the dietary supplements that are promoted like crazy at health clubs.

Chapter 17

Yoga and Pilates

• •

In This Chapter

▶ What yoga and Pilates can give you that weight training can't

▶ How to fit yoga or Pilates into your fitness program

▶ How to find quality instruction

• •

*I*f you read fitness magazines or belong to a health club, you've probably been hearing a lot lately about yoga and Pilates, activities touted to increase strength and flexibility and make you look and feel younger than Britney Spears. You may be wondering: What are the benefits of these activities compared to weight training? Do I need to incorporate all three modes of exercise into my fitness program? How many days a week should I do each one? Will I go broke doing all of these activities? Will my body collapse from exhaustion? This chapter answers all of these questions and more.

What's the Difference Between Yoga and Pilates?

We explore each mode of exercise in detail later in the chapter, but here's the answer in a nutshell.

Yoga, developed in India more than 5,000 years ago, consists of a series of poses, known as *asanas,* that you hold anywhere from a few seconds to several minutes. The moves, which require a blend of strength, flexibility, and body awareness, are intended to promote the union of the mind, body, and spirit. Most yoga styles include the same basic poses but differ in terms of how quickly you move, how long you hold each pose, how much breathing is emphasized, and how much of a spiritual aspect is involved. Some styles offer more modifications for beginners. Other styles are for people who can already fold themselves in half like a piece of foam rubber.

Pilates (pih-LAH-teez) is an exercise form named after Joseph Pilates, the former carpenter and gymnast who invented the technique for injured dancers at the turn of the twentieth century. Many Pilates moves were inspired by yoga, although some were patterned after the movements of zoo animals, such as swans, seals, and big cats. Pilates mat classes involve a series of specialized calisthenics exercises; rather than hold the positions, as in yoga, you're constantly moving. Private lessons are taught on medieval looking machines with names such as the Cadillac and the Reformer. The Cadillac looks like a four-poster bed that's been rigged for torture, with its array of springs, straps, poles, and bars. The Reformer looks like a weight bench souped up with assorted springs, straps, and pads.

What Will Yoga and Pilates Give You That Weight Training Won't?

Some yoga and Pilates practitioners claim that yoga and Pilates are superior to weight training because these disciplines can make you stronger without creating bulky muscles. It's true that yoga and Pilates can build strength without bulk — but, in reality, so can strength training with free weights or machines. The only way to end up with barrel-sized biceps is to train for it by lifting super-heavy weights and performing a minimal number of repetitions. So, choosing yoga or Pilates simply because you're trying develop strength without bulk is buying into a fitness myth. However, there are plenty of other excellent reasons to take up these alternative modes of exercise. Here's a rundown.

Yoga and Pilates engage your whole body

Weight training tends to emphasize individual body parts; you think about working your chest muscles or your shoulders or your hamstrings. Magazines promote "The Ultimate Ab Workout" or "Eight Moves for a Better Butt." With most weight training exercises — especially with those performed on machines — you work one or two muscle groups without involving any others. Yoga and Pilates take a different approach. Both disciplines require you to engage virtually your whole body at once. For instance, when performing a thigh exercise, you don't simply straighten and bend your leg, as you would in a traditional weight training exercise for your quads. Instead, you must engage your butt muscles in order to sit evenly in the seat, use your abs and lower back to avoid wiggling back and forth, work your upper body muscles to keep your back and neck in alignment, and so on. Every movement is a thoughtful process, and you learn to take into account how every part of your body must respond and contribute to even the smallest movements.

The benefit of working so many muscle groups simultaneously is that this is the way you're likely to use them in everyday life. It may not seem that laying on your stomach and arching your chest off the floor is a position you often assume during your life, but if you think about it, the way you use your lower back in an exercise like this is pretty similar to the way your lower back muscles spring into action whenever you have to screw in a light bulb that's just within your reach or when you put something back up on a high shelf.

Not only do yoga and Pilates offer the benefit of engaging your whole body, but they also place a particular emphasis on your "core" muscles — your abdominals, lower back, and dozens of small spinal muscles that don't get much action in a weight machine workout. This is a type of strength worth developing: It can help you stand up straighter and move more loosely and comfortably. When all of those small, internal muscles are optimally strong, they also lend support, stability, and added strength to your weight room activities. You may find that you can up your poundage in the weight room if you include regular yoga or Pilates sessions in your repertoire.

Yoga and Pilates increase your flexibility

Weight training has an undeserved reputation for making your muscles tight; in reality, lifting weights can actually increase your flexibility somewhat if you go through the entire range of motion. However, strength training — even under the best of circumstances — isn't going to make a big difference in how freely your muscles and joints move. (That's why we strongly recommend stretching on a regular basis. See Chapter 19.) However, yoga and Pilates can do remarkable things for your flexibility. You may never be able to fold yourself into a human half sandwich, but if you put time and effort into these pursuits, you will be surprised by how pliable your body becomes.

Yoga and Pilates can improve your balance, coordination, and concentration

Some weight training moves, such as the Squat and the Lunge (and other advanced moves not included in this book), do require a fair amount of balance and coordination. But for the most part, strength training simply gives you strength. Lying facedown on a hamstring machine and kicking your legs up doesn't exactly train you to float down a flight of stairs without having to look at your feet.

But yoga and Pilates moves tend to be more complicated. Consider a Pilates move called the Teaser. You lie on your back with your arms overhead and your legs straight and off the ground at a 45-degree angle. Then you lift your upper body and torso off the floor and try to reach your fingers to your toes.

This requires more balance, strength, and flexibility than you could possibly think. When you first try this move, you typically tip over sideways. It can take several years just to start to perform this move with grace and fluidity. These disciplines require a lot of concentration and body awareness. You can't simply go through the motions and expect to get much out of the technique.

Can Yoga and Pilates Replace Weight Training?

Probably not. One of the best reasons to lift weights is to maintain and build bone density so that you'll have enough bone in reserve to prevent osteoporosis later in life. Currently, no studies show whether yoga and Pilates strengthen bones. But we suspect that the bone-building benefits of these exercise modes are, at best, minimal. For the most part, you don't work against nearly as much resistance during a yoga or Pilates routine as you do during a challenging weight workout. By the way, this doesn't mean that yoga and Pilates are easier than weight training; the challenge is simply different. Also, don't think that the mere act of lifting a dumbbell guarantees you bone-building benefits. Many people lift such dinky weights that their bones don't even notice.

Also, it's not clear whether yoga and Pilates can build as much muscle as a good, solid weight training program. It's important to build muscle for the same reason it's crucial to build bone: to bank it away for the future, when, inevitably, you will have less of it.

For these reasons, we think of yoga and Pilates as complimentary to — not replacements for — weight training.

How Can I Fit Yoga and Pilates into my Fitness Program?

First, realize that you can't do everything in life! You can't be a full-time investment banker *and* a professional TV critic *and* a world-class pole vaulter. There just isn't enough time in the day. Besides, your brain would explode. By the same token, you can't devote yourself to weight training, yoga, *and* Pilates — especially when you're also (we hope) doing cardiovascular exercise. You'll feel like your body has been dragged through the spin cycle.

That said, we do think it's a good idea to incorporate either yoga or Pilates into your workout program. Which one? Try out both and see which one you like best.

This may take a while to figure out because there are so many different styles of yoga and different Pilates contraptions and because various instructors may teach the same class differently. From our experience, Pilates mat classes tend to be similar nationwide, whereas yoga classes seem to vary more. During this tryout period, drop to two weight training sessions a week and take a third day to try an alternative exercise. Or, take a two-week break from weight training (don't worry; your muscles won't disintegrate) and try a number of different yoga and Pilates classes and/or instructors.

Then decide which weight training alternative you'd like to try for a while, whether it's private Pilates lessons or a power yoga class at your gym or an Ananda yoga (defined below) class at a studio. This isn't a lifetime commit-ment, of course. But we think it's a good idea to choose one route and stick with it for at least a couple months. This should give you enough time to see whether you enjoy this type of workout and are getting benefits.

As for your weekly schedule: We recommend lifting weights twice a week and doing either yoga or Pilates twice a week. Doing any of these activities just once a week typically isn't enough for a beginner to see results and get the hang of proper technique. For weight training, yoga, and Pilates, repetition is extremely important.

These are not hard-and-fast rules. Some yoga and Pilates classes are more demanding than others. You'll have to experiment and see what type of weekly schedule your body thrives on. Just make sure you don't overdo it. The first time Liz did Pilates, she thought it would be a breeze. After all, she had been lifting weights for a long time and considered herself strong as a team of oxen. But she quickly learned that you can't just muscle your way through Pilates. The discipline requires more coordination, flexibility, and balance than Liz had developed in the weight room. She found herself strug-gling to complete the most basic movements, such as rolling up into a sitting position without relying on momentum. The first few times she overshot the movement and went rolling across the room like an errant bowling ball. There were 65 year olds in the class who had been studying the technique for years and who performed tough moves with ease and grace while Liz struggled to keep up. It was a humbling and enlightening experience for Liz. And the next day, she felt muscles in her abs and hips that she didn't even know existed.

More Details About Yoga

Yoga classes have become amazingly popular as people search for ways to complement the pounding and pumping they do in the gym. But this doesn't mean that yoga is easy. Yoga can be extremely demanding, both in terms of flexibility and strength. Even if you can bench press a heavy load in the gym, you may find yourself lacking the strength to hold a yoga pose for a minute (see Figure 17-1). A good rule to follow: Don't try to keep up with anyone else.

Figure 17-1:
The Active Cat is a classic yoga posture.

Different styles of yoga

You can choose from many different types or styles of yoga. Ananda yoga, for instance, requires less strength and flexibility than most other styles. The moves are fairly straightforward; for instance, you may practice something as simple as sitting up straight or standing with good posture. Ananda, which doesn't involve much chanting, may be a good place for beginners to start. On the other hand, Astanga, sometimes called Power Yoga, is one of the most physically demanding forms of yoga in terms of flexibility, strength, and stamina. You move from one posture to another without a break. For beginners, this may be more discouraging than invigorating.

Though some yoga styles retain spiritual elements such as chanting or burning incense, others have been Westernized and are taught using the same techniques and language that you'd find in a body sculpting class. Liz recently checked out a Disco Yoga class that had her and her classmates bopping through yoga poses to the beat of Donna Summer, Cher, and the Saturday Night Fever sound track. We suspect that several ancient yoga masters were turning over in their graves. This same studio also offered Yoga for Runners and Urban Yoga, which is aimed at reducing the stress of city life and improving the posture of those who sit slumped over their computers all day.

Most gyms and workout studios don't advertise the style of yoga practiced, and the gym staff probably won't know much about what's being taught. Your best bet is to ask the instructor what her style and teaching philosophy is. Look for a class with the word *beginner* or *novice* in the title. If you accidentally wander into a more advanced class, you may wind up feeling like one of those tangled necklaces that mysteriously appear in your jewelry box.

Although your gym is a good place to start, you'll find a wider variety of styles at yoga-only studios. Typically, studios charge $5 to $20 per class depending on the teacher, the style, and the region of the country. You'll also find classes aimed at different experience levels.

Finding a qualified yoga instructor

There's no national yoga certification, so we can't list certain credentials to look for in a teacher. Rely on your own judgment and recommendations from friends. Look for yoga instructors who wander around the room correcting class members' techniques and offering modifications for less flexible people. In a class that Suzanne once took, the teacher instructed the class to sit with their legs outstretched and bend from the hips. "Put your chin to your shins!" he kept repeating. Suzanne, a complete novice, could not even come close, but the instructor refused to accept this and kept pressing down on Suzanne's back. Suzanne's hamstrings were so sore after the class that she could not ride her bike for four days. Of course, this is probably what Suzanne deserved for agreeing to try out her sister's advanced yoga class.

Another good introduction to yoga: videos. The good ones take you step-by-step through a series of traditional poses. Only your VCR will have to witness your lack of strength and flexibility. Many of the tapes offer different levels of the same moves so that you can progress over a long period of time without having to buy a new tape. We especially like the videos starring yoga master Rodney Yee and those produced by the Yoga Zone. Kathy Smith's yoga tapes, featuring yoga expert Rob Striker, offer a Westernized, accessible approach to the discipline. All of these tapes are available through www.collagevideo.com.

The Lowdown on Pilates

Like yoga, Pilates emphasizes correct form rather than brute strength. Many of the moves look easy but are deceptively tough (see Figure 17-2). There is a series of leg exercises that require no equipment at all, yet Liz could barely get through the first time she took a Pilates class. One of these moves involves lifting your leg up and then moving it in tiny circles. The exercise didn't look that tough until Liz tried to do it with her knee held just so, her foot in the correct position, and the circles perfectly symmetrical. Keep in mind Liz runs, does leg strength training, and rock climbs on a regular basis.

Most Pilates moves emphasize the principle of opposition: while you are strengthening one muscle, you are stretching the one on the opposite side of the joint. For instance, the mat class move known as the Hundred, involves pumping your arms up and down as you lie on your back with your legs lifted off the floor straight out in front of you. The purpose of the Hundred is to strengthen your abs, front of thighs as you stretch out your lower back, back of thighs, and arms.

We also love that, like weight training and yoga, Pilates is progressive. Although you can't add an extra 5-pound weight plate every time an exercise becomes easy, whenever you master a move, another slightly different, slightly harder version of it is there to take its place. It can take months to learn the basics and years to become a real expert.

Figure 17-2:
The Single Leg Kick is part of the Pilates mat class.

The Pilates controversy

If you start taking Pilates, you may discover a lot of confusion about what exactly qualifies as Pilates. This discipline may go by several other names, such as The Method or Stott Conditioning. That's because the Pilates trademark is being contested in a heated lawsuit. Currently, the name is trademarked and owned by one man, who charges a hefty fee to instructors who wish to refer to their classes and instruction as Pilates. Until the legalities are straightened out, look for workout descriptions that use the term "Pilates-inspired." Two Pilates-inspired workouts we recommend are Jennifer Kries's The Method and Elise McNearny's IM=X. Both classes are offered nationally and cannot use the Pilates name outright. We also like Stott Conditioning, spearheaded by Moira Stott.

How to find Pilates instruction

Pilates classes and private instructors aren't tough to find in most cities. There are nearly 500 Pilates studios nationwide. Instructors of the official Pilates Method must complete a rigorous training program that includes more than 600 apprenticeship hours. Other Pilates factions have created their own certifications, which may or may not be just as rigorous. Some only require instructors to attend a two-hour seminar, which we feel is inadequate. To find a good Pilates instructor, get recommendations from people you trust, and ask the instructor a lot of questions about his or her training, certification, and experience.

Just be aware: Pilates is expensive. Private lessons run from $40 to $200 a session. Mat classes are a relative bargain at $12 to $25 per session, but that's still more than many monthly gym memberships. Some gyms offer Pilates classes to members at no additional charge and offer private instruction at a discount.

If you can't afford Pilates instruction, you can try several excellent videos. We like a series of tapes called The Method as well as the Stott Conditioning exercise video series, which comes with resistance bands you need for the workout. Surprisingly, we don't like the official workout tape created by the owner of the Pilates trademark. It is short on instruction and long on warnings about not messing with the Pilates name. All of these tapes can be purchased through the Collage Video catalog and Web site at www.collagevideo.com.

Chapter 18

Whipping Your Heart and Lungs into Shape

Maybe you've taken up weight training so that your bones don't disintegrate later in life. Or maybe your goal is to become strong enough to unscrew the cap of a stubborn pickle jar. But for all the effort you are putting into your chest presses, arm curls, and leg extensions, we suspect you have another agenda, too: You'd like to *see* your muscles. When you look in the mirror, you'd like some good, solid evidence that you actually do have pecs, biceps, and quads.

This isn't going to happen if you have an extra layer of fat covering your muscles. Weight training makes your muscles firmer and larger, but you can't see these results unless you reduce that blanket of fat. The best strategy for fat loss is to combine aerobic exercise with weight training workouts and a sensible, low fat diet. *Aerobic workouts* — walking, jogging, bicycling, and the like — are the best way to burn lots of calories in a relatively short period of time.

Of course, aerobic exercise is important for other reasons, too. This type of exercise strengthens your *cardiovascular system:* your heart, lungs, and blood vessels. When your heart is stronger, it beats fewer times per minute because it's capable of pumping out more blood per beat. Over time, a slower resting pulse rate saves wear and tear on your heart. Aerobic workouts also enable your lungs to suck in more air per breath — and to more efficiently extract oxygen, the fuel that provides you with energy. The end result: You have more stamina. You're able to get through your workouts and your day with more energy and less effort. What's more, aerobic exercise — also called cardiovascular exercise or *cardio* — can lower your blood pressure and your level of "bad" cholesterol while increasing your "good" cholesterol count. These are all important reasons why, on your way to the weight room, you shouldn't walk past those funny machines with blinking red lights, belts that go round and round, and pedals that go up and down.

In this chapter, we answer all your questions about aerobic exercise. We explain how often you need to do these workouts, how long your sessions should last, and how hard you need to push yourself. We also give you lessons in cardio machine etiquette.

What Type of Activities Count as Aerobic Exercise?

Aerobic exercise is any rhythmic, repetitive activity that involves your large muscles (like your butt, legs, and back) and lasts longer than a minute and a half. For example, the cyclist in Figure 18-1 is engaging in aerobic exercise. Weight lifting doesn't fit the bill; you break the rhythm when you stop to rest between sets. The only type of weight training that is moderately aerobic is circuit training: You move from one weight lifting exercise to another with little or no rest in between. (We describe this technique in Chapter 15.) In general, however, activities such as weight training or the 50-yard dash are not considered aerobic; they're anaerobic.

Figure 18-1:
Cycling is an
example of
an aerobic
activity.

If you're wondering where these terms come from, *aerobic* means *with air,* and *anaerobic* means *without air.* Because weight lifting exercises and sprinting take only a few seconds to complete, your body has enough stored energy to get through these actions. But to sustain any activity that lasts longer than 90 seconds (the type of activity necessary to strengthen your heart and lungs), your body needs an outside source of fuel, which it gets in the form of oxygen from the air you breathe.

How Many Days a Week Should I Do Aerobic Exercise?

The answer depends on your goals. If your aim is to maintain good health — to reduce your risk for heart disease, diabetes, high blood pressure, and other serious conditions — experts recommend 30 minutes of physical activity per day on most days. However, this doesn't mean you need to jog for 30 consecutive minutes; instead, you can piece together short bouts of exercise. You could walk for 10 minutes before work, walk the stairs at your office for 3 minutes a day, and take a 15-minute walk at lunch. Any type of activity counts, as long as you're slightly winded. If you can't fit in a half hour of activity every day, you may be able to make up for it by accumulating extra activity on the days that you do exercise.

However, don't fool yourself: To build significant stamina and achieve significant weight loss, a leisurely 5-minute walk here and there isn't going to cut it. You may need to do four to six longer workouts a week, putting in 45 minutes to an hour of aerobic exercise. (However, 45 minutes is not a starting point. Beginners should start with 10 to 20 minutes and gradually build up.)

Should I Do Aerobic Exercise Before or After My Weight Workouts?

Again, the answer depends on your goals. If you're serious about building big muscles or getting as strong as you possibly can, lift weights first, while you feel fresh and full of energy. (However, before you pick up a single weight, you need to warm up with at least five minutes of aerobic exercise, as we explain in Chapter 2.) On the other hand, if burning calories or building stamina is your priority, do your aerobic routine first, before your muscles get tired from pushing around weights.

If you give equal importance to weight training and aerobic exercise, you can do your workouts in either order. Some people like to break up their aerobic workouts; for example, they may do 15 minutes on the treadmill, a 30-minute weight lifting routine, and then 30 minutes on the stairclimber. How you arrange your workout is a matter of personal preference. Depending on your schedule, you may want to do your aerobic and weight training workouts on different days.

Is It True That I'll Lose More Weight If I Exercise at a Slower Pace?

No. For years, fitness magazines trumpeted the advantages of exercising in your *fat-burning zone.* The theory was that, because your body uses fat as its primary fuel during long, slow aerobic workouts, you'd burn more body fat exercising at a slower pace than you would at a faster pace, which uses carbohydrates as the primary source of fuel.

It's true that when you exercise slowly, a greater percentage of the calories you burn are fat calories, as opposed to carbohydrate calories. (No matter what your pace, you always burn both fat and carbohydrates.) But the percentage of calories you burn from fat doesn't matter. What matters most is how many total *calories* you burn. If you walk for a half hour you might burn 120 calories; if you jog for a half hour you might burn 300 calories. If you choose a slower pace, you'll have to spend more time exercising; on the other hand, you may find exercise more enjoyable at a comfortable pace. You're more likely to stick with your exercise program if you don't consider it torture. In the next section, we give you more details on selecting your pace.

So How Hard Should I Work Out?

To challenge your cardiovascular system, you need to get your heart pumping faster than normal and your lungs sucking in more air than when you sit around watching *Bass Fishing Today* on The Nashville Network. But how do you know if you're working hard enough? And how do you measure your effort?

The simplest (although least precise) way to gauge your huff-and-puff factor is the *talk test.* You simply open your mouth and see how tough it is for words to come out. If you're so breathless that you can't even say "Tom Cruise deserves an Oscar" without gasping for breath, you're working too hard. On the other hand, if you're able to engage in a heated debate about the merits of boxers versus briefs, you need to pick up your pace. In other words, your goal is to be slightly winded.

Obviously, the talk test is not exact science. A more accurate way to gauge how hard you're working is to measure your *heart rate*. The harder you exercise, the faster your heart beats — up to a point. At some point, your heart rate reaches its maximum; even if you *try* to exercise harder, your heart won't beat faster. Max heart rate can vary greatly from person to person. During exercise you don't want to come *too* close to your maximum. Instead, you want to stay in your target training zone — a range between 50 percent and 90 percent of your maximum heart rate.

How do you know if you're in the zone? First, of course, you need to know your maximum heart rate. The easiest way is to use a mathematical formula that estimates your maximum based on your age. (In general, the older you are, the slower your maximum.) To find your max, simply subtract your age from 220. If you're 40 years old, your estimated maximum is 180 beats per minute. We say estimated because, in reality, your personal maximum may vary as much as 15 beats in either direction.

To find the top end of your target training zone, simply calculate 90 percent of your max. So, if your maximum heart rate is 180, multiply this number by 0.9. The top end of your training zone is 162 — you don't want to exercise so hard that your heart beats faster than 162 beats per minute. (Actually, you may not want to exercise this hard at all. The 90-percent level is reserved for very limited, specific training. You visit that upper range for short spurts one or two times a week — only if your goals warrant doing so and only if you're very fit. If you are training for an event or to move up a level in fitness, you might go to 90 percent during certain cycles of your training.)

To find the low end of your zone, simply calculate 50 percent of your max. Fifty percent of 180 is 90. So you want to exercise hard enough that your heart beats at least 90 times per minute.

Calculate your own target zone, and then write down the high number and the low number. Next time you exercise, take your pulse (we show you how in the next section) and see whether your heart rate falls between those numbers. If your heart rate is too slow, speed up your pace, and vice versa. Keep in mind that this method of finding your target training zone is nothing more than an estimate. A doctor or physiologist can determine a more precise, personalized zone by testing your fitness level on a treadmill or other piece of cardiovascular apparatus. Many gyms and trainers can also do a less strenuous version of the medical evaluation to help you find your training zone.

How Do I Take My Pulse?

Knowing your target training zone is of no use if you don't know how fast your heart is beating at any one moment. Here's how to measure your heart rate:

✔ The low-tech way is simply to take your pulse the way the nurse does it at the doctor's office. Place two fingers (not your thumb) on your wrist directly below the base of your thumb and feel for the thumping. See Figure 18-2. Count how many times your heart beats in 15 seconds and multiply this number by four. Now you have your pulse — the number of times your heart beats in one minute.

If you have trouble locating your pulse at your wrist, you can find it at your neck. Slide your fingers into the groove on either side of your Adam's apple until you feel the beat. Just don't press too hard; otherwise, you may artificially slow your heart rate and think that you're not working as hard as you really are.

✔ A more convenient and more accurate way to gauge your pulse is to buy a heart rate monitor that straps around your chest. The chest strap sends your heart rate readings to a special wristwatch, which translates the information into a number. Suppose that your target zone is between 90 and 162; if you're walking on the treadmill and you glance at the wrist-watch and see 125, you know you're doing fine. Good heart rate monitors are as accurate as medical EKG monitors.

Heart rate monitors are much cheaper than they used to be. You can buy one for as little as $40, about half the price of a decent pair of work-out shoes. We think they are an excellent idea for beginning exercisers. They teach you how your body reacts to all levels of exercise intensity. The more sophisticated monitors — albeit the more expensive ones — allow you to download your workouts into your computer so you can chart your progress. Let's say you do your favorite neighborhood run in 30 minutes with an average heart rate of 140. Two months later, you do the same 30-minute run with an average heart rate of 120. That's when you know it's time to pick up the pace.

Our favorite brand of heart rate monitor is Polar, although we also like Cardiosport. The basic $50 model, known as the Beat, simply measures your heart rate. For $300 you can buy a fancy model that does every-thing but walk your dog. It beeps when your pulse is too high or too low, times your workouts, and stores your average heart rate from several previous workouts.

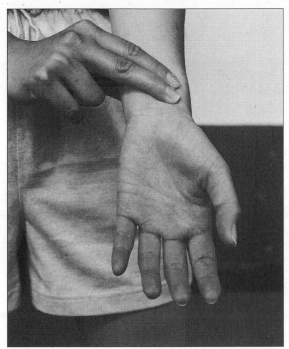

Figure 18-2:
You can take your pulse at your wrist.

If I Do Aerobic Workouts Regularly, When Will I Start Seeing Results?

Chances are, you'll have more energy and stamina within a few weeks of starting regular aerobic workouts. Those stairs at the office won't make you want to keel over anymore. You may even feel like playing ball with your kids when you get home from work. Your *vitals* such as heart rate and blood pressure probably will improve, too.

As for weight loss: This depends just as much on your eating habits, your metabolism, and your genetic makeup as it does on your commitment to exercise. So we can't give you a schedule of how quickly those pounds can melt away. And if you're lifting weights, you may not lose weight at all because the muscle you're gaining weighs more per square inch than fat does. Don't worry about what the scale says; it's fat loss you're after, not weight loss. Know that fat loss is a long-term project, and you can't expect to keep the fat off unless you continue to exercise regularly.

The same goes for improving your health. From the moment you step onto a treadmill, you're doing your body some good. But if you stop working out, those benefits diminish. Most people begin to lose aerobic power within a week. Within a couple of months, you're basically starting from scratch. Think of aerobic exercise — as with all healthy habits, including weight training — as a lifelong pet project.

What Is the Best Cardiovascular Machine?

Forget the TV commercials that claim one machine is better than another: The best aerobic contraption is the one you use, whether it's the treadmill, the bike, the elliptical trainer, or the stairclimber. So try them all to see which ones float your boat. Some people can spend hours on the stairclimber; others would rather be locked in a cell with their boss than climb on that thing. In the calorie-burning department, what really matters isn't so much the machine itself but how long and how hard you work out. Running on the treadmill can burn twice as many calories as walking on the machine, but you can make up the difference by walking twice as long.

Can I Make Cardio Exercise Machines Less Boring?

We're not going to pretend that stepping, running, and pedaling in place are thrills on par with, say, riding the Viper at Six Flags' Magic Mountain amusement park. But using cardio machines need not be drudgery.

Listening to music can be a great motivator; most people last longer on the machines if they're rocking out to their favorite tunes. Other people prefer to read, whether it's *People* magazine, the stock listings, or a crime novel. If you exercise at home, park your cardio machine in front of the TV and schedule your workout when there's something to watch other than reruns of *The Dukes of Hazzard*.

Varying the intensity of your workout also helps. You can do intervals — for example, pedal the bike at 100 rpm for 30 seconds and then recover for two minutes at 80 rpm; then repeat the sequence. Or alternate five minutes at Level 3 with five minutes at Level 5. Learn how to use the variety of programs available on computerized cardio machines. And consider placing your towel over the machine's console so that you're not constantly reminded of how many minutes you have left.

Some gyms have "Exertainment systems" that combine a TV, VCR, CD player, radio, and Internet access all in one unit. The two most common brands are Net pulse and E-Zone. The more sophisticated models allow you to sample MP3 music or pull up a movie out of the archives.

With so many distractions, it's simply impossible to get bored during your workout. But there's a catch: Some of these systems are compatible only with a special pair of headphones. Although the headphones are given away free, you have to fill out an extensive questionnaire, revealing everything from how old you are to the brand of toilet paper you prefer. To use the headphones, you must punch in your access code, at which point the system begins gathering information about you that is in turn is sold to advertisers.

The makers of these systems are pretty quiet about the fact they gather this information and, frankly, it makes us feel uncomfortable. For instance, Liz doesn't want anyone to know that her secret guilty pleasure is watching "The Nanny" while she runs on the treadmill — let alone have someone try to sell her a car while she does so. (Now that you know this about Liz, you're sworn to secrecy.) Another downer is that you are forced to watch up to three minutes of advertising before you can access all other programming. And ads are programmed to flash across the screen throughout your workout. If this amount of commercialism bothers you when you exercise, you may want to stick to the old-fashioned approach of bringing your own headphones and listening to plain old music.

Chapter 19

Stretching: The Truth

· ·

In This Chapter

▶ Why stretching is so controversial

▶ Stretching rules

▶ Pros and cons of the five major stretching methods

▶ Sample stretches

· ·

Stretching seems like such a straightforward topic that you may expect us to explain it in a sentence or two and then show you a stretching routine. Well, as it turns out, stretching is so controversial that even the American College of Sports Medicine (ACSM), one of the most respected sports and fitness organizations in the world, didn't offer official guidelines on how to stretch until recently. And the organization still admits that a lot more research is needed to determine exactly what stretching can and cannot do for you. In this chapter, we explain why stretching is the subject of so much debate. We outline the new ACSM guidelines for stretching and describe other stretching methods that are considered promising by exercise experts. We also show you several excellent stretches.

Why Stretching Is So Controversial

The purpose of stretching is to lengthen your muscles and to loosen up the joints they connect to so that you can move more freely. When your muscles and joints are flexible, you can walk without stiffness, reach down to tousle a toddler's hair, or turn around when someone calls your name — everyday movements that you take for granted until you have trouble doing them. The problem is this: No one has determined with certainty the best way to accomplish these results.

It seems logical that the longer you hold a muscle in a stretched position, the more flexible it becomes — that holding a stretch for one minute would be more effective than holding a stretch for two seconds. But some research suggests that the opposite may be true. In fact, several recent studies have shown that the optimal amount of time to hold a stretch is about 30 seconds. Holding a stretch for 60 seconds doesn't seem to make you more flexible or do anything for you except waste 30 seconds of your time. And stretching several times a day doesn't appear to be better than stretching once a day.

Another area of controversy: Stretching is supposed to prevent injury and ease muscle soreness, but many recent studies have found that traditional methods of stretching may accomplish neither goal and may in fact *cause* injuries, such as muscle tears from overstretching. One University of Hawaii study of more than 100 runners found that the non-stretchers performed better, reported fewer injuries, and experienced less muscle soreness after their running workouts than did those runners who stretched regularly. Why? Perhaps tighter muscles better stabilize the joints, thereby protecting knees and hips from the trauma of running.

However, this may be true only to a point. If muscles are *too* tight, the risk of injury appears to increase. For instance, runners who sit a lot during the day — and therefore have tight hamstrings — are prone to herniated disks because their hamstrings pull on the pelvis, rotating it backward. Over time this creates a flat-back posture; the disc fluid moves toward the back of the disc, creating pressure and a bulge. Inflexible runners aren't the only ones who can be troubled by inflexibility. One recent study found that, two and three days after moderately heavy weight lifting, less flexible exercisers feel more muscle tenderness than more flexible subjects

Keep in mind that these are just a few studies among many, and that there is little research that attempts to prove or disprove previous studies. So, we're left with a hodgepodge of studies that seem to compare apples and oranges.

The bottom line about stretching

So what's the upshot? If the benefits of stretching are so ambiguous, is it a big, fat waste of time to try reaching for your toes? According to the ACSM, no.

The ACSM's position stand, last published in 1998, states that, despite conflicting research, there is a mounting body of evidence in support of stretching, as well as substantial "real life" reports to make a good case for its importance. Because the scales seem to tip in favor of stretching, the ACSM has issued the following guidelines on how to stretch:

- ✔ Hold each stretch for 10 to 30 seconds.
- ✔ Do at least one stretch for each major muscle group.
- ✔ Stretch at least twice a week, preferably almost every day.

✔ Stretch to the point of discomfort but not beyond.

✔ Don't hold your breath while stretching.

Although the ACSM recommends holding each stretch for 10 to 30 seconds, some experts believe that holding a stretch this long can cause injury. The theory is that after about two seconds, something called the *stretch reflex mechanism* kicks in. This mechanism is a muscle's defense against over-stretching and tearing, and it signals the muscle to shorten and tighten; so if you hold a stretch too long, the theory goes, the muscle may actually wind up tighter than when you started.

Two stretching methods we describe below, active isolated and PNF, address the problem of the stretch reflex. With these methods, you hold stretches for a shorter period of time than you do with traditional stretching, and you work to tire the muscle so that it has no choice but to relax. The ACSM acknowledges that these methods of stretching may be viable but states that there simply isn't enough evidence yet to make a judgment call.

To date, most stretching studies have looked at traditional stretching. The other varieties of stretching, which we describe later, show some promise in the areas of preventing injuries and easing muscle soreness. But no major studies that we know of have compared the various stretching methods head to head. Until researchers come up with a definitive answer on the best way to stretch, we suggest that you experiment with a variety of stretching methods and find out which stretches feel most comfortable to you. You may even want to combine a number of stretching methods. You may find, for example, that you enjoy doing Active Isolated stretches for your *hamstrings* (rear thigh muscles) but traditional stretching for your shoulders.

Traditional Stretching

What it is: You hold each stretch for 10 to 30 seconds without bouncing. (Traditional stretching is also called *static* stretching because you hold your body still.) As you hold the position, you feel a pull that spreads up and down the length of the muscle. Traditional stretching is the method performed at the end of many exercise classes and in exercise videos. Right now, it's the stretching method most accepted by fitness professionals.

Pros:

✔ Almost anyone can perform at least some static stretches; you can easily modify the position to suit your level of flexibility.

✔ Many people find this method of stretching a good way to relax and to cool down after a workout.

✔ If you perform traditional stretches at least three days a week, you'll probably notice an increase in flexibility after a few weeks.

Cons:

✔ Static stretching is supposed to prevent injury and muscle soreness, yet evidence to this effect is inconclusive.

✔ If you're inflexible, this type of stretching may be far from relaxing. In fact, it may be so uncomfortable that you end up skipping your stretches altogether.

✔ Separating one muscle group from another with traditional stretches is difficult; you often are forced to stretch several different muscle groups at once. This situation is a problem if one of the muscles being stretched is a lot tighter than the others.

The rules of stretching

Follow these simple stretching rules, which apply to all methods of stretching:

✔ **Aim to stretch daily, but make sure you stretch at least three times per week.** You improve your flexibility the same way you get to Carnegie Hall: practice, practice, practice. Your muscles will "remember" to stay loose and flexible if they're reminded often enough.

✔ **Stretch after your workout, not before.** Follow this rule whether you're doing aerobic exercise, weight training, or both. On days when you do only weight training, you need to do at least five minutes of rhythmic, low-intensity aerobic exercise such as walking, jogging, cycling, or stepping. Warming up gets your blood flowing and raises your body temperature so that your muscles are more receptive to the stretch. Never stretch a cold muscle. (This rule does not apply to Active Isolated stretching, which can safely be included as part of a warm-up.)

✔ **Never force a stretch.** Stretch to the point at which you're right on the edge of discomfort; never to the point of "Ouch!" Don't get into a contest with your friends to see who can touch their tongue to their shoulder blade. There's no optimal amount of flexibility, so stretch within the limits of each individual joint.

✔ **Don't forget to breathe.** Deep, natural breathing increases your flexibility by helping you to mellow out and by sending oxygen-rich blood into your muscles. Inhale deeply just before you go into a stretching position, and then exhale through your mouth as you move into the stretch. Breath deeply several times as you hold the stretch.

✔ **Don't just go through the motions and declare, "There, I've stretched."** Concentrate. Focus. Do you feel the stretch where you're supposed to? Are you using correct form? Do you need to back off or push a little further? However, there's no need to quiz yourself with the intensity of a prosecutor; stretching is supposed to be relaxing, after all.

✔ **Give priority to the muscles you use the most in your workouts and in everyday life, but don't neglect any major muscle group.** For instance, cyclists should perform a few extra sets of stretches on their thighs, calves, and lower back, but they shouldn't skip upper body stretches altogether. You want your entire body to be flexible so that you can reach across the bed to snag the remote control from a spouse who inexplicably watches reruns of *The Iron Chef* on the Food Channel.

Traditional stretching workout

Contrary to popular belief, you should never perform traditional stretching before you warm up. Stretching in and of itself does *not* constitute a warm-up. See the sidebar, "The rules of stretching," to learn what does constitute a proper warm-up.

Hold each of the following positions for 10 to 30 seconds. If you're a stretching neophyte, start with 10 seconds and gradually work your way up to the full 30 seconds. Do not bounce. Jerky movements may actually make you tighter. Get into the proper stretching position slowly and smoothly and then stay there. After you've held the stretch for a few seconds, slowly stretch a bit further.

Quadriceps (front thigh): Lie on your left side with your legs out straight and your head resting on your outstretched arm. Bend your right knee so that your heel is close to your butt, and then grab your ankle or toes with your right hand. Pull your heel back and away from your butt, taking care to keep your hips stacked directly on top of one another. Try to keep knees together, not separated. Don't arch your back or allow your butt to stick out. Use the image of trying to press your pocket forward and flat. After you stretch your right quadriceps, turn over (to lie on your right side) and stretch your left. See Figure 19-1.

Figure 19-1:
Don't arch
your back.

Hamstrings (rear thigh): Lie on your back with your left knee bent and your left foot flat on the floor. Straighten your right leg out in front of you along the floor and flex your toes toward yourself. Slowly raise your right leg off the floor as high as you can without allowing your back or butt to lift up. As you hold this position, you feel a stretch through the back of your thigh. Clasp your hands or wrap a towel around your thigh above your knee to help raise your leg. Lower your leg slowly and repeat the stretch with your left leg. Using your hands or a towel to help is an especially good idea if you are not very flexible. See Figure 19-2.

Figure 19-2:
Hold this
postion to
feel the
stretch.

The Pretzel Stretch (butt, lower back, and outer thigh): Lie on your back and bend your knees. Lift your legs up so that your knees are directly over your hips and your calves are parallel to the floor. Cross your left ankle over the front of your right thigh. Clasp both hands around the back of your right thigh and pull back with gentle, steady pressure. Keep your butt in contact with the floor. Don't round hips up and off the floor. As you hold this position, you should feel the stretch spread through your left buttock and outer hip and through the center of your lower back. Repeat this stretch on your other side. See Figure 19-3.

Figure 19-3:
Pull back
with gentle,
steady
pressure.

Reach Up (entire upper body and lower back): Sit up tall either cross-legged on the floor or in a chair. Make a loose fist with your hands and raise your arms directly over your shoulders. Lengthen your right arm upward, as if you're trying to touch an object above you that's just out of reach. Hold this position for two to four slow counts. Without relaxing your right arm, stretch your left arm upward. Sit up tall and keep your shoulders relaxed as you alternate stretching each arm upward five times. Try to reach a little higher each time — without hunching your shoulders up to your ears. You should feel this stretch throughout the length of your spine, in the "wings" of your upper back, and in your shoulders and arms. See Figure 19-4.

Figure 19-4:
Keep your
shoulders
relaxed.

Hand Clasp (chest, shoulders, and arms): Sit up tall either on a chair or cross-legged on the floor. Lean a few inches forward from your hips and clasp your hands behind your back. Drop your shoulders and shoulder blades downward as you lengthen your arms out behind you. You should feel the stretch across the top of your chest, in your shoulders, and along the length of your arms. If you don't have enough flexibility to clasp your hands together, hold an end of a towel in each hand. See Figure 19-5.

Figure 19-5:
Lean
forward a
few inches.

Assisted Stretching

What it is: Traditional-type stretches that require a partner. Your partner helps you into position and then gently helps you stretch further than you can by yourself. As with traditional, or static, stretching, you hold the position for 10 to 30 seconds without bouncing. The best way to learn assisted stretches is from an experienced fitness trainer. While the new ACSM position stand does not offer guidelines for this type of stretching, the organization does reference it as promising and possibly effective.

Pros:

✔ Having someone else do a lot of the work for you is relaxing. This technique is particularly valuable for a tight muscle that you have trouble stretching yourself.

✔ If have trouble mastering some of the common stretching positions, assisted stretching can help you learn the techniques while you develop enough flexibility to do them more comfortably on your own.

✔ A partner tends to push you a bit further than you can push yourself.

Cons:

✔ If you don't have a partner, you're out of luck (although some assisted stretches can be mimicked by using a towel or rope).

✔ If your partner overstretches you, you may end up injured.

✔ Assisted stretching requires less muscle awareness than the other techniques, so you may not learn much from doing it. (We discuss muscle awareness in the PNF section that follows.)

Sample Move: This stretch focuses on your lower back and butt. Lie on the floor with your partner standing in front of your feet; relax your arms at your sides and keep your head on the floor. Lift your legs and bend your knees into your chest. Your partner should place his or her palms on your thighs and gently press down and in so that your knees move even closer to your chest. As you hold this position, you should feel the stretch spread from your butt into your lower back. See Figure 19-6.

Figure 19-6:
An assisted
stretch.

PNF: Proprioceptive Neuromuscular Facilitation

What it is: The term *Proprioceptive Neuromuscular Facilitation* sounds like some high-tech, life-saving medical procedure used by doctors on *ER,* but really, it's a simple method of stretching: You get into a stretch position, tighten a muscle for about four seconds, and then allow it to relax. The theory is that when the muscle exhausts itself from the tightening, it is too tired to resist the stretch and therefore stretches further than normal. Some PNF stretches work best with the assistance of another person; others you can perform yourself. The best way to learn PNF stretches is from a trainer who is familiar with the technique.

Pros:

✔ Many studies, including some referenced by the ACSM, show that PNF stretching is a good way to increase your flexibility.

✔ The tightening part helps strengthen the muscle being stretched. This is especially true if the muscle is injured and you can't do the bending and straightening necessary to perform strength-training exercises.

✔ Some studies have found that PNF stretching increases blood flow into joints and muscles, especially if they've experienced a recent injury.

✔ PNF teaches you about your muscles. If you are doing a PNF hamstring stretch, you need to know where your hamstring is and how it feels to tighten this muscle. This knowledge also comes in handy when you perform weight training exercises.

Cons:

✔ Many people find PNF stretching uncomfortable or even painful.

✔ You need extra motivation to tighten a muscle as hard as you can for four seconds. Not everyone has the strength or the patience for this.

✔ If you do PNF stretches with a partner, your buddy may be overenthusiastic and try to force the stretch beyond your capabilities, and then *snap*! Pay attention so that this doesn't happen. If you have high blood pressure, avoid PNF stretches because they may result in sharp, sudden increases in blood pressure.

Sample PNF Stretch: This PNF stretch loosens up your hamstrings. Lie on your back with your left knee bent and left foot flat on the floor. Your partner should kneel on one knee in front of your feet. Raise your right leg and place the back of your heel on top of your partner's shoulder. Your partner should place one hand on your thigh, just above your knee, and the other hand on top of your shin. Forcefully press your heel down into your partner's shoulder and concentrate on tightening your hamstring as much as possible for three to five seconds. Then relax the muscle and have your partner gently push your leg up and back without allowing the knee to bend. Hold the stretch for five slow counts and repeat the stretch three to five times. Then switch legs. To do this stretch without a partner, wrap a towel around your ankle or the back of your calf, and then pull your leg toward you as you tighten your hamstring and press it downward. See Figure 19-7.

Figure 19-7:
A PNF
stretch.

Active Isolated Stretching

What it is: *Active Isolated (AI) stretching* involves tightening the muscle opposite to the one that you're planning to stretch and then stretching the target muscle for two seconds. You repeat this process 8 to 12 times before going onto the next stretch. By stretching for such a brief period of time, the theory goes, you don't give the muscle enough time to trigger its stretch reflex. (We define the stretch reflex earlier in this chapter, in the "Why Stretching Is So Controversial" section.) What's the purpose of tightening the muscle opposite the one you're stretching? When a muscle tightens, the opposing muscle has no choice but to relax.

Although active isolated stretching has been around since the 1950s, it's just now gaining popularity, largely through the efforts of father-and-son physiologist team Phil and Jim Wharton, authors of *The Whartons' Book of Stretching* (Times Books). This method is also favored by many sports teams and elite athletes, including one of the world's fastest humans, sprinter Michael Johnson, who won two Olympic gold medals in 1996. Researchers are currently studying this method and may soon offer more insight into its benefits.

Pros:

✔ Many active isolated stretching exercises do a good job of isolating one muscle group at a time. For example, with an AI stretch, you can stretch the hamstrings without involving the lower back and hip muscles.

✔ If you are particularly weak in one area or are rehabilitating a muscle from injury, the tightening may help strengthen that muscle.

✔ Many people find AI stretches less painful than traditional stretches.

Cons:

✔ The technique is harder to learn than traditional stretching and some of the positions are difficult to get into.

✔ AI stretching is time-consuming. You need about 20 minutes to stretch your entire body, whereas you can do an adequate traditional stretch routine in 5 to 10 minutes.

Sample Active Isolated Stretch: This move stretches your calf muscles. Hold one end of a belt or towel in each hand. Sit on the floor, and lift your left leg a few inches off the floor, positioning your right leg however it's most comfortable. Loop the center of the belt around the instep of your left foot. Point your toes away from you to tighten your calf muscles and then pull your toes back to stretch your calf muscles. Hold the position for two seconds. Repeat 8 to 12 times and then stretch your right calf. See Figure 19-8.

Figure 19-8:
An AI
stretch.

Chapter 20

Improving Your Balance and Coordination

In This Chapter

▶ Why balance training is important

▶ Three great exercises to improve your equilibrium

▶ Nifty balance gadgets

*U*nless you're training to be a circus tightrope walker or a gymnast with a specialty in the balance beam, you probably haven't given any thought to improving your sense of equilibrium. The payoffs aren't obvious; after all, balance exercises don't strengthen your bones, give you buns of steel, or turn you into a calorie-burning inferno.

So why bother? Here's why: One out of every three people over age 65 falls at least once a year, and about 50 percent of those who break their hips never regain full walking ability. These trips and falls are associated with a reduced sense of balance. But what if you're only 30 years old and haven't fallen since that bully in fourth grade tripped you on the playground? Well, think long-term. Just as it's wise to take preventive measures against osteoporosis and muscle-wasting, it's important to act now to preserve your sense of equilibrium for the future. Better balance also serves you well in dozens of sports, from mountain biking to rock climbing to in-line skating. You'll catch on to these activities more quickly and avoid injuries that would befall those with a shakier sense of balance.

This message is slowly going mainstream: Many health clubs now offer classes that use props such as physioballs, balance beams, and wobble boards. One club in New York City has a "rebounding" class in which exercisers jump up and down on a miniature trampoline to sharpen their balance, coordination, and agility. In this chapter we show you three simple moves to improve your balance and tell you about some nifty gadgets that you can use to expand your repertoire of coordination exercises.

Losing Balance with Age

Special receptor cells located in your skin, muscles, joints, and tendons — the fancy term for these cells is *proprioceptors* — process information about your body's orientation as it moves through space. For instance, when you walk across a lawn, your proprioceptors tell you things like "Okay, I'm putting my feet here now. The ground is spongy because it's grass. It has a little give and isn't completely uniform." As you age, these proprioceptors become less sensitive, giving your brain less information and feedback to work with. Now when you walk across a lawn, you don't get quite so much input about the texture or give of the surface, and you're more likely to stumble on little inconsistencies of terrain. Slower reflexes and decreased muscular strength, combined with deteriorating eyesight and depth perception, also contribute to a diminished sense of equilibrium.

A fear of falling may be another reason that older people experience a loss of balance. Ironically, this fear may increase the risk of falling. When people worry about taking a tumble, they try to compensate by standing with their feet farther apart and walking with smaller steps. However, these adjustments actually prevent you from judging subtle cues from the environment, like the firmness of the ground and small changes in height of the surface you're walking on.

What's more, poor balance results in a shaky, unsteady gait. It becomes harder to go up or down stairs or negotiate high curbs and other obstacles that you might not otherwise give a second thought. You may find it more difficult to reach for objects on overhead shelves or to stand in tight spots on trains, in line, and in crowds with your feet close together.

Fortunately, you can do a lot to reduce or reverse some of these problems and, as a result, you can become less accident-prone. One study looked at 110 men and women with an average age of 80. After three months of performing balance exercises regularly, most of the subjects had the body control of people three to ten years younger.

Balance Exercises

We think that balance exercises are best taught one-on-one or in small groups supervised by a trainer or physical therapist with a practiced eye and in-depth knowledge of anatomy and body alignment. However, you can also do a number of excellent drills on your own.

Keep in mind that balance exercises are about quality rather than quantity. Focus hard when you perform the following moves, and don't get frustrated if you're not graceful at first. For example, walking across a low wooden beam (see Figure 20-1) requires a constant correction of knee, hip, and head alignment. All of your muscles from head to toe must work in synch in order for you to glide across the beam without extending your arms in the air or wandering off the edge. This can be tough at first, but with practice, you can master this move in just a few sessions. After a while, balance exercises awaken reflexes and teach body awareness and control on a subconscious level. This can translate into lasting improvements in posture and overall quality of movement.

Do these exercises two or three times a week at the end of your regular weight training sessions. Start with one set of each exercise and gradually work up to three sets. If you feel that you need more work, try an additional session or two each week. This type of training is deceptively challenging and can leave you feeling exhausted and sore if you overdo it at first. Even if you learn other balance exercises, don't do more than four moves in a session.

- ✔ **Balance Beam Walk:** Walk slowly across a low wooden beam while maintaining a tall posture, keeping your knees forward and your hands relaxed at your sides. (If you don't have a balance beam, draw or tape a straight line 6 to 12 feet long on the floor.) Place one foot directly in front of the other and stay as steady as possible. If you fall off the beam or wander off your line, simply get back on and continue from that point. It helps to focus your eyes on the end of the beam. Easier version: Extend your arms out to the side, but only as much as is necessary. Aim to make three back-and-forth trips. Here's a tougher version to try when this gets easy: Walk backwards. See Figure 20-1.

- ✔ **Fulcrum:** With your arms relaxed at your sides, stand on one foot with your other leg extended behind you and a few inches off the floor. Lean a few inches forward and maintain your balance for up to one minute. Then slowly bring your foot back to the floor, and repeat with your other leg. Do three to five repetitions with each leg. Easier version: Rest your fingertips lightly against a wall, chair, or other sturdy object. Tougher version: Lean forward a few inches more. When you get really good, you can lean forward until your torso is perpendicular to the floor. See Figure 20-2.

- ✔ **Ostrich:** With your arms relaxed at your sides, stand on one foot with your opposite knee bent and your opposite foot a few inches off the floor directly in front of you. Hold this position for up to a minute, slowly return your foot back to the floor, and then repeat with the other foot. Do three to five repetitions with each leg. Easier version: Rest your fingertips lightly against a wall, chair, or some other sturdy object. Tougher version: Do the exercise with your eyes closed. See Figure 20-3.

Figure 20-1:
Focus your
eyes on
the end of
the beam.

Figure 20-2:
Try to
maintain
your
balance for
up to one
minute.

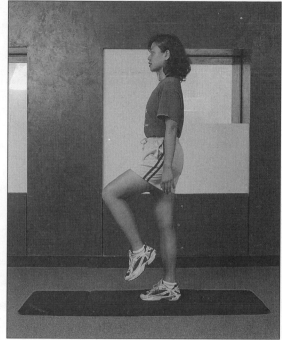

Figure 20-3:
For a real challenge, do this exercise with your eyes closed!

Nifty Balance Gadgets

If you want to expand your repertoire of balance exercises, you can find some helpful gadgets at equipment specialty stores. Two catalogs, OPTP (888-819-0121) and Flag House (800-793-7900), also sell these gadgets, many of which come with manuals that demonstrate exercises. One of our favorite tools is a balance board, a round board balanced on a knob or a ball. You stand on this and balance in a variety of one- and two-legged positions. Other items we recommend: foam rollers, physioballs, low balance beams, and "traffic" cones. Many are used in an excellent video called *Mat Exercises with Small Apparatus,* by Elizabeth Larkam. Whoever thought of the title should not attempt a career in show business, and the video itself is short on personality. However, the tape features a whole host of killer exercises. To order, call (800) 240-3539.

Chapter 21

Pills, Powders, and Potions: Nutrition in a Nutshell

A few years back, Doris Shafran, Liz's mother-in-law, became very ill. She felt almost constantly nauseous, her skin was flushed, and she lost a lot of weight very quickly. When she began having fainting spells, she was admitted to the hospital. Test after test showed nothing out of the ordinary; her doctors were baffled. Finally, a sharp resident discovered that for more than 11 years, Doris had been taking niacin, an over-the-counter vitamin supplement that has been shown to lower blood cholesterol levels. But the niacin had built up to such toxic levels in Doris' body that it caused all the aforementioned symptoms, plus some serious impairment of her liver. She stopped taking the niacin supplement and recovered completely.

Mind you, niacin has a scientifically proven track record of reducing blood cholesterol levels, and doctors often recommend it to their patients. If you can get in this much trouble with a supplement that's well-researched and may have the approval of your physician, imagine the potential dangers of taking a substance that scientists know virtually nothing about. And yet, many people are popping the latest "miracle supplement" like breath mints or blindly following the newest diet in an effort to (a) burn body fat, (b) gain muscle, (c) increase energy, (d) get stronger, or (e) all of the above.

Gym weight rooms in particular tend to double as research labs. News about the latest supplements is often bandied about like gospel, often by the guys with backs as big as barn doors. You may find yourself tempted to run down to the local health food store and stock up on the supplement du jour.

In this chapter, we give you the lowdown on some of today's popular nutritional supplements and diets, along with some sensible tips for healthy eating. No matter what substances you ingest or diets you follow, remember this: If you use your body as a research lab, you run the risk that the experiment will go awry. You may end up with unwanted hair, liver damage, or even, in extreme cases, a new address six feet underground. And some of the side effects and after effects may not be immediate. Ten years from now, the supplements you've sworn by may turn out to be the pills about which scientists say, "We hope you never took *that*."

The Scoop on Fat-Burning and Muscle-Building Supplements

We recently read a newspaper article in which teenagers were asked why they smoke. "If cigarettes were really so bad for you," one kid said, "they wouldn't be legal." Many dieters and weight lifters resort to the same rationalization when they buy dietary supplements of dubious value. If these pills were harmful, these people figure, the government would have pulled them off the market.

Not necessarily. The U.S. Food and Drug Administration (FDA) has limited power to regulate dietary supplements. Manufacturers don't have to prove that a supplement is safe; the onus is on the FDA to prove that a product is dangerous before it can be yanked from the shelves. As a result, bogus or potentially dangerous supplements can be sold for years before the FDA gathers enough complaints to launch an investigation. Furthermore, the Federal Trade Commission (FTC), which is in charge of enforcing truth-in-advertising laws, cannot sue every manufacturer of bogus supplements. So when you see a pill bottle that says "Reduces body fat and increases lean muscle!" don't assume that the claim is true.

You can't always believe what you read in magazines, either. One popular muscle magazine recently ran an ostensibly objective article about supplements, stating as fact that "protein powders can be considered superior to food because their consistency and texture make them soluble in water and easier for the body to digest." No legitimate nutritionist would tell you that protein powders are superior to food. Not surprisingly, the company that owns the magazine in which the article appeared also manufactures a whole line of protein powders — which are advertised heavily in the magazine.

So if you can't trust advertising and you can't be sure that the government has identified all unsafe or useless dietary supplements, where should you get your nutritional advice? Certainly not from the most muscular lifter in the weight room or from the leanest member of your body sculpting class. Instead, seek out advice from reputable sources, such as registered dietitians and the FDA. (Even though the agency can't yank every bogus supplement, the FDA does try to warn the public when products are being investigated.) The following sections look at some of the popular supplements promoted in health clubs.

Chitin

Steve Garvey and Kendall Carson have found not one but two weight-loss supplements they claim to believe in. Their Exercise in a Bottle infomercial also features a pitch for Fat Trapper, a pill that contains chitin.

- ✔ **What it is:** Chitin is a substance found in the exoskeletons of shrimp, crab, and other shellfish.

- ✔ **The claims:** Garvey claims that Fat Trapper "literally traps fat before it gets into your system." In other words, he is saying that chitin attaches to fat in the stomach and prevents its absorption in the digestive tract. To demonstrate the effectiveness of this pill, Garvey pours bacon grease into a glass of water and then adds the contents of four Fat Trapper pills. When globs of fat form and fall to the bottom, he declares that this demonstrates Fat Trapper's ability to absorb up to 120 grams of fat.

  Several Web sites promoting chitin, and a similar compound called chitosan, make incredible weight-loss claims. One site boasts about a Finnish study in which subjects lost 8 percent of their body weight in four weeks.

- ✔ **The reality:** Garvey's bacon grease demonstration is impressive — until you remember that oil and water separate naturally, anyway! In reality, the few studies that have been done on chitin and related substances show that they absorb only 3 to 5 fat grams, the equivalent of a pat of butter. And these studies were performed on rats. The only research we could find that was conducted on human beings and published in a legitimate scientific journal found that, after four weeks, subjects who took chitosan supplements did not lose *any* more weight than subjects who took a phony pill. Furthermore, speculate that long-term use of the supplements may lead to nutritional deficiencies because they may prevent the body from absorbing fat-soluble substances such as vitamin D, vitamin E, and essential fatty acids.

Creatine

When creatine first became popular, this strength-building supplement was primarily marketed in powder and pill form. Now it has become so popular that it can be found in energy bars and even smoothies.

- ✔ **What it is:** Creatine is a nitrogen-containing substance that's produced naturally in your body and is found in meat, poultry, and fish. Creatine is a building block for several amino acids, which are themselves the building blocks for protein.

- ✔ **The claims:** Creatine is said to give you more energy during high-intensity exercise so that you can work out longer and harder, thereby building more strength and muscle mass. (One of the more cleverly titled brands is called *Kick Some Mass.*)

> ✔ **The reality:** This stuff actually seems to have some value — under certain circumstances. Several, but not all, creatine studies suggest that the substance can help weight lifters and sprinters build muscle and gain strength. The substance may also help tennis players, football players, and others who play sports that require short bursts of energy (generally less than 30 seconds).

But creatine can work only if you stick to a serious weight lifting program. If you take creatine every day but don't work out, you won't get any more muscular than if you drink lemonade. Also, if you don't have the genetic predisposition toward building huge muscles, you can suck down a truckload of creatine and lift weights six hours per day, and you *still* won't be Mr. Olympia. Also, individual response to creatine supplementation can vary greatly.

The Lowdown on Protein

Protein has always been an obsession with bodybuilders, but recently high-protein diets have become the craze among average people who are trying to lose weight. Here's a look at what protein can and cannot do for you, whether you're trying to slim down or bulk up.

The high-protein diet craze

High-protein diet's popularity has been bolstered by several best-selling diet books and some inaccurate reporting in major newspapers. Advocates claim that high-carbohydrate diets — the type of diet promoted by the majority of the medical community — have made us fatter as a nation now than at any other point in history. ("Pasta Makes You Fat" blared a *New York Times* headline that was later retracted.)

High-protein diet gurus tell us that eating pasta, bagels, fruit, and other high-carbohydrate foods make us fat because they cause a condition called insulin resistance. Here's the deal: After you eat carbohydrates, your body breaks them down into a substance called *glucose,* which floods the bloodstream and triggers your pancreas to release the hormone insulin. One job of *insulin* is to deliver glucose from the blood to the muscles, where the glucose is used as energy. However, according to high-protein proponents, a diet high in carbohydrates triggers *insulin resistance* — a condition that blocks the delivery of glucose and keeps insulin floating around in the blood. This excess insulin, diet books say, leads to weight gain in two ways: by causing people to crave more carbohydrates (and therefore overeat) and by triggering the body to store excess calories as fat.

Now, this theory has a few problems. For one thing, research has not proven that high-carbohydrate diets cause people to overeat. True, eating sugary foods can cause people to crave more sugary foods, and some people are more prone to this phenomenon than others. However, you can't lump all carbohydrates into the same category, as many diet books do. Potatoes, whole-wheat bagels, and apples don't trigger the same type of sugar rush as doughnuts. If you're sensitive to carbohydrates, you may need to cut back on sugary foods and you may respond well to a diet that's relatively high in protein, but this doesn't mean spaghetti is off limits. We all should aim for a mix of carbohydrate, protein, and fat at each meal. For each person, the ideal ratio of protein to the other nutrients may differ.

As for the notion that insulin causes the body to store excess calories as fat: Realize that *any* excess calories you eat — whether from carbohydrates, protein, or fat — gets stored as fat. You can't cast insulin as the evil creator of body fat any more than you can blame the supermarket checkout person for the high price of coffee. Insulin resistance is a real condition with serious health consequences, such as diabetes and high blood pressure, but it has not been proven to *cause* weight gain (and it's not as common as some high-protein diet gurus would have you believe). On the contrary, many experts believe that being overweight is what appears to cause insulin resistance. When people who are insulin resistant lose weight and exercise, the condition often disappears.

One major problem with many of the so-called high-protein diets is that many are too high in fat, particularly saturated fat (the artery-clogging kind), and low in fiber. Dr. Atkins, father of the whole protein diet craze, even recommends bacon, sausage, and pastrami as "risk reducing" foods! This diet is so wacky that Dr. Atkins recommends limiting your intake of most types of fruits and vegetables. (Atkins was recently booed at a government-sponsored diet debate when he said he would not spend any money to research his questionable theories.)

So why do some people lose weight (at least temporarily) on these diets? It's the calories, stupid. What none of these books tell you is that the eating plans are also low in calories — some call for less than 1,000 calories per day. If you eat fewer calories than you burn, you're going to lose weight no matter what type of food the calories come from. But beware: Chances are you're going to gain the weight back. Very low calorie diets tend to slow your metabolism and make you feel deprived. And in fact, upping your protein intake, especially if you have been eating low protein for a while, may initially help you satisfy your hunger more quickly. We have nothing against protein. In fact, protein can help make a meal more satisfying so that you're not tempted to overeat. And some people do need more protein and less carbohydrate than others. But don't rely on one of these high-protein diets as a magic bullet for weight loss.

Can protein pump you up?

Ironically, while many people turn to protein to lose weight, another segment of the population turns to protein for the opposite reason: to gain weight. Bodybuilders, football players, and skinny guys who want to go up a few shirt sizes guzzle high-protein shakes, pop protein pills, and mix up amino acid concoctions. "Get Big Now!" boasts an ad for a chocolate-flavored powder that contains 42 grams of protein per serving.

Do these guys have the right idea? Not really. Serious athletes do need slightly more protein than the average person. They need more carbohydrates and fat, too. However, most Americans eat twice the amount of protein they need anyway, so the chances of a weight lifter not getting enough protein are pretty slim. In fact, if you eat too many calories, your body stores these calories as fat, even if many of the calories came from "Ripped Fuel Thermogenic Protein Drink."

Although mountains of research debunk the idea that high-protein diets build muscle, this theory is alive and well in most gyms.

Our friend Mike Spike, a long-time bodybuilder, remains a staunch believer. "These theories (that high-protein diets do not help build muscle) are from a bunch of pencil-neck book writers," he says. "Theory does not always translate to reality, and there's the reality of millions of bodybuilders out there to back up that it does work." Mike says he has never met a successful bodybuilder who hasn't been on a high-protein diet. "If guys weren't doing well on high-protein diets, they (the diets) would have been abandoned years ago," he says. Spike is a pretty big guy, so we don't want to argue with him. However, we wonder how bodybuilders would perform if they didn't dose up on protein but continued with the same training program.

Just know that eating too much protein can cause kidney problems. Also, keep in mind that getting your protein in powder or pill form is expensive. One can of protein powder we saw in a health food store costs $20, which works out to $1.18 for a serving containing 16 grams of protein. A ¼-cup serving of tuna also contains 16 grams of protein — and costs about 23 cents. (The powder and the tuna had roughly the same number of calories.)

Do Energy Bars Really Give You Energy?

Just a few years ago, the only people who gobbled down energy bars were hardcore athletes who bought them in gyms or health food stores. Now PowerBars are as mainstream as Hershey bars. You can find them — along with Clif Bars, Steel Bars, Met-RX bars and countless others — at the convenience store checkout counter. At one recent trade show, we counted 27 different energy bar companies marketing at least 8 varieties each! You may be wondering: Are they just high-priced candy bars, or do they have any nutritional value? And do they all taste like moldy chalk dust?

You may also wonder which nutrient mix is best. Some bars contain almost entirely carbohydrate. Others are high in protein and very low in carbs. Still others have an equal balance of carbs, protein, and fat. Here's the lowdown on energy bars.

Are energy bars good meal replacements?

No! One trade show marketer told Liz that his company's bar was the perfect food, better than anything nature has ever come up with. He made this claim despite the fact that the bar tasted like wet shoe leather and contained zero grams of fiber. The truth: Energy bars can be a nutritional source of supplemental energy — say, either before or after a workout — but they're certainly no substitute for a well-balanced meal. Even bars that contain vitamins and minerals don't offer phytochemicals and other disease-fighting nutrients found only in food.

The main benefit of energy bars is convenience. You can keep a bar in your gym bag or the glove compartment of your car, and it won't turn into some biological experiment. Be sure to drink 12 to 16 ounces of water whenever you eat a bar. Otherwise, the bar may sit like a rock in your stomach and cause nausea. The carbohydrate has to be diluted so it can better be digested and absorbed into the bloodstream.

Which ingredients should I look for?

If you use bars to fuel up before a workout or to refuel right afterward, your best bet is a bar high in carbohydrates, the energy source that your body can use most quickly. (These bars usually contain 40 to 45 grams of carbs, about 70 to 80 percent of their total calories.) High-protein bars are popular among weight lifters, but contrary to popular opinion, wolfing down 30 grams of protein after a killer workout isn't going to speed up the process of muscle repair. Mixing a small amount of protein with your postworkout carbs can indeed help your muscles refuel, but the majority of your postworkout calories should still come from carbs.

What about those bars containing 40 percent carbohydrate, 30 percent protein, and 30 percent fat? Some of them may taste better than the high-carb carbs because of the added fat, but the extra fat also takes longer to digest. (And some still taste like spackle.) These bars may be most helpful for long aerobic workouts, such as a three-hour bike ride, because they will keep you satisfied longer than a high-carb bar. Just know that they provide energy less efficiently than carbohydrate-dense bars.

Part VI

The Part of Tens

The 5th Wave — By Rich Tennant

"When exactly was it discovered that fun house mirrors had accidentally been installed in the body sculpting room?"

In this part . . .

We perpetuate the notion that all the important information in the universe fits neatly into groups of ten. (Although we never really got the hang of the metric system, we do like the concept of tens.) We discuss ten ways for you to educate yourself about weight training, such as reading fitness magazines, browsing the World Wide Web, and spying on fellow health club members. We clear up ten myths about lifting weights, and we demonstrate ten common weight training mistakes — goofs that could leave you with some serious medical bills or simply rob you of good results. Also in Part VI, we describe ten great (G-rated) exercises that you can do with a $3 piece of latex rubber and tell you about the best and the worst exercise products on the market. Not every manufacturer is trying to fleece you, but we found no shortage of hucksters.

Chapter 22

Ten Ways to Educate Yourself about Weight Training

You can't find out everything there is to know about fraternizing with members of the equine species by reading *A Horse Around the House,* even though it's considered the horse owner's bible. You need more than one source of information about weight lifting, too. Once you get your bearings in the world of weight training, we suggest that you expand your horizons by trying new exercises, keeping up on the latest research, and communicating with other weight training enthusiasts. In this chapter, we offer ten ways to get smart about lifting weights. We steer you toward the reliable fitness magazines, Web sites, and television shows, and we help you identify the misleading mumbo jumbo. Technology has triggered a flood dubious information, so you do need to be selective about what exactly you let into your brain.

Read Fitness Magazines

A decade ago, you could read about weight lifting in only a handful of magazines, and the articles featured headlines like "Five Delt Trashers! Learn How to Get Wider than a Virginia Sunrise!" (We didn't even make that one up.) You still can find hard-core bodybuilding magazines, but in recent years, weight training has gone mainstream. Plenty of fitness magazines aim at people who want to lift weights and still be able to fit through your average doorway. Even general-interest men's and women's magazines, such as *GQ* and *Redbook,* are touting the benefits of pumping some iron.

Of course, you can't always believe what you read. We recently picked up a bridal magazine that encouraged readers to slim down for the big day by using a body wrap. "Cheat your way to a better body by toning up the easy way and using an inch-loss treatment," the article advised. That's like suggesting that you cheat your way to becoming a lawyer by hanging a diploma on your wall. Many of the men's magazines are no better. One of them featured an article titled, "Lose That Gut: A No-Sweat Program." Yes, the program involves no sweat — it's simply a bunch of abdominal exercises. But, as we explain in Chapter 12, ab exercises won't flatten a flabby belly.

Don't assume that the models in fitness magazines developed their perfect bodies by performing the workouts pictured. Most of these people are among the small minority who are genetically programmed to carry minuscule amounts of body fat — and they may starve themselves on top of that. Furthermore, many photographs are doctored. One prominent fitness magazine slimmed down the hips of a world-class female tennis star. You know that if one of the best athletes in the world can't even grace a magazine cover with her body as is, the magazine's standards are absurd.

Fitness magazines we like

For weight training information, we tend to favor mainstream fitness magazines over general-interest publications. Typically, the articles are more accurate, and the exercise instructions are more complete. Here's a look at the weight training coverage of some better (and larger) fitness magazines. This list is limited to publications that cover weight training in every issue.

- ✔ *Men's Health* (www.menshealth.com): This magazine is subtitled "Tons of Useful Stuff" and lives up to its name, even if the cover headlines — "Rock Hard, Right Now," for example — tend toward the preposterous.

- ✔ *Men's Fitness* (www.mensfitness.com): You may find inspiration from this magazine's Success Story department; each month the column chronicles one guy's odyssey from fat to fit and lists his weekly workout schedule.

- ✔ *Shape* (www.shapemag.com): *Shape* is serious about educating its readers; you not only learn how to perform an exercise but also learn the names of each muscle group involved. Each issue includes at least three weight training stories.

- ✔ *Heart & Soul*: Aimed at African-American women, this health and fitness magazine urges women to set realistic goals and stop wanting waif-like bodies. Our only concern: strength-training workouts that aren't challenging enough. One routine included biceps curls without weights, which won't do a darned thing for you.

✔ *Fitness* (www.fitnessmagazine.com): This is one of the few celebrity-oriented magazines that report accurately on weight training and exercise in general. You won't find any wacky diets or silly workouts here.

✔ *Self* (www.self.com): We like *Self*'s "Move of the Month" section, which demonstrates a single weight training exercise in great detail. The magazine also covers fitness Web sites, books, videos, and research.

✔ **Other magazines:** The following magazines cover strength training fairly regularly: *Cooking Light*, *Health*, *Men's Journal*, *Outside*, *Prevention*, and *Walking*. Even some of the most general interest women's magazines, such as *O* (Oprah's new magazine), *Good Housekeeping,* and *Family Circle,* are now featuring weight training routines that you can do at home with little equipment. We particularly like *O* because it represents women of all different shapes and sizes, not just skinny models.

Be a Voyeur

In the gym, voyeurism is not only legal but may actually keep you out of trouble. Watching other people is another good way to learn new exercises. If you've been curious about how to use a machine but are afraid to ask, you can wait for a fellow club member to put the contraption in motion. You may be relieved to find out that, if left to your own devices, you would have strapped the wrong body part into it. We've picked up some good spotting techniques by watching others. And we admit that we've even saved a few bucks by eavesdropping while trainers advise their clients. Of course, the people you're spying on may not appreciate being watched, so at least be a discreet peeping tom.

Also know that you may be witnessing some mighty bad form. Just recently we watched a guy bounce the weight up and down on the 45-degree Leg Press Machine (see Chapter 13) by folding his legs into his chest so that his knees were practically in his mouth, and then exploding his legs straight up with such force that you could actually hear them snapping. As a beginner, you may not feel confident enough to distinguish good form from bad. In reality, worthless (or dangerous) exercises share a number of characteristics that are easy to spot. Use these clues to help determine whether a movement you're witnessing is one that you should forget you ever saw.

Don't emulate a fellow club member if . . .

✔ **Grunting appears to be an essential part of the exercise.** A person should be able to move a weight without letting loose sounds that rival Tarzan's call to the wild elephants.

✔ **You hear more clanging and banging than you would in the kitchen of the trendiest restaurant in town.** A person who is performing an exercise correctly moves the weights with control and without sound effects.

- **The lifter engages in extreme bodily contortions.** We once saw one guy shimmy into a machine backwards, stretching his arms way behind him to grab the handles. All he had to do was turn around.

- **You ask which muscle an exercise is supposed to strengthen and the lifter replies, "I don't know, but I sure feel it in my lower back."**

- **The exercise involves grand sweeping gestures that appear to threaten the safety of others.** When you see people ducking to avoid the guy in the corner moving a heavy barbell in expansive arcs, this is a good tip-off that you don't want to include the move in your repertoire.

Browse the Web

Browsing the World Wide Web is a great way to find out about all aspects of weight training, from performing the perfect Deadlift to lifting while pregnant. It's also a good way to waste four hours sifting through a bunch of self-promoting gobbledygook. Sometimes the Internet can seem to be the mother of all infomercials. Any yahoo with a home computer and the right software program can serve up a Web site. A recent Internet search yielded more than 100,000 hits for the phrase *weight training*. You could spend the rest of your life sorting through the nonsense.

Because fitness Web sites come and go faster than sitcoms on the WB network, we're not going to give you specific recommendations. Instead, we offer these tips on how to judge the weight training information you read online:

- **Don't consider FAQs the gospel.** One of the most inconsistent sources of information on the Web are FAQs, or *frequently asked questions*. These pages answer common questions about a particular topic, such as training your abdominals, designing your workout routine, and taking nutritional supplements. One Web site lauded creatine as the secret to weight loss and muscle building while another site deemed the substance totally useless. (See Chapter 21 for our take on creatine.) Just because "FAQ" sounds like "FACT" does not mean the information provided is accurate.

  The authors of one fitness FAQ touting high-protein diets stated that they "assume no responsibility for errors or omissions, or for damages resulting from the use of information contained herein." You should read this as: "Take our information with a grain of salt." Keep in mind that no respectable magazine or newspaper would provide information and then say, "What you just read may or may not be true, and if it's not true, it's not our fault."

- **Be wary of product recommendations.** You can trust the product recommendations in *Weight Training For Dummies,* 2nd Edition because we, the authors, do not make money off of the products that we recommend. (The only exceptions are other books that we have written, but we tell you straight out that we are the authors.) However, you can bet that most fitness Web sites do have a financial interest in the product that they tell you about, especially if you can purchase the product directly through the site.

One fitness Web site, which contains plenty of accurate training tips, provides a lengthy list of weight training books. Some are excellent; others are lousy. One book touts the wacky theory that the more lactic acid you produce by lifting weights, the more growth hormone you produce, which, in turn, speeds up fat loss. Fourteen of the book's 88 pages are essentially advertisements for a nutritional supplement company. The bottom line: Even if a Web site appears to be offering sound advice, don't assume that you can trust the products it recommends.

✔ **Put more trust in nonprofit sites than those trying to make money.** In general, you're more likely to find accurate, unbiased information on sites that are sponsored by major fitness organizations, such as those listed in Chapter 5, or by government organizations, such as the President's Council on Physical Fitness (`www.surgeongeneral.gov/ophs/pcpfs.htm`). Many university physical education programs have their own fine Web sites that offer the latest in exercise research; look for sites with names that end in .edu or .org, signaling that they are run by accredited schools or legitimate not-for-profit organizations.

✔ **Use your common sense.** Don't let the Web be your only source of weight training information. Back up any advice you get with other sources, such as magazines or qualified trainers.

Read Books

Naturally, we feel that books are an excellent way to find out about weight training, or we wouldn't have bothered to write one. A weight training book can offer the depth that a magazine article, TV show, or video can't. Weight training books are especially helpful for learning new exercises and new ways to organize your weight routine. The best books are those that don't promote a particular program and instead offer you a variety of exercises and routines to choose from.

Weight training books we like

We offer this glance at some of our favorite weight training books that are excellent for rookies.

✔ *A Woman's Book of Strength,* by Karen Andes (The Berkley Publishing Group) is aimed at level-headed women who aren't trying to achieve physical perfection — women who don't relate to the "timid, anorexic-looking waifs that flood the fashion pages."

- *The Complete Book of Abs* and *The Complete Book of Butt and Legs,* by Kurt Brungardt (Villard) manage to live up to their names, demonstrating more than 70 exercises for the aforementioned body parts.

- *Keys to the Inner Universe,* by Bill Pearl (Bill Pearl Publishing) contains every free weight exercise known to humankind. Let's just say that, when you stand on this book, you can reach the top shelf in your closet.

- *The Complete Home Fitness Handbook,* by Ed Burke (Human Kinetics) offers no-nonsense advice on how to choose a multigym, a free weight bench, or other pieces of home weight training (and cardiovascular) equipment.

- *The Return to Glory Days,* by Morton Dean and Benjamin Gelfand, P.T. (Pocket Books) is a head-to-toe guide to treating and preventing sports injuries. It should be on every weight lifter's bookshelf.

Signs of a lousy weight training book

The aforementioned books are some of the good ones. Unfortunately, a lot more bookstore shelf space is taken up by volumes that are better used as kindling. The least useful are those written by authors who claim to have developed the world's best routine. One author says that he has "invented . . . a fitness methodology that is more effective than *anything* in existence."

Here's a handful of other misleading statements we found in a recent trip to the bookstore:

The statement: "It doesn't matter what your genetic tendency is. You'll overcome it with this program."

The reality: Nothing, except perhaps drugs, can change the way your body responds to weight training. Even if Regis Philben followed precisely the same program as the reigning Mr. Universe, he is not going to win any bodybuilding contests.

The statement: "Three-pound weights are all you need."

The reality: The book in question is devoted entirely to routines that use three-pound dumbbells. But this violates one of the major rules of weight training: You need to challenge each muscle group in order for it to get stronger. Three pounds might fatigue your rotator cuff muscles, but to your back muscles, lifting three pounds will feel like lifting a cup of yogurt. To firm up your body, you need to lift heavy enough weights so that your muscles fatigue within 15 repetitions.

The statement: Giant sets are "better than aerobics or jogging."

The reality: As we explain in Chapter 16, a *giant set* involves stringing together one set each of three different exercises without resting between the sets. Giant sets are a terrific way to challenge your muscles, and eliminating the rest period between sets does get your heart pumping faster than it otherwise would. However, as a workout for your heart, giant sets are vastly inferior to aerobics or jogging. In Chapter 18, we explain what constitutes a legitimate cardiovascular workout.

Hire a Cyber Trainer

Hiring a real-live personal trainer is one of the best ways to learn about weight training; that's why we've included trainers in our chapter about weight training deals and duds (see Chapter 26). There's no substitute for the sharp eye and hands-on experience of a qualified personal trainer. However, if you don't have access to a flesh-and-blood fitness professional, you can still learn a lot from a cyber trainer — a trainer who offers advice and routines online.

Like many fitness sites found on the Web, cyber trainers are a mixed bag. Some are run by reputable, knowledgeable professionals and offer safe, sound training advice. Others are run by charlatans looking to bag big bucks from gullible consumers. Here are some tips to help you distinguish the sensible from the schlocky:

- ✔ **Look for sites staffed by certified and experienced fitness professionals rather than famous athletes or well-known bodybuilders.** See Chapter 5 for a list of legitimate certifying organizations. Some certifications sound important but in fact require nothing more than the ability to type in your credit card number over the Internet.

- ✔ **Choose a site that assigns one trainer to you for your entire tenure.** Some sites put all of their trainees in one "barrel," and you get your training and advice from whichever trainer happens to be on duty that day. This breaks up the continuity of your training. If you hired a live personal trainer, wouldn't you expect the same person to show up each session?

- ✔ **Look for personalized attention.** The good cyber trainers ask you to fill out a health history questionnaire, ask your goals and experience, and tailor a routine specifically to your needs.

- ✔ **Try before you buy.** Many of the reputable sites allow a trial period before you commit. By the way, don't assume that the cheaper sites are the bargain they appear to be. (Fees generally range from $8 to $100 per month.) The low-cost and free sites survive on advertising and sales and tend to heavily promote dubious supplements and cheapo exercise products.

> ✔ **Look for extra features like charts that track your progress and motivational e-mail reminders.**
>
> ✔ **Look for a site that features an exercise technique library.** This is a graphic catalog (some sometimes containing audio and video) depicting the exercises included in your routine.

Watch Fitness TV Shows

Chalk it up to the brilliance of television producers: They've found a way to combine the ultimate couch potato device (the TV) with the ultimate health practice (exercise). Cable channels in particular are home to that oxymoron of oxymorons, the television exercise show. The cable explosion has dramatically expanded air time for fitness shows. National cable channels such as ESPN2 and Lifetime now have fairly extensive weight training lineups. Some shows also feature question-and-answer segments in which the hosts answer viewer mail. Fit TV runs fitness programming 24 hours a day in some markets.

Exercise programming can fill in the gaps on days when you can't get to the gym or when you've done every video in your library so many times that your VCR has begun rejecting them. We know some people who have compiled a taped collection of their favorite exercise show episodes. Taping these shows is a great — and cheap way — to add variety to your workouts.

We know one group of guys who schedule their health club workouts when fitness programs are showing on their club's TVs. One guy actually began performing the Lat Pulldown correctly after he watched Kiana, the sexy star of an ESPN2 program, lecture about the importance of keeping your torso still as you pull the bar down.

Surprisingly, many TV weight training shows are worth watching. True, you feel a little lost during commercial breaks. But most of the shows offer a safe, sane approach to fitness. Heaven knows these shows are a giant step up from those infomercials masquerading as fitness information programs.

Hook Up with an Advice Board

An online advice board posts questions and answers about a particular topic, whether it's *The Sopranos,* tattoos, or weight training. Advice boards aren't in "real time," as we say in Internet lingo for events that are happening right now. You submit a question and then other people post an answer to you on the same board (or sometimes directly to you via e-mail). An advice board can be a great place to ask questions that you're too shy to ask at a health club, such as what sports bra to wear at the gym if you're a size 38EEE. Many people write in and ask for advice on working out at home. For instance, we see people exchanging weight training video names all the time. They even ask for advice if they are getting bored with their routine. Also, you get the benefit of a variety of viewpoints. For instance, if you're find yourself lacking in motivation, dozens of people will write in with their suggestions about how to get back on track.

However, an advice board can also be a place to get lousy opinions. Liz runs a board for iVillage.com, a lifestyle Web site for women. She constantly has to go in and warn participants against advice that readers give to each other about useless or even dangerous weight loss plans. (One woman suggested fasting for 10 days every month.)

The best advice boards are patrolled by experts so they can help make sense of the information flying back and forth. Experts also answer many of the questions themselves. We think advice boards are a great way to get support from others, but be sure to let common sense — not wishful thinking — prevail.

Many advice boards also have accompanying chats led by experts in real time. You can log on at the appointed time, ask your questions, and get immediate feedback. Because the other chatters are also interested in the same topics you are, this is a good way to get camaraderie and motivation from fellow exercisers. Many fitness enthusiasts even find Internet pen pals and workout partners through organized chats.

Advice boards related to weight training can be found virtually everywhere on the Web. Stick to large, reputable sites that use experts and screen their boards daily. IVillage.com, women.com, oxygen.com, and fitnessonline.com are good sites that offer a host of good fitness information and plenty of health and fitness boards for you to pick and choose from.

Hire a Registered Dietitian

Sometimes, in our quest to get fit, we go nuts with a new exercise routine and forget that working out is only part of the equation; nutrition is equally important. If you're short on iron or protein or some other nutrient, you may run out of gas during your workouts. If you're eating too much, you'll have a hefty layer of fat covering the muscles that you're working so hard to tone. Most of us have little insight into our own eating habits. Think about it: Do you have any idea how much fiber or folic acid you ate today? Do you even know which foods contain these nutrients?

A dietitian can assess your eating habits and suggest ways to reach your goals. Most dietitians ask new clients to keep a three-day food diary before the first meeting. You have to write down everything you consume — every Oreo, every glass of apple juice, every handful of peanuts. The dietitian punches this information into a computer program that spits out your average daily intake of important nutrients.

How to find a qualified dietitian

To make significant changes in your eating habits, you may need more than a single counseling session. We suggest signing up for three to five. A session costs $50 to $100. Make sure you consult a registered dietitian — not simply a "nutritionist," a term that implies no particular qualifications. Registered dietitians must pass a tough exam and put in hundreds of hours of internship time in a clinical or hospital setting before they are let loose in the real world. Many R.D.s also have master's degrees. To find a qualified dietitian, get a recommendation from a friend or a good gym. Or, you can find a list of registered dietitians in your area through the American Dietetic Association (call 800-366-1655) or www.eatright.org. The Web site lets you do a zip-code search and search for registered dietitians with specialties such as weight control, vegetarian eating, pregnancy, and sports nutrition.

Signs of a sharp dietitian

As with trainers, education doesn't mean everything. A good dietitian should

- ✔ **Ask you what foods you like and what foods you don't like, and tailor your eating plan to these preferences.** A dietitian should not insist that you include or eliminate a particular food. If you love chocolate or detest broccoli, your dietitian should be able to work within those guidelines. (Just don't expect to eat three chocolate bars a day or to eliminate vegetables from your diet.)

- ✔ ***Not* attempt to sell you any dietary supplements or products.** If your dietitian tries to sell you anything, find a new one, pronto.

- ✔ **Help you make gradual changes in your diet.** If you suddenly stop eating fat or drastically cut back on calories, you'll feel deprived and probably give up.

- ✔ **Educate you.** A dietitian needs to do more than suggest that you eat oatmeal with blueberries for breakfast. She needs to explain why those foods make for a nutritious breakfast — and teach you the components of a good meal so that you can put one together on your own.

✔ **Urge you to be patient and set realistic goals.** If you tell your dietitian that you're going on a Caribbean cruise in a month and want to lose 16 pounds before you set sail, he or she should tell you to stop dreaming.

✔ **Assess your progress.** If you don't seem to be gaining energy or slimming down, your dietitian should re-examine your eating habits and figure out where you've gone wrong.

Keep a Training Log

Elsewhere in this chapter, we discuss ways of learning about weight training through other people, including authors, health club members, and online fitness enthusiasts. But you also can learn a great deal from *yourself* by keeping a diary of your weight training workouts. In Chapter 3, we describe in detail what information to record. Here's just some of what you can learn from your notes:

✔ **Whether you're making progress:** If you log how much weight you're lifting, you'll notice when you come to a plateau. If your Lat Pulldown has been stuck at 40 pounds for three months, perhaps it's time to make some changes in your routine.

✔ **Whether you're working out as often as you think you are:** Telling everyone you lift weights three times a week is impressive cocktail party banter, but it won't do you any good if it's not true. Your log is a good reality check.

✔ **Whether you're getting a balanced workout:** Even if you are lifting weights three times a week, you may be neglecting a muscle group or two. Perhaps you've been training your abdominals only once a week. If you glean this bit of information from your log, you might want to perform your ab exercises first for a while, to get yourself back into the habit of doing them.

Get Certified as a Trainer

This suggestion may seem too advanced for a weight training rookie. And indeed, we're not suggesting that after one month in the weight room, you're ready to become a trainer to the stars. However, you may want to keep certification in mind as a future option. At some point, you may find that you really dig weight training and you want to get a real education — either to improve your own workouts or to train other people.

For the typical fitness enthusiast, we recommend aiming for the Personal Trainer certification by the American Council on Exercise (www.ACEfitness.org). This certification is attainable to just about anyone who devotes time to studying, although if you're starting from ground zero, you'll need at least six months of preparation. This certification is in a different league than the high-level credentials offered by the American College of Sports Medicine and the National Strength Conditioning Association, which require at least a college degree in a fitness-related field and a more-than-working knowledge of important concepts.

You can purchase the organization's thorough, hardcover textbook, *The ACE Personal Trainer Manual,* for about $40. This hefty volume outlines everything you need to know to pass the test, although you may have to ask a knowledgeable trainer to clarify some of the information. The book covers the basics of anatomy, physiology, nutrition, injury prevention, weight training program design, and much more. The test itself costs about $150 and consists of more than 100 multiple-choice questions.

You must answer questions such as, "In the performance of a Standing Barbell Curl, the muscles of the hip, back and shoulders act as: a) stabilizers, b) co-contractors, c) antagonists, and d) prime movers." (Answer: a.) You can purchase a sample test for $15. If you're an experienced lifter but have no formal fitness education, give yourself at least a few months to study for this exam and bone up on your knowledge with a weekend prep course approved by ACE (Cost: about $100). You must have a valid CPR certificate in order to even take the exam.

Chapter 23

Ten Myths and Misconceptions about Weight Training

Human beings finally stopped believing the earth is flat and that you get warts from frogs. Now we'd like to push the human race yet another step forward by clearing up the misconceptions and misinformation related to weight training.

This is actually important stuff. If people had the straight dope on weight training, they'd suffer fewer injuries and see results more quickly, and they'd better understand what weight training can and cannot do for them. They'd be less likely to waste money on a schlocky product or buy into a bogus concept.

In this chapter we clear up ten of the most prevalent myths related to weight training. Many of these are based on what we like to call "gym science." The reasoning behind the myth may have a grain of truth or contain some official-sounding mumbo jumbo. But when you dig underneath the surface, even just a little, the theories don't hold weight.

Myth #1: You'll Get Huge Unless You Lift Light Weights

Perhaps the single most common weight training myth is that unless you lift very light weights, your muscles will bulk up to Mr. Olympia proportions. Suzanne recently worked out with a bike racer named Garth, who had the typical cyclist's physique: powerful legs and a narrow, wimpy upper body. When Suzanne took Garth to the weight room, he was apprehensive about lifting anything heavier than a shaving cream bottle. "I don't want to get too big," Garth said, to which Suzanne replied as politely as possible: Get real!

Here's the reality: The only way your muscles will burst the seams of your dress shirts is if you regularly lift extremely heavy weights — so heavy that you can perform only about three to five repetitions — *and* if you have a body type that will even allow for the development of mega muscles. Most of us — men and women — couldn't build enormous muscles even if we devoted several hours a day to this pursuit and we took illegal steroids.

The reason we're making such an issue of this myth is that it prevents many exercisers from pursuing an effective weight training program. If you lift dinky weights, you won't preserve or build enough bone density to help prevent osteoporosis. You won't get much in the way of muscle toning benefits, either. Some people perform 30 to 40 repetitions (or 10 repetitions with a weight so light they actually could perform 20 more). But when you can lift something 30 or 40 times, it doesn't challenge your bones or muscles enough to make a difference.

If you have a muscle-growth phobia, do one or two sets for each major muscle group. Use a weight heavy enough so that your last repetition — in the 8 to 15 range — is particularly challenging.

Myth #2: You're the Only One in the Gym Baffled by the Equipment

Trust us: Nobody is born knowing how to operate the Assisted Dip Machine or how to perform a Decline Chest Fly! Weight training equipment can baffle even the sharpest of minds. We consider Liz's mother to be a highly intelligent person, yet the first time she encountered the Triceps Extension Machine she sat down backwards. Both of us have made similar mistakes ourselves, and we like to think we know a thing or two about weight training.

It may *seem* like weight training is second nature to everyone at your gym, but that is not the case. Those who know how to use the equipment properly were *taught* to do so. And many of the people who swagger around with confidence actually have no clue what they are doing. We have seen large bodybuilders use machines in ways that would almost seem creative if they weren't so dangerous.

So, rather than stare in wonder at the machinery, simply ask a trainer to teach you how to use it. If you feel shy about asking a trainer, discretely observe other members using the equipment. Or, hire a trainer for a session or two to show you the ropes. Soon, *you'll* be one of the people that gym newcomers seek out for help.

Myth #3: Lifting Weights Is Dangerous

If Dr. Ruth tried to hoist a 300-pound barbell overhead, that would be dangerous — no argument there. But if you follow the safety precautions explained in Chapter 2, you will find that strength training is perfectly safe.

In fact, not only is only is strength training safe, but pumping iron can actually *prevent* injuries. With stronger muscles, tendons, ligaments, and bones, you're less likely to fall and sprain an ankle or fracture a wrist. And if you do fall, a strong body can limit the damage.

The key to safe weight training is good technique. Most injuries happen when someone uses poor form, either because they were lifting too much weight or not paying attention. Chapter 24 describes in detail ten common mistakes that frequently lead to injury. If you avoid these mistakes and use common sense, you're very likely to remain injury-free.

Myth #4: Thigh Exercises Will Slim Your Thighs, and Ab Exercises Will Whittle Your Middle

We wish we could afford to purchase prime-time TV commercials that would set the public straight on this issue. The truth is you cannot melt the fat off of any particular body part by performing exercises that target that area. Abdominal exercises will strengthen your abs, but they will do nothing to reduce the layer of fat sitting on top of your abdominal muscles. The Butt Blaster will tone your tush, but it will not diminish the size of your derriere.

There simply is no such thing as spot reducing. In other words, you can't selectively zap fat from your abs, thighs, arms, or any other body part. In fact, the calories you burn from doing abdominal crunches may help you lose weight in your arms if that is how your body is genetically programmed.

Even though you can't spot reduce, you *can* strengthen and firm up specific areas. Stronger, well-toned muscles always look better than weak, flabby ones, even if there happens to be a bit of extra fat covering them.

Myth #5: The Best Trainers Are Those with the Best Bodies

At Suzanne's gym, there is a trainer whose muscles are so perfectly sculpted that he looks like a replica of Michelangelo's David. Gym members flock to this guy, hoping — presumably — that he can help them develop the physique he has built for himself. Yet when Suzanne observes this trainer with clients, he barely pays attention to them. Often he is watching college basketball on the club's TV while his clients perform their exercises with atrocious form.

Just because a trainer has a phenomenal body doesn't mean that he has good teaching skills or the knowledge to tailor a program to the more genetically challenged clients who hire him. Screen your trainers carefully, following the tips we offer in Chapter 5.

Myth #6: Lifting Weights Won't Help You Lose Weight

Wrong! Lifting weights is an essential part of a weight-loss program. Developing muscle is the only way to boost your metabolism, which can help you lose fat and keep it off. When you lose weight by dieting alone — or by combining a diet plan with cardiovascular exercise — you tend to lose muscle along with fat. With less muscle, your metabolism slows down, making it easy for you to gain back the weight. However, when you add weight training to the mix, you preserve muscle mass as you shed fat.

If you lift weights two or three times a week, you're likely to gain about 1 pound of muscle per month for about six months, after which the rate of increase slows down. Adding muscle is well worth the effort: For every 3 pounds of muscle you build, research shows, you increase your resting metabolic rate by about 7 percent. So if your body burns 1,200 calories per day (not counting exercise or any other movement), you'd burn an extra 84 calories per day.

Myth #7: There's One Best Weight Training Program

Many exercisers perform three sets of 10 repetitions for each exercise as if that routine had been written into federal law. Others blindly follow the programs of their favorite athletes or models, as described in fitness magazines.

In reality, there is no ideal program — and no one program that works best for everyone. There are countless ways to build strength and firm up your body, as we explain in Chapters 15 and 16. No matter what you read in magazines, see on infomercials, or hear from your best friend, weight training is part art, part science. You've got to fiddle around with your program until it suits your goals, your body type, and your time schedule. Of course, you've got to stay within the parameters we give you in this book; if your ideal program involves lifting once a month, that's not going to cut it.

There are so many different training techniques that researchers will never be able to compare them all. So try 'em all and see which seem to work best for you. Keeping a weight training log and periodically testing your strength (see Chapter 3) can help you determine if your program is working.

Myth #8: Stretching Is a Good Warm-up for Weight Lifting

We strongly believe in warming up for weight training, but stretching is not the way to do it. Before lifting weights, do at least a few minutes of easy cardiovascular exercise such as brisk walking or stationary cycling. These types of activities increase blood flow to your muscles and literally warm them up so that they will be more pliable.

You can stretch your muscles after your warm-up or after your weight training session; we prefer stretching at the end of our entire workout because it's a great way to relax and transition into the rest of our day. Another option is to stretch during the rest periods between weight training sets. This way you won't be tempted to blow off stretching at the end of your workout.

Although you do need to warm up before you stretch, there is one exception to this rule: active isolated stretching. This form of stretching, described in detail in Chapter 19, calls for you to tighten the muscle opposite the one you are stretching and then stretching the target muscle for two seconds. You repeat this tighten-stretch combination 8 to 15 times before moving on to the next stretch. Active isolated stretching is acceptable as a warm-up because it is designed to increase blood flow and raise the temperature of a muscle. You don't have the same risk of injury that you do when you hold a stretch position for 10 to 30 seconds as you do in traditional stretching.

Myth #9: Free Weights Are for Muscleheads and Machines Are for Beginners

Many novice lifters think the free weight room of a gym is some kind of special club for bodybuilders and steroid-pumping football players. In reality, everyone is welcome to work out there, and novices should make a point of learning to use the equipment.

Sure, dumbbells and barbells are a bit more risky than weight machines, but if you follow the simple safety precautions explained in Chapter 2, you should have no problem. Free weights enable you to do dozens, if not hundreds, more exercises than you can do with machines, and the variety will help you stay motivated. You may find that you prefer certain movements on machines and other movements on free weights. So, unless you have certain physical limitations — such as extreme muscle imbalances or poor coordination — we recommend that you mix free weights into your weight training program.

We also recommend a mix for advanced lifters, too. Some weight room veterans develop inflated egos and think their muscles will instantly shrink if they use equipment that involves a pin and a stack of weight plates. But there are many exercises — such as the Seated Row and Leg Curl — that simply cannot be duplicated with free weights.

Myth #10: Not Everyone Needs to Strength Train

Some people may think they're "not the weight training type." Perhaps they enjoy hiking or biking or tennis and feel that they are getting plenty of exercise already. Maybe they feel they are in tip-top shape because they can run a marathon or cycle 100 miles without getting tired.

But cardio exercise is only part of the equation. As scientists learn more about aging and the human body, it's clear that muscle and bone strength are just as important for good health and quality of life as a fit heart and lungs. There simply is no substitute for strength training, which is the only way to slow down the inevitable deterioration of muscle and bone as you age. Walking, jogging, and other "weight bearing" activities do help preserve bone, but they are not enough.

We believe that every adult should pursue some sort of strength training program, whether it's at home or at the gym, whether it's a one-set routine twice a week or a periodized split routine six days a week (for an explanation of all that gobbledygook, see Chapter 16).

You may have to nudge yourself to start a program, but once you get into the habit of lifting weights, you'll feel so strong and energetic that you'll never want to quit.

Chapter 24

Ten Major Weight Lifting Goofs

*W*e witness some awfully strange things in weight rooms. Not long ago we saw a guy attempting the Shoulder Shrug (see Chapter 8), but instead of shrugging his shoulders, he simply bobbed his head back and forth. We saw another guy performing the Lat Pulldown (see Chapter 8) in a way that resembled an attempt to slice a giant wedge of cheese. And we saw a woman doing some martial arts-type punching movements with 8-pound weights in her hands. One wrong move and she would have flown into the mirror. Some of these mistakes simply make the exercises ineffective; other goofs can result in serious injury. Avoid the following ten weight training mistakes.

Cheating Your Abs

To listen to abdominal gadget infomercials, you'd think that it was impossible to perform an abdominal crunch correctly without some sort of machinery. The truth is, you are perfectly capable of crunching correctly without any equipment.

The wrong way to crunch

Many people complain that crunches cause neck pain. They do — but only if you yank your head and neck instead of lifting your torso by the power of your abdominals. Another mistake is lifting your torso straight off the floor, rather than curling it upward. How do you know whether you're curling or just lifting? Do the Basic Crunch, described in Chapter 12, and freeze at the top of the movement. Your torso should be in a slightly rounded, almost C-shaped position. A third Crunch error: forgetting to breathe. See photo A of Figure 24-1.

The right way to crunch

To avoid jerking your neck, place your hands behind your head, but do *not* lace your fingers together. Hold your elbows out wide, but not too wide. Your arm placement is correct if you can barely see the points of your elbows out of the corners of your eyes. As you curl up, keep your head, neck, and arms frozen in position. When you curl the right way, your head, neck, and lower back feel nearly weightless. Finally, breathe correctly. As you lift your torso, exhale forcefully through your mouth; as you lower, inhale through your nose. See photo B of Figure 24-1.

Figure 24-1:
As you curl up, keep your head, neck, and arms frozen in position.

Squatting Too Far

The Squat strengthens virtually every muscle in your lower body: your butt, front thighs, rear thighs, and lower back. The Squat even improves your sense of balance. That's pretty good for a move that essentially mimics getting in and out of a chair. But if you don't do this exercise correctly — and many people don't — you're asking for injury.

The wrong way to squat

We know one guy who would spread his legs practically into the splits and lower his butt all the way to the floor. Then he'd pop back up into a standing position so forcefully that he was close to being airborne. After a few months, this guy began showing up at the gym with ace bandages wrapped around his knees. Small wonder! Another common error is leaning too far forward, letting your knees shoot out past your toes. Two other problems: dropping your knees inward or letting them bow to the outside. These mistakes put incredible pressure on the delicate tendons, ligaments, and cartilage that hold the knee in place. See photo A of Figure 24-2.

The right way to squat

Start with your feet hip-width apart and point your toes either straight ahead or angled slightly outward, whichever foot position you find more comfortable. As you squat down, your knees should travel in a straight line, in the direction that your toes are pointed. Never squat so low that your legs are lower than parallel to the ground. When you stand up, press through your heels, and finish with your legs straight but relaxed. Snapping your knees places pressure on your knees and sends your lower back into an extreme arch. See photo B of Figure 24-2.

Don't lean forward; instead, stand up tall.

Figure 24-2:
Never squat so low that your legs are lower than parallel to the ground.

A) B)

Arching Your Back

We recently heard a trainer approach a guy who had just finished bench-pressing and ask, "Hey, is your name Archie?" "No," the guy replied. "Why do you ask?" "Because you arched your back so high off the bench that a Mack truck could have driven under it."

The wrong way to bench press

Some people figure that anything they can do to pile on poundage — including arching their back and squirming around — is fair game. In reality, how much weight you can hoist above your chest is not necessarily related to how strong your chest muscles are. When you arch your back, you simply increase your mechanical advantage (and your injury risk); more muscles are pitching in to move that bar upward. We know one guy who was convinced that the arch was an essential part of the Bench Press. We had to produce several anatomy textbooks before we could convince him that we had not fabricated this bit of information. See Figure 24-3.

Figure 24-3: Keep your back in contact with the bench throughout the exercise.

The right way to bench press

Keep your back in contact with the bench throughout the exercise. You need not force your back into an unnaturally flat position — it's okay to have a small, natural arch. If you can't plant your feet flat on the floor because the bench is too high, place your feet on the bench.

Lowering Your Elbows Too Far

We hate to pick on chest exercises again, but they're often the victim of multiple mistakes. The mistake we discuss in this section applies to the Dumbbell Chest Press, the Bench Press, and the Chest Fly, all described in Chapter 9.

The wrong way to lower your arms

When doing chest exercises, some people drop their elbows so low that they practically touch the floor. The resulting stretch in your chest muscles may feel good, but at this point your chest muscles are in danger of snapping, much like a rubber band that has been pulled too far. Also, when you lower your arms too far, you shove the head of your big arm bone, the humerus, way up into your shoulder socket. The rotator cuff muscles and nearby ligaments and tendons must twist themselves in unspeakable ways to accommodate this unnatural position. You may not feel pain immediately, but sooner or later, all of this twisting may catch up with you. See photo A of Figure 24-4.

The right way to lower your arms

When you perform the Dumbbell Chest Press, Bench Press, or Chest Fly, stop when your elbows are slightly below chest level. Depending on the way your body is built, the bar may or may not touch your chest on the Bench Press. See photo B of Figure 24-4.

Figure 24-4:
When you perform chest exercises, stop when your elbows are slightly below chest level.

A)
B)

Pulling a Fast One

Pulling a bar down to your chest isn't as simple as it might appear. To give your back muscles a good workout and to protect yourself from injury, you need to make sure the bar travels in a specific path. Here are tips for performing a perfect Lat Pulldown (described in Chapter 8).

The wrong way to pull down a bar

One common mistake is to pull the bar straight down toward your lap, rather toward your chest — a mistake that places your shoulder and rotator cuff muscles in jeopardy. A second error is pulling the bar down unevenly; one end of the bar may be a good six inches lower than the other. But perhaps our biggest pet peeve is leaning waaaaay back as you pull the bar down and then rocking forward as the bar travels upward. Generating this type of momentum helps you move lots of weight but doesn't improve your back strength. See photo A of Figure 24-5.

The right way to pull down a bar

Choose a weight that's challenging but not so heavy that you feel like you're dangling off the end of a helicopter ladder. Sit down — taking the bar with you — and wedge your thighs under the thigh bar. Then lean just a *few* inches backward. Pull the bar toward the top of your chest, lifting your chest to meet the bar. Take your time so that the bar remains level throughout the movement. Don't sway back and forth: Rock and roll is dead here. When you've completed your set, stand up and gently deposit the bar back where it belongs. If you open your hands and let the weight plates come crashing down, we will personally hunt you down and give you forty snaps with a wet towel. See photo B of Figure 24-5.

Figure 24-5:
Don't sway
back and
forth as you
pull down
the bar.
Rock and
roll is dead
here.

A)   B)

Sticking Your Butt Up

The Leg Curl, described in Chapter 13, is the most popular hamstring (rear thigh) exercise; unfortunately, performing this exercise incorrectly is also quite popular.

The wrong way to use the Leg Curl Machine

Watch people do this exercise and you'll see that as they kick their legs toward their butt, their hips lift off the support pad, and their butt sticks up about two inches. This is a subtle mistake, but it's a sneaky way of taking work away from your hamstrings and transferring the effort to your hip muscles. See photo A of Figure 24-6.

The right way to use the Leg Curl Machine

To prevent your hips from popping off the pad, raise your upper thighs just a hair off the pad before you bend your knees for the kick upward. In this position, you feel your hamstrings working a lot harder. See photo B of Figure 24-6.

A)

B)

Figure 24-6: Don't let your hips pop off the support pad.

Exaggerating the Row

If you sit hunched over in a chair most of the day, you're a good candidate for goofing up the Seated Cable Row, described in Chapter 8.

The wrong way to row

One common mistake is to round your back or allow your shoulders and neck to droop forward. This slumped posture puts your neck and lower back in a pressure cooker. Another problem: leaning way back like someone involved in a game of tug of war. See photo A in Figure 24-7.

The right way to row

Sit up tall with your abdominals pulled in. Your upper body, from the top of your head to your belly button, should be perpendicular to the floor. Bend your knees as much as you need to in order to maintain good posture. Allow your arms to stretch fully out in front of you without losing that perpendicular posture. Then when you pull the bar toward your chest, sit up even taller and bring your hands into your body, just below your chest. Squeeze your shoulder blades together as you go, and drive your elbows straight back behind you. See photo B in Figure 24-7.

Figure 24-7: Don't lean way back like someone involved in a game of tug of war.

Carrying a Weight Plate Too Casually

We often listen to exercisers gripe that their backs hurt after they perform the Bench Press. Yet when we go to check out their technique, it looks impeccable. We're baffled — until these people pop off the bench, slide the weight plates off the bar, and put them back on the weight tree. Ah ha! Mystery solved. It's not the Bench Press or any other exercise that's giving them an aching back; it's the way they carry around those big, heavy weight plates. (See Chapter 1 for descriptions of weight plates and weight trees.)

The wrong way to carry a weight plate

Sometimes we see people carrying weight plates around the gym floor as if the plates were super-size Frisbees. Other lifters tuck plates under their arms as if they're clutching a purse. Or, they hold the plate on the edge of their finger tips with a straight arm and locked elbow, as if they're carrying a bowling ball. Carrying around a lot of weight with one hand tied behind your back may be the ultimate display of macho, but this sort of behavior puts your body in a terribly unbalanced position, even if you're a big, strapping fellow. Your elbows and shoulders bear more of the burden than they're designed to handle. See photo A of Figure 24-8.

The right way to carry a weight plate

Hold the plate close to your chest with both hands. Stand as close as you can to the bar, line up the hole in the plate with the bar, and then slide the plate on. Don't just extend your arms out straight and toss the plate like you're performing some sort of ring-tossing circus act. When you pick up a plate off the floor or from a low rung on a weight tree, bring the weight in close to your chest, and stand up. All this advice goes for light weights, too. See photo B of Figure 24-8.

Figure 24-8: Always hold weight plates close to your chest with both hands.

A)   B)

Finishing an Exercise the Wrong Way

Liz was spotting a woman who was performing a textbook-perfect set of the Dumbbell Chest Fly (see Chapter 9). The set was truly a thing of beauty — until right after her final repetition. Suddenly she extended her arms straight out, lowered the weights toward the floor, opened her hands and let the weights roll off her palms. She then jerked herself upright and popped up off the bench. Overall, she managed to make about a half dozen mistakes on movements that weren't even part of the actual exercise. Realize that you can't let up your guard until you have safely gotten yourself out of the exercise position.

Sitting up the wrong way

In this book, we show you many exercises that you perform while lying on your back on the floor or on a weight bench. When you sit up after doing these exercises, don't jerk straight back up into a sitting position, especially if you're holding weights. Another no-no: bringing your arms straight out to the sides and dropping the weights, or twisting to either side to drop a weight. See photo A of Figure 24-9.

Sitting up the right way

To protect your lower back when you get up off the floor, roll to the side and then use both arms to push up into a sitting position. Or hug one knee into your chest and gently rock yourself up. After performing an exercise involving dumb-bells, such as the Chest Fly, bring the weights down into your chest, and then roll up. (When you begin the exercise, do the opposite: Bring the weights into your chest and rock yourself back onto the bench.) See photo B of Figure 24-9.

Figure 24-9:
After an exercise, don't jerk straight back up into a sitting position, especially if you're holding weights.

A)   B)

Spotting Too Much — Or Not Enough

Most weight training mistakes you make don't affect anyone but you. However, if you mess up while spotting someone, you may be putting your friend (or ex-friend) at risk for injury. Or, at the very least, you may be depriving your buddy of an enjoyable and effective workout. When acting as a spotter, you need to walk that fine line between not helping enough and getting too involved.

The wrong way to spot

Don't zone out while you're spotting someone. This is not the time to contemplate peacekeeping solutions in the Middle East. If your buddy poops out in the middle of a set and you're even a split second too late to grab the weight, your friend may get clunked on the head, chest, or some other body part. Or your spottee may tear a muscle or ligament while trying to do your job for you (that is, save the weight from crashing). See Figure 24-10.

Some spotters take their job too seriously. They clutch onto the bar and practically perform the exercise *for* their spottees. Too much help is frustrating for the people being spotted; it denies them the glory of completing repetitions on their own.

Figure 24-10: When acting as a spotter, walk that fine line between not helping enough and getting too involved.

The right way to spot

Tune out everything in the universe other than your spottee. Put your hands in the right place (see Chapter 2 for details) and watch your buddy like a soldier guarding the Vatican. Don't wait for your spottee to scream, "Dude! Where *are* you?!"

At the same time, don't hover over your charge like a doting grandmother. Give the lifter the freedom to lift the weight under his or her own power. Offer only as much assistance as is necessary.

Chapter 25

Ten (G-Rated) Things You Can Do with Latex Rubber

In This Chapter

▶ Excellent reasons to invest in exercise bands

▶ Tips on using bands safely

▶ Ten great band exercises

*W*hen it comes to firming up your muscles, a strip of latex rubber is a lot more useful than you may expect. You're not going to build a Mr. Universe-type body by pulling on an exercise band, but you can develop a surprising amount of strength and muscle tone. In this chapter, we present ten band exercises and offer tips for using bands safely.

Bands on the Run

Bands are particularly helpful if you want to keep up your strength work when you travel. You can't very well lug around a complete set of chrome dumbbells in your suitcase. (And we hate to imagine how an airport metal detector would react.) Even if you're booked into a hotel that has a gym, we suggest that you bring along a band.

Liz recently stayed in a luxury hotel that boasted a state-of-the art weight room in its brochure. After she arrived, she found a broken-down multigym. Luckily, she had a few of her trusty exercise bands tucked in her suitcase.

Make sure that you use a band designed for exercising. Don't just grab anything made of rubber. Halloween masks, strips of old tire, and office rubber bands are not suitable for working out. Besides, exercise bands cost next to nothing — you can purchase a set of three bands for less than $10 from manufacturers such as Spri, DynaBand, LifeLine, and StretchCordz or from catalogs such as *The Complete Guide to Exercise Videos,* available from Collage Video Specialties (call 800-433-6769).

If you really want to get fancy, you can buy a band with cords or plastic handles attached. The handles make it easier to hold an end in one or both hands, such as when you perform the Band Biceps Curl, described later in this chapter. However, the handles aren't practical for exercises (such as the Band Butt Blaster) that require tying your band in a circle. Because bands are so inexpensive, we recommend investing in several. Some are flat and wide; others resemble surgical tubes. In general, the shorter and/or the thicker the band, the harder it is to pull and the more resistance it provides.

Tips on Using an Exercise Band

Experiment with different shapes, sizes, and thicknesses to determine which band you like best for each exercise. Have all your bands within reach as you begin your workout so that you don't need to waste time hunting under the couch for the right one. Here are some tips for working out with bands:

- Check frequently for holes and tears by holding your band up to a light. If you find even the slightest tear, replace the band immediately.

- If an exercise calls for you to hold the end in each hand (and your band doesn't have handles), loop the ends *loosely* around the palms of your hands. Leave a little slack so that, as you pull on the band, it doesn't tighten up around your hand and cut off the circulation to your fingers.

- If an exercise calls for you to stand on the band with your feet together, place both feet on the center of the band and then step one foot out to the side so that you have about six inches of band between your feet. This prevents the band from sliding out from under you.

- Make sure that the band is securely in place before each set. Liz was demonstrating the Band Row exercise to a class when the band slipped off her feet and popped in her face. Ouch! Without missing a beat, she informed the class that this was how *not* to use a band and went on to warn them about the dangers of misusing a band. She would have gotten away with it, too, if the band hadn't slipped off and popped her in the face again 20 minutes later while she was demonstrating another exercise.

- Long-term care: If you use the flat bands frequently and on sweaty skin, periodically rinse them in clean water, towel or drip dry, and store in a zip lock bag with a little baby powder. Just shake off the powder before your next use.

Ten Excellent Band Exercises

Integrate your favorite band exercises into your regular weight training routine. If you plan to use a band when you travel, practice these exercises beforehand so that you don't waste time trying to figure out what to do. As with all other resistance exercises, do 8 to 15 repetitions per set and do at least one set per muscle group. (We tell you which muscle group each band exercise strengthens.) When you can perform 15 repetitions easily, make the exercise tougher by using a shorter or thicker band.

Band Squat

The Band Squat is an excellent way to add resistance to the Squat in lieu of free weights. This exercise strengthens your butt, quadriceps, and hamstrings. Use caution if you're prone to **lower back, hip,** or **knee** pain.

Getting Set: Hold the end of a band in each hand and stand on top of the center of the band so that your feet are hip-width apart. Clasp your hands together and then raise them in front of your chest so that your elbows point down and the band wraps around behind your elbows. Stand tall with your abdominals pulled in and shoulders square. See photo A in Figure 25-1.

The Exercise: Sit back and down, as if you're sitting into a chair. Bend your knees and lower yourself as far as you can without leaning your upper body more than a few inches forward. Never go lower than the point at which your thighs are parallel to the floor, and don't allow your knees to move out in front of your toes. After you feel your upper body fold forward over your thighs, stand back up, pushing through your heels and taking care not to lock your knees. Throughout the exercise, keep your head up and your eyes focused directly in front of you. See photo B in Figure 25-1.

Figure 25-1:
Never go lower than the point at which your thighs are parallel to the floor.

A) B)

Don't let your knees shoot past your toes.

Band Butt Blaster

JOINT CAUTION

The Band Butt Blaster does a better job of working your butt than many of the butt machines you find in gyms. Use caution if you have **lower back** problems.

Getting Set: Tie a foot-long band in a circle and place it around both feet at the instep. Next, kneel on your elbows and knees. Flex your left foot. Pull your abdominals in. See photo A of Figure 25-2.

The Exercise: Keeping your knee bent, lift your right leg and raise your knee to hip height. Slowly lower your leg back down, taking care not to let the band go slack. Your knee should almost, but not quite, touch the floor between repetitions. Do the same number of repetitions with each leg. See photo B of Figure 25-2.

A)

Figure 25-2:
Your knee should almost, but not quite, touch the floor between repetitions.

B)

Band Outer Thigh Lift

The Band Outer Thigh Lift is a challenging outer thigh exercise. Make sure that you keep your abdominals pulled in to protect your **lower back.**

Getting Set: Tie an exercise band (1- to 2-feet long) in a circle. Lie on the floor on your left side with your legs a few inches in front of you, knees slightly bent, and head resting on your outstretched arm. Place the band around your thighs, just above your knees. Bend your right arm and place your palm on the floor in front of your chest for support. Align your right hip directly over your left hip and pull your abdominals in so that your back isn't arched. See photo A of Figure 25-3.

The Exercise: Keeping your knee slightly bent, raise your right leg until your foot reaches shoulder height. Hold the position for a moment, and then slowly lower your leg back down, keeping tension on the band the entire time. Switch sides, and do the same number of repetitions with your left leg. See photo B of Figure 25-3.

A)

Figure 25-3:
Pull your abdominals in so that your back isn't arched.

B)

Wrap the band above your knee.

Band Calf Press

The Band Calf Press targets your calf muscles. As a bonus, it also strengthens your shins, upper back, and biceps, especially if you keep tension on the band as your toes move both toward you and away from you.

Getting Set: Holding one end of a flat band in each hand at waist level, sit on the floor with your legs straight out in front of you and wrap the band around the ball of your right foot. Bend your right knee slightly and lift it up in the air. Sit up straight and bend your left knee if you want to. Just don't round your back. See photo A of Figure 25-4.

The Exercise: Point your toe as you pull back on the band. Hold this position a moment and, while maintaining your pull on the band, flatten your foot and pull your toes back as far as you can. Complete the set and then do the exercise with your left foot. See photo B of Figure 25-4.

A)

Figure 25-4:
While maintaining your pull on the band, flatten your foot and pull your toes back as far as you can.

B)

Band Lat Pulldown

The Band Lat Pulldown mimics the Lat Pulldown you do on a machine. Like the machine version, the Band Lat Pulldown works your upper back muscles with some emphasis on your shoulders and biceps. Be especially careful with form if you're prone to **neck** discomfort.

Getting Set: Sit in a chair or stand with your feet hip-width apart and hold an end of the exercise band in each hand. Raise your arms over your head with your left palm facing in and your right palm facing forward just above shoulder level. Your elbows should be slightly bent. Stand tall with your abdominals pulled in and your knees relaxed. See photo A of Figure 25-5.

The Exercise: Keep your left arm still. Bend your right elbow down and out to the side, as if you're shooting an arrow straight up into the air. Keeping your wrist straight, pull the band until your right hand is to the side of your right shoulder, the band is tight, and your right elbow points down. Slowly straighten your arm. Switch sides, alternating arms as you complete the set. See photo B of Figure 25-5.

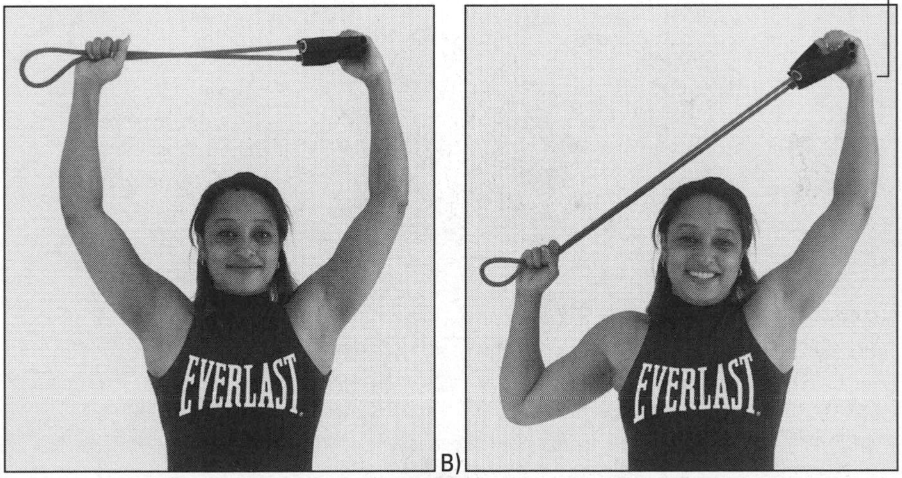

Keep your wrist straight.

Figure 25-5:
With your left arm still, bend your right elbow down and out to the side, as if you're shooting an arrow straight up into the air.

A)

B)

Band Push-up

The Band Push-up is a unique way to make the Push-up more challenging. This exercise strengthens your chest, shoulders, triceps, and abdominals. If you have **lower back, neck,** or **elbow** problems, you may want to skip this Push-up variation.

Getting Set: For this exercise, use a band that's at least three feet long. Wrap the band around your back and over your shoulder blades, and hold an end in each hand. Lie face down on the floor with your elbows bent and your palms on the floor in front of your shoulders. Bend your knees and cross your ankles. Tilt your forehead toward the floor and pull your abdominals in so your back doesn't sag. See photo A of Figure 25-6.

The Exercise: Straighten your arms and press your body up. (Adjust the band so it's taut when your arms are straight.) Slowly bend your elbows and lower yourself down until your elbows are just above your shoulders. Your chest may or may not touch the floor, depending on the length of your arms and the size of your chest. See photo B of Figure 25-6.

Figure 25-6: Lower yourself down until your elbows are just above your shoulders. Whether your chest touches the floor depends on your arm length and chest size.

A)

B)

Band One-arm Shoulder Press

The Band One-arm Shoulder Press strengthens your entire shoulder muscle, with additional emphasis on your triceps. Pay special attention to your form if you have a history of **lower back** or **neck** problems.

Getting Set: Stand on top of one end of the band near the handle so that your feet are hip-width apart. Hold the other handle in your right hand and place your left hand on your hip, palms facing forward. Raise your right hand to shoulder height so that your elbow is bent, your upper arm is parallel to the floor, and your palm is facing forward. Keep your head centered between your shoulders, pull your abdominals in, and relax your knees. See photo A of Figure 25-7.

The Exercise: Straighten your arm overhead and then slowly bend your arms until your elbows are slightly below shoulder height, but no lower. After you've completed a set with your right arm, do an equal number of reps with your left. See photo B of Figure 25-7.

Figure 25-7:
Bend your arms until your elbows are slightly below shoulder height but no lower.

A)   B)

Keep your knees relaxed.

Band External and Internal Rotation

The Band Internal and External Rotation is very effective at strengthening the rotator cuff muscles.

External Rotation, Getting Set: Tie a band around a stable object. Hold one end of the band in your hand with your palm facing in. Bend your elbow 90 degrees. See photo A in Figure 25-8.

External Rotation, The Exercise: Keeping your elbow in place, move your hand a few inches away from you to increase tension in the band and then slowly move it back to the starting position. See photo B in Figure 25-8.

Internal Rotation, Getting Set: Turn around and hold the band in your other hand. Hold your arm as in the External Rotation. Pull your arm toward you to create more tension. See photo C in Figure 25-8.

Internal Rotation, The Exercise: Pull your arm toward you to create more tension. Move your arm out again. See photo D in Figure 25-8.

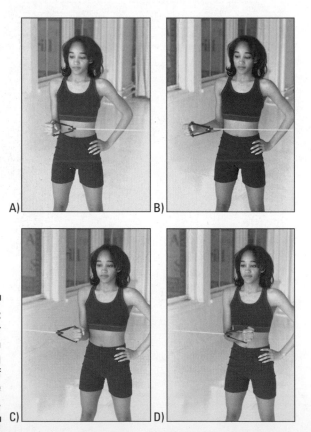

Figure 25-8: Keep your elbow in place during both of these exercises.

Band Double Biceps Curl

The Band Double Biceps Curl, an excellent imitation of the Barbell Biceps Curl, targets your biceps. Use caution if you're prone to **elbow** injuries.

Getting Set: With an end of the band in each hand and palms facing up, stand on top of the center of your exercise band so that your feet are hip-width apart. Straighten your arms down at your sides. Stand tall with your abdominals pulled in and your knees relaxed. See photo A of Figure 25-9.

The Exercise: Bend your elbows and curl both arms up until your hands are in front of your shoulders. Don't permit your elbows to travel forward as you curl. The band should be taut at the top of the movement. Slowly straighten your arms. See photo B of Figure 25-9.

Don't lean back as you curl your arms.

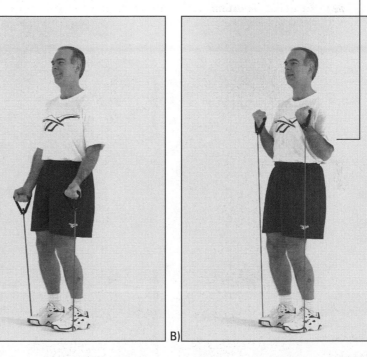

Figure 25-9:
Don't let your elbows travel forward as you curl.

A)   B)

Band Triceps Extension

As you might guess, the Band Triceps Extension strengthens your triceps muscle. Go easy on this one if you experience **elbow** discomfort.

Getting Set: While holding onto one end of the band with your left hand, stand with your feet as wide as your hips and place your left palm over the front of your right shoulder. Hold the other end of the band in your right hand with your palm facing inward. Bend your right elbow so that it's at waist level and pointing behind you. You can lean slightly forward from your hips if you find that position comfortable, but always keep your abdominals in and your knees relaxed. See photo A of Figure 25-10.

The Exercise: Keeping your elbow stationary, straighten your right arm out behind you so that the band gets tighter as you go, but don't allow your elbow to lock. Then bend your elbow so that your hand travels back to your waist. Reposition the band to work your left triceps. See photo B of Figure 25-10.

Figure 25-10:
Keeping your elbow stationary, straighten your right arm out behind you so that the band gets tighter as you go.

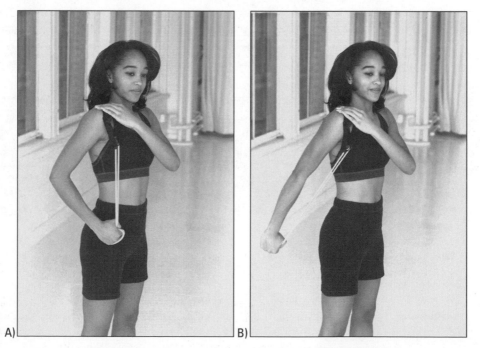

A)   B)

Chapter 26

Ten Weight Training Deals and Duds

· ·

In This Chapter
▶ Five great weight training investments
▶ Five weight training rip-offs

· ·

Suppose that a used car salesman walked up to you wearing a leisure suit, gold chains, and a pinky ring and said, "I've got a '92 Mercedes in mint condition for $999 — it's a steal. It's a deal!" Would you whip out your checkbook? We think not. And yet millions of Americans open their wallets right up when infomercial personalities and magazine ads make equally dubious offers for muscle-toning gadgets. All the same warning signs may be there — the outlandish claims, the cheesy outfits, the smarmy smiles — and yet for many people, wishful thinking seems to overcome good judgment.

Fortunately, not every weight training product is less reliable than your average psychic hotline. In fact, a number of them are quite clever and useful. The good gadgets can make your workouts safer and more fun and help you get better results. In this chapter, we describe some of the best and worst of weight training products and services.

Five Great Weight Training Values

Throughout this book we mention some of our favorite weight training bargains — videos, health club memberships, and fitness magazine subscriptions, to name a few. We've chosen to highlight the following investments because they bring an exceptional return on your money.

An adjustable weight bench

Although you can perform dozens of exercises with dumbbells alone, a weight bench gives you far more versatility. With a flat weight bench, you can perform exercises while sitting, kneeling, or lying on your back. An adjustable weight bench is an even better option, allowing you to work your muscles from even more angles. An adjustable bench is like a padded chair with a seat back that you can slide down so that you're leaning back or even lying all the way flat on your back. Some adjustable benches, like those made by Tuff Stuff, also adjust to a decline position so that you're lying with your head below your feet. The decline feature isn't as important as the incline; if you opt for a bench that doesn't decline, don't lose too much sleep over it.

In addition to Tuff Stuff, high-quality brands of home weight benches include Hoist, York, and Icarian. Some benches come with stanchions (either fixed or detachable) to hold a barbell. If you have a choice, go with detachable stanchions; otherwise, make sure that the upright bars don't impede your motion when you perform dumbbell exercises. See Chapter 4 for more tips on buying a weight bench.

Hand protection

Weight training does nice things to your muscles but isn't particularly kind to the skin on your palms. Calluses and blisters are common among people who lift weights regularly. The following two products can prevent these annoying problems:

  ✔ **Weight lifting gloves:** You've probably seen people in the gym wearing gloves with padded palms and the finger tips cut off. Not only do these gloves protect the skin on your palms, but they also give you a firmer grip on the dumbbells, bars, and handles. If you plan to do more than a quickie machine workout, we recommend investing in a pair.

By the way, bicycling gloves, which also have the fingertips cut off, aren't a good substitute because they have too much padding. Also, the fingers are shorter than those on most weight training gloves, so the fabric tends to dig into the palm side of your knuckles when you grab onto a weight.

Some hard-core weight lifters wear gardening gloves instead of those designed for weight training. Although these gloves make you look like a telephone repair person, they cost around three bucks and can adequately protect your hands. However, if you don't cut off the fingertips, your hands may feel too hot.

✔ **Hand pads:** You place these flexible neoprene pads in your palms and then grab onto a weight. The pads act as a sort of pot holder between your hands and the weights so that you don't lose your grip and develop calluses. These pads cost around $4 a pair and are sold at many fitness equipment stores and gyms. Are they better than gloves? It's a matter of personal preference, just as some people like oven mitts while others prefer pot holders for grabbing a hot casserole out of the oven.

A personal trainer

We know people who have been performing the Bench Press incorrectly for 20 years because they didn't learn to do it properly in the first place. Some of these people have suffered injuries related to their sloppy technique. But if you dare suggest that they alter their form, they respond with an indignant "I know what I'm doing — I've been lifting weights for 20 years."

To make sure that you develop good weight lifting habits, we suggest that you begin your weight training career with at least three personal training sessions. Expect to pay $30 to $75 per session. A qualified and gifted trainer can get you over the learning curve in a hurry and, in just a few sessions, teach you technique tips that last a lifetime. You may want to check in with the trainer three or four times a year for a technique tune-up and creative ideas for updating your routine. Read Chapter 5 for tips on finding a qualified trainer.

Exercise tubing

As much as we love dumbbells and a free weight bench, they're kind of heavy to lug with you to the train station or the airport. Exercise tubing fits easily into your carry-on bag or your desk drawer at work and gives you a better strength workout than you might imagine. You can buy a decent set of tubing for under $10; the wide flat bands are sold at sporting goods and exercise equipment specialty stores for pennies a yard. Even if you go the super-deluxe route, you'd be hard pressed to spend more than $100. If tubing is your primary weight training equipment or you use it frequently when you travel or you can't get to the gym, we recommend buying a band set with several attachments. Look for a kit with a hook that fastens over a doorknob, under the doorway, or in the edge of the doorway. This attachment will increase your exercise options tenfold. You can mimic many of the exercises performed on a cable crossover machine because you can attach one end up very high or very low. For more tips on purchasing tubing, flip to Chapter 4. In Chapter 25, we show you an entire tubing workout.

A weight-training diary

How much has your Bench Press increased over the last three months? Are you giving your hamstrings and your quadriceps equal time on the weight machines? Can you squat more weight when you warm up with two sets or three?

If you have to search your brain for these answers, your weight training routine probably isn't as effective as it could be. Tracking the details of your workouts provides you with valuable information and feedback.

A training log keeps you honest. You may brag to your coffee shop buddies that you lift four times a week, but if your diary says otherwise, you know it's time to stop talking and get to the gym. A diary keeps you motivated, too, because you can flip back through the pages and see your improvements. If you reach your goals successfully, you've got a written step-by-step guide outlining how you got there. If you're stuck in a rut, you usually can find the problem with a careful read of your log. For tips about what to write down in your diary, see Chapter 3.

You can use a plain notepad to record your weight training workouts, but since workout diaries cost less than $15, why not treat yourself to a log specifically designed for lifting? You can find these logs at the bookstore. Our personal favorite is *The Ultimate Workout Log, Second Edition.* But that is probably because Suzanne wrote it.

If your computer keyboard has become an extension of your hands, you can record your lifting sessions online. Many online training logs are free or extremely cheap. For instance, Net Pulse, an entertainment system that is commonly available in gyms today, offers a complimentary exercise log that lets you track how much weight you lifted for each exercise and how many sets and reps you performed. Online and electronic logs are generally excellent and can analyze your workout data in countless ways. However, they're hard to tote around. We personally like to take our log with us so we can jot notes after each exercise. That way, you're not struggling to remember everything when you get back to your computer. If you're feeling really ambitious, you can carry around a paper log and take a few moments to transfer the information into an electronic medium.

Five Weight Training Rip-offs

We know of so many bogus weight training products that we had a hard time whittling our list to five. We chose the following items either for their outrageously misleading ads or for their potential to hurt you.

Electrical stimulation devices

"You quickly shape up doing nothing at all!" That's the pitch for a $99 electronic muscle stimulation belt that looks like an accessory that might have been popular in discos in the seventies. According to the ad, which was featured in one of the country's top-selling fitness magazines, the belt sends electrical impulses to your muscles, causing them to expand and contract repetitively, as they would in a normal workout. "No sit-ups," the ad says, "No sweat."

Electronic stimulation devices have legitimate uses, but building muscles are not among them. (Physical therapists use these gizmos to help relax muscle spasms in the back and neck.) This gadget does stimulate your muscles to contract, but it won't give you a better body. In order for your muscles to become stronger and firmer, they must both contract *and* work to overcome a force such as gravity, a weight, or a rubber band.

Electronic stimulation devices aren't just a waste of money; they're also potentially dangerous. Not long ago, Liz's friend Norman bought one of these gizmos after undergoing knee surgery. A doctor that he knew (not the doc who operated on him) told Norman that the stimulation would help him regain strength in his knee. Norman was afraid of this thing, so he asked Liz to try it first. She placed the electrodes along the side of her knee and cranked up the dial to the "maximum voltage" setting. Her thigh jumped like the frog's leg that she had experimented on in tenth-grade biology. She ripped off the pad, but not in time to stop the formation of two deep red splotches on her thigh. Liz later learned that the doctor who had sold Norman the stimulator was a scam artist. He was selling these gadgets to his patients for $20 and then charging their insurance company more than $300 for physical therapy.

Electrical stimulation devices are becoming so popular that the American Council on Exercise recently commissioned the University of Wisconsin to test a model sold on infomercials. After eight weeks, the subjects who underwent electrical stimulation three times a week experienced no changes in weight, body-fat percentage, or strength. What's more, using the gizmo was painful and time-consuming; each session took about 45 minutes, even after weeks of practice. (Hmmm, about the same amount of time it would have taken to do a workout.) Also, the model used in this study cost more than $500. (Hmmm, the same as most yearly gym memberships.)

Weight belts

According to the conventional gym wisdom, wearing a weight belt is a smart way to protect your back when you're hoisting dumbbells and barbells. But research has proven otherwise. In fact, wearing a belt may actually increase your risk of injury.

When you wear a belt, your lower back and abdominal muscles don't have to work as hard to support your body. As a result, they never develop the strength necessary to assist you with heavier lifts. You may end up with muscular imbalances that set you up for injuries when you're not wearing a belt. Let's say you have powerful legs and go to kick a soccer ball; if your abs and back are not strong enough to support your body during this forceful kick, that loud ripping sound you'll hear is the sound of your back muscles pulling. Dozens of studies show that people who wear belts have weaker abs and lower back muscles than those who don't.

A strong argument can also be made for going beltless when you already have a lower back injury. You're better off lifting only as much weight as your back can tolerate without artificial help. The belt may allow you to lift past your safety point without feeling pain — until it's too late. Plus, you're better off taking the time to properly rehabilitate your injury before you start seriously hitting the weights again.

High-rep classes

These days, more and more health clubs are offering choreographed strength training classes that are set to music and involve performing dozens and dozens of repetitions with very light weights. One of the most popular is Body Pump, a New Zealand import that claims to be "the fastest way in the universe to get in shape." According to the Body Pump Web site. "You don't get big. Just toned and strong."

This claim is misleading. For one thing, it perpetuates the myth that traditional weight training — performing, say, 8 to 12 reps — will make you big and bulky. As we explain in Chapter 23, that is ludicrous. Also, it is just plain wrong to say that performing 40 repetitions of an exercise will give you strength. You know that the Body Pump promoters are reaching when the "evidence" they cite on their Web site is a study published in 1968! According to this research, subjects who trained for endurance (by performing lots of reps with light weights) gained as much strength as those who trained for strength. "The authors suggested that the choice of weights and repetitions was not of prime importance providing the repetitions were continued to the point of fatigue."

Well, at one point, scientists thought the earth was flat, too! No reputable exercise scientist today agrees with the conclusions of that 1968 article. In high-rep classes, the weights are too light to make any real difference in muscle strength or shape. The Body Pump Web site claims that you will increase your "fat burning ability," but the only way to increase your metabolism is to add muscle mass, which a high-rep, light-weight routine is not going to accomplish. (Not surprisingly, no studies on the Body Pump Web site show strength and metabolism gains from this program.)

Finally, we're concerned that performing dozens of repetitions may be unsafe, especially for the delicate elbow and shoulder joints. Rather than waste an hour with these classes (or videos that provide similar workouts), spend 20 minutes with a set of dumbbells and a weight bench performing routines that we describe in Chapters 15 and 16. Or, if you prefer a class setting, find a body sculpting instructor who follows the sensible guidelines that we outline in those chapters.

Ab gizmos

We were hoping that when the Ab Roller industry crashed and burned, we had seen the last of abdominal infomercial gadgets that claim to help you "go from flab to abs" and "whittle your middle." We were wrong! The American public seems to be obsessed with using gadgets to trim their tummies. Reality: You cannot exercise a specific spot on your body and then expect the flab to disappear from that spot any more than you can expect to get smarter by massaging your head.

But with American consumers, it seems, hope springs eternal. The latest entrepreneur to take advantage of this hope is Suzanne Sommers, the same former sitcom star who has sold more than $20 million worth of ThighMasters and authored half a dozen useless exercise and diet books (including one that warns against foods that rot in your stomach!). Sommers endorses a product called the Torso Track, which has spawned a slew of imitators. Essentially, this contraption is a long track of metal with handles on one end and a pad at the other. You kneel on the pad, grasp the handles, and then push the handles forward and back as your torso slides along the track.

Sommers implies that this motion will melt fat away from your body faster than you can say "More money in Suzanne Sommers' pocket." In reality, using this machine may be the perfect way to wreck your back, especially if you are overweight. At best, this $200 gadget is a waste of money. You can do dozens and dozens of more effective abdominal exercises, such as the ones we describe in Chapter 12. (Interesting side note: When you read the fine print about Sommer's personal guarantees for the product, you learn that all she is really promising you is that your machine will be delivered in less than 10 days and that she will warranty it for 90 days.)

Terrible trainers

Earlier in this chapter, we mention that a personal trainer is one of the best fitness investments you can make. Absolutely true. However, there are a few bad apples out there, and you should know how to spot them. You cannot trust that every health club screens its trainers for knowledge and experience.

In a recent issue of *Women's Sports & Fitness* magazine, a writer showed how easy it is for an unqualified trainer to get hired. The writer "earned" a cheap certification off the Internet by answering questions such as, "Does a biceps curl work the triceps, deltoid, or biceps muscle?" A few days later her certification card arrived, "licensing" her to teach kickboxing as well, even though she had never even taken a kickboxing class! The writer then applied for a job at eight health clubs in New York City. It's a good sign that six of them turned her down. It's pretty scary that one of them offered her a job on the spot, and the other was eager to consider her application.

If you inadvertently hire a lousy trainer, don't be shy about unhiring him or her. In Chapter 5, we discuss trainers in detail. But, briefly, you need to say sayonara to your trainer if he or she . . .

- **Doesn't have reputable credentials.** Just because someone claims to be a "trainer to the stars" or a "nationally recognized personal trainer" doesn't mean that he or she has any education or teaching skills. See Chapter 5 for a list of legitimate credentials.

- **Fails to custom-design a program for you.** We know one trainer who has all his clients — whether they're 25-year-old triathletes or 60-year-old novices — hop up and down off benches and squat so low that their butts touch the floor. His name has been mentioned more than once in operating rooms where knee surgery is a specialty.

- **Forces you to perform a movement that feels uncomfortable or painful.** For every exercise a trainer suggests, he or she should know several alternative exercises that work the same muscles.

- **Doesn't teach you to be independent.** If you want to work out with a trainer three times a week for the rest of your life, great. But don't think that you should *need* a trainer forever. Three to five sessions should get you up and running.

- **Fails to monitor your technique.** We know a trainer who spends most of a session gazing at himself in the mirror instead of watching his client. One time he leaned backward just as his client was straightening his arms on a triceps machine, and the trainer got clanked in the head.

- **Steps outside the boundaries of your professional relationship.** If this happens, terminate your session immediately and find another trainer. If the trainer is part of the gym staff, file a complaint with the management. If the trainer is an independent trainer, file a report with any organization that he or she is certified by so that the organization won't recommend this trainer to anyone else.

Index

• C •

• F •

• *M* •

 # WWW.DUMMIES.COM

YOUR ONLINE RESOURCE

Discover Dummies Online!

The Dummies Web Site is your fun and friendly online resource for the latest information about *For Dummies* books and your favorite topics. The Web site is the place to communicate with us, exchange ideas with other *For Dummies* readers, chat with authors, and have fun!

Ten Fun and Useful Things You Can Do at www.dummies.com

1. Win free *For Dummies* books and more!
2. Register your book and be entered in a prize drawing.
3. Meet your favorite authors through the Hungry Minds Author Chat Series.
4. Exchange helpful information with other *For Dummies* readers.
5. Discover other great *For Dummies* books you must have!
6. Purchase Dummieswear exclusively from our Web site.
7. Buy *For Dummies* books online.
8. Talk to us. Make comments, ask questions, get answers!
9. Download free software.
10. Find additional useful resources from authors.

Link directly to these ten fun and useful things at
www.dummies.com/10useful

For other technology titles from Hungry Minds, go to
www.hungryminds.com

Not on the Web yet? It's easy to get started with *Dummies 101: The Internet For Windows 98* or *The Internet For Dummies* at local retailers everywhere.

Find other *For Dummies* books on these topics:
Business • Career • Databases • Food & Beverage • Games • Gardening
Graphics • Hardware • Health & Fitness • Internet and the World Wide Web
Networking • Office Suites • Operating Systems • Personal Finance • Pets
Programming • Recreation • Sports • Spreadsheets • Teacher Resources
Test Prep • Word Processing

 Hungry Minds™

FOR DUMMIES
BOOK REGISTRATION

Register This Book and Win!

We want to hear from you!

Visit **dummies.com** to register this book and tell us how you liked it!

✔ Get entered in our monthly prize giveaway.

✔ Give us feedback about this book — tell us what you like best, what you like least, or maybe what you'd like to ask the author and us to change!

✔ Let us know any other *For Dummies* topics that interest you.

Your feedback helps us determine what books to publish, tells us what coverage to add as we revise our books, and lets us know whether we're meeting your needs as a *For Dummies* reader. You're our most valuable resource, and what you have to say is important to us!

Not on the Web yet? It's easy to get started with *Dummies 101: The Internet For Windows 98* or *The Internet For Dummies* at local retailers everywhere.

Or let us know what you think by sending us a letter at the following address:

For Dummies Book Registration
Dummies Press
10475 Crosspoint Blvd.
Indianapolis, IN 46256

...FOR DUMMIES™

**BESTSELLING
BOOK SERIES**